MW01535172

A STUDENT'S OBLIGATION

A STUDENT'S OBLIGATION

Advice from the Rebbe of the Warsaw Ghetto

RABBI KALONYMUS KALMAN SHAPIRA

translated by Micha Odenheimer

𝒜

JASON ARONSON INC.
Northvale, New Jersey
London

The translation of this volume,
which was made possible in part by a
grant from Miriam and Nachman Futterman,
was a project of Zecher Naftoli,
Rabbi Eli Chaim Carlebach, ל״ז, Director and Founder.

Production Editor: *Adelle Krauser*
Editorial Director: *Muriel Jorgensen*

This book was set in 11 point Weiss
by NK Graphics of Keene, New Hampshire.
It was printed and bound by Haddon Craftsmen
of Scranton, Pennsylvania.

Library of Congress Cataloging-in-Publication Data

Kalonimus Klemish ben Elimelekh, 1889–1944.
    [Kuntres hovat ha-talmidim. English]
    A student's obligation : advice from the rebbe of the Warsaw Ghetto /
Kalonymus Kalman Shapira.
      p. cm.
    Translation of: Kuntres hovat ha-talmidim.
    ISBN 0-87668-653-6
    1. Jewish Students—Religious life. 2. Jewish Students—Conduct
of life. 3. Motivation in religious education. 4. Jewish religious
education—Philosophy. 5. Hasidism—Study and teaching. I. Title.
BM727.K35 1991
296.7—dc20   90-28118

Manufactured in the United States of America. Jason Aronson Inc. offers books
and cassettes. For information and catalog write to Jason Aronson Inc., 230 Liv-
ingston Street, Northvale, New Jersey 07647.

To my mother
Golde bat Yehudah Avigdor (Goldie Futterman), 1901-1987

A sensitive and beautifully delicate woman with a deep commitment to building a Jewish home and community. She always supported those in need. She gave to her children a deep appreciation for the love of Hashem, the power of prayer, honoring parents and grandparents, and doing what one says one is going to do. She was a loving and loved wife, mother, grandmother, great-grandmother, aunt, and friend. May the reading of this sefer be a merit for her soul.

Nachman Yirachmiel Futterman

To my father
Yehudah Leib ben Menachem Manes (Louis Futterman), 1896-1987

A peacemaker and healer, using a smile, a joke, a song, laughter, and dance. He was a man who served God with joy *(simchah)*. He gave to his children a deep appreciation for not speaking badly about another person, always being joyous *(besimchah)*, and always looking at the positive side of life and people. He was a loving and loved husband, father, grandfather, greatgrandfather, uncle, and friend. May the reading of this sefer be a merit for his soul.

Nachman Yirachmiel Futterman

To my mother
Fraidle bat Chaim (Fannie Lessow Chavin), 1914-1989

"She envisions a field and buys it. From her earnings she plants a vineyard."
(Proverbs 31:16)

A woman of grace and beauty, a lover and dancer of life. Filled with a rich Jewish spirit that touched and helped people of all ages and needs. With skill and determination she brought forth and manifested visions that deeply supported and nourished her family and Jewish community. She was a loving wife of fifty-four years, a devoted mother, sister, grandmother, aunt, and friend. May her soul continue to radiate its love and blessings in our lives.

Miriam Chavin Futterman

CONTENTS

CONTENTS

CONTENTS

FOREWORD

KALONYMUS KALMAN SHAPIRA, REBBE OF THE WARSAW GHETTO

by Aharon Sorasky

Rabbi Kalonymus Kalman Shapira, the Rebbe of Piaseczno, was 55 years old when he was burned in a Nazi death chamber in a final, consummating act of sanctification of God's name.

At the age of 34 he had established a yeshivah where thousands of chasidic children and young adults were educated and sustained. At the age of 24 he had been appointed Chief Rabbi of the town of Piaseczno. Four years earlier, he had already begun to serve as Rebbe—master and guide—to a large chasidic following; this was a post he had both earned and inherited. But his distinctive characteristics—brilliance, holiness, warmth, piety—were discernible in him from a much earlier age.

Kalonymus Kalman was born in Grodzisk, Poland, on the 19th day of Iyar, 5649 (1889). His father, Reb Elimelech of Grodzisk, was a great chasidic master, one of the leaders of Polish Chasidism, and already one of the elders of his generation when Kalonymus was born. Reb Elimelech was a descendant of numerous great teachers and rebbes, including the Maggid of Kozhnitz, one of the great teachers and wonder-workers in the early history of Chasidism. Kalonymus Kalman Shapira was named after his father's grandfather, Reb Kalonymus Kalman of Krakow, one of Reb Elimelech of Lyzhensk's greatest disciples and the author of the chasidic Torah commentary *Maor VaShemesh*.

Reb Elimelech was devoted to his young son, Kalonymus Kalman, from the moment he was born. He showered him with affection, guarded and protected him with special care, and began to educate him in spiritual practices from his early infancy. Reb Elimelech went so far as to appoint someone to wash Kalonymus's hands each time he woke up and to make sure that he always had his head covered—disciplines a child is usually initiated into only when he has become able to practice them himself.

During infancy, Kalonymus contracted scarlet fever. Piaseczno chasidim who were alive at the time later told of the great distress his son's illness caused Reb Elimelech. When the child became so sick that his life was in danger, Reb Elimelech took off his *kolpack*, which is a special kind of hat signifying the wearer's status as rebbe, and declared that he was no longer a rebbe and would neither teach nor counsel chasidim until his son recovered.

The entire population of Grodzisk assembled to pray for Kalonymus's recovery. As the fever intensified, Kalonymus began to convulse in seizures. His mother, crying bitterly, gathered him into her arms, brought him into her husband's study, and said, "Take your baby." The Rebbe sat near his son's crib all night, praying and crying continuously. In the middle of the night, the child's yarmulke fell off. His father placed it back on his head and said, "A future leader of Israel should keep his head covered."

In order to cure his son's seizures, Reb Elimelech bound his fingers with fronds from the *lulav* that he had used on Succot. Immediately, the child calmed down. Reb Elimelech had also asked that his son's name be mentioned to the holy Maggid of Trisk. The Maggid sent back to Grodzisk the silver seder plate that had been used by Rav Yitzchok of Nezchiszh, one of the great rebbes of an earlier generation, with instructions to feed the baby warm soup from the seder plate. This, he said, would cure him—and it did, according to the chasidim who witnessed the events. Reb Kalonymus would use this seder plate for the rest of his life during his Shabbat meals.

Reb Elimelech's belief in his son's future potential influenced his disciples: Kalonymus was viewed with awe by great numbers of Grodzisk chasidim. Many times Reb Elimelech would tell people who came to him with difficult problems to leave a written account of their requests under the pillow of his 2-year-old son.

Before the boy turned 3, his father passed away. Kalonymus was an exceptionally sensitive child, and years later he recalled how he had felt his mother's grief during the days following his father's passing. One can see in this book—the English version of *Chovat HaTalmidim*, Reb Kalonymus's book on education, first published in Warsaw in 1932—how deeply his father's special belief in him affected his life and philosophy. This book is permeated by an effort to inculcate in every Jewish young person a belief in his or her spiritual potential. It is as if Reb Kalonymus were attempting to take the feeling he had received about himself from his father and pass it along to the children of an entire generation.

According to Reb Kalonymus's own testimony, he was able to remember many details about his father, many of his words, deeds, and practices. Once, he later told his friends, his father was in the middle of the seven encirclements, which are part of the services for Hoshana Rabba. The prayer services on Hoshana Rabba (the last day of the Succot festival) were performed with great awe and devotion in Grodzisk and lasted virtually the entire day. From time to time the rebbe would stop in the midst of his devotions and speak words of Torah to the chasidim. "This particular Hoshana Rabba," Reb Kalonymus related, "when I was 2 years old, I burst into tears and began calling for my father. He himself was at that moment weeping and praying, as he carried the four species in circular procession. He immediately turned to face me and said, "You are calling your father? I am also calling my Father!"

From the age of 3, Kalonymus showed evidence of being gifted with an ability to see into the spiritual dimension of reality. Chasidim witnessed how, during the first year after his father's death, Kalonymus was brought in to say Kaddish for his father during prayer services. At one particular Minchah service, he refused, explaining that he could clearly see his father sitting in his customary chair.

After Reb Elimelech's death, the Grodzisk chasidim, who numbered in the tens of thousands, began to seek guidance from the Rebbe's descendants and disciples. The Rebbe had several grandchildren who were already grown men; among them was Rav Yisroel of Grodzisk, and some of the chasidim attached themselves to his court. Others began to travel to Rav Chaim Yechiel Meir of Ostrowiec, or to the holy Rav Yechiel of Ravo. Many of the older chasidim, including a number of great scholars, sought the leadership of Rav Yerachmiel Moshe of Kozhnitz, a grandchild of Reb Elimelech (the son of a daughter born to Reb Elimelech years before the birth of Kalonymus Kalman), who had been an especially close disciple of his grandfather. But regardless of which rebbe a particular group chose to follow, Grodzisk remained a center for various groups of chasidim. Many chasidim lived in Grodzisk. Others came to visit and to pray at the tomb of Reb Elimelech and in his synagogue, and to see his two young sons—Kalonymus and his brother, Yeshayahu, who was a year and a half younger. And on the first day of the month of Nisan, the anniversary of Reb Elimelech's passing, thousands of his chasidim from all corners of Poland thronged into Grodzisk and filled the sanctuary where he had prayed.

Kalonymus grew into a child who was famous for his brilliance and his diligence. It was often said that he didn't waste a minute of his day, even as a young boy. He had an unquenchable thirst for Torah and for mitzvot. He arose at dawn and studied Torah until late at night. Although he was very serious, he also had a pleasant disposition and turned a kindly face to all. He had a highly developed inner spiritual life from his childhood onward, and his prayers were fervent and filled with fire. His maturity, thoughtfulness, and piety brought him a reputation for righteousness.

Kalonymus had many teachers. The greatest of his father's disciples took him under their wing and devoted much time and effort to educating him on the chasidic path. His mother would often travel with her children to her father, Reb Chaim Shmuel Halevy Hurwitz Sternfeld, the Rebbe of Chentzin, who was a grandson of the Seer of Lublin and of the Good Jew of Neustadt and who was himself one of the great chasidic masters of that generation.

Reb Chaim accorded his grandson much honor and spent many hours initiating him into the mysteries of Chasidism.

Most of all, perhaps, it was his nephew—Reb Yerachmiel Moshe, the Rebbe of Kozhnitz—who must be considered Kalonymus's main educator. Reb Yerachmiel Moshe, being the son of Reb Elimelech's daughter from a previous marriage, was much older than his uncle Kalonymus. Rav Yerachmiel Moshe was extremely concerned with both the material and spiritual welfare of the two young boys and would travel to Grodzisk from time to time to see them and to make certain that their needs were being fulfilled in all areas. Kalonymus developed a particularly close relationship with Reb Yerachmiel Moshe, who became his teacher in the study of the hidden secrets of the Torah.

When Kalonymus Kalman was 13, he was brought even closer into the circle of Reb Yerachmiel Moshe's family. He became engaged to Reb Yerachmiel Moshe's daughter, Rachel Chaya Miriam.

In Kozhnitz

Reb Yerachmiel Moshe was one of the great men of his generation and had thousands of chasidic followers. The paths leading to Kozhnitz were always crowded with people. Reb Yerachmiel Moshe was a precious link in the dynastic chain of Kozhnitz, Magelnitza, and Grodzisk, and he was considered a real exemplar of this glorious chasidic tradition. "If you want to witness the kind of light the holy Maggid of Kozhnitz radiated," people would say, "go see Reb Yerachmiel Moshe."

Kalonymus was only 16 years old when he married Reb Yerachmiel's daughter and went to live in Kozhnitz, near his father-in-law. He lived close to his father-in-law for four years. During that time he absorbed and internalized his father-in-law's teachings to such an extent that he was said to have learned more in his four years of discipleship than other chasidim managed to learn in forty. He struggled to acquire every possible good trait and to learn from everyone. Guided by his father-in-law, he calculated plans for every minute of the day in order to find time to study both the hidden and the revealed portions of Torah. He attained much by hard work and added to his knowledge by learning from every move his teacher—his father-in-law—made. His discipleship in Kabbalah, with his father-in-law as guide, continued to broaden and intensify.

Reb Kalonymus's years of spiritual discipleship were not fated to last long; during the fourth year after Reb Kalonymus's marriage and his move to Kozhnitz, Reb Yerachmiel Moshe began to hint that this own days were numbered. In 1909, on Shavuot, Reb Yerachmiel Moshe declined to lead his chasidim in reciting the special *Akdomot* prayer, which he had done every year, and instead indicated that he wished to bestow this honor on his son-in-law. Reb Kalonymus refused to accept this or any other symbol of leadership during his father-in-law's lifetime. The chasidim, however, saw in the offer a sign that Reb Yerachmiel Moshe was passing on the royal scepter to Reb Kalonymus—that the guards were changing.

In the summer of that year, on the 13th day of Elul, Reb Yerachmiel Moshe passed away after returning home from a health spa in Krenitz. Reb Kalonymus had accompanied his father-in-law on this last trip and did not leave his bedside when Reb Yerachmiel Moshe was sick and dying. He eulogized his father-in-law with a play on the numerical value of the letters in the biblical passage describing Moses' ascent to the mountain where he died: "And Moses ascended from the plains of Moav to Mount Nevo. The numerical value of Moav is forty-nine, and Nevo, which begins with the letter Nun, whose numerical value is fifty, alludes to the fiftieth and final gate of wisdom."

Reb Yerachmiel Moshe was 49 when he passed away. He was laid to rest among his ancestors in the old cemetery in Kozhnitz. After his death, his chasidim split into two groups. Half of them followed his son, Reb Aharon Yechiel, and half followed his son-in-law, Reb Kalonymus Kalman, who became Rebbe in the town of Piaseczno.

In Piaseczno

Although he was only 20 in 1909 when he became Rebbe, Kalonymus Kalman struck an impressive figure from the very beginning of his tenure. His appearance was enchanting, his personality charismatic; he commanded the respect and admiration of everyone who met him. Throngs of followers clung to him with great love and devotion, seeking his counsel and guidance. To his chasidim and all who encountered him, he seemed a true embodiment of holiness and a symbol of Jewish spiritual glory.

Among the thousands of chasidim who began to flock to Piaseczno were many of the elder disciples of both his father, the Rebbe of Grodzisk, and his father-in-law, the Rebbe of Kozhnitz. Many chasidim of the saintly Rebbe of Ostrowiec also began to look toward Piaseczno for leadership, after being explicitly commanded by their rebbe before his demise to seek out Reb Kalonymus Kalman and his teachings.

Many other towns and villages invited Reb Kalonymus Kalman to set up headquarters and establish his residence within their borders, but Reb Kalonymus chose to remain in Piaseczno for several reasons. First, it contained a major concentration of Grodzisk chasidim who recognized Reb Kalonymus as his father's spiritual heir. In addition, Rav Noach, one of the elders of Gerrer Chasidism, the Rabbi of Piaseczno and a talmudic master of renown, held Reb Kalonymus in very high regard. He went to great lengths to ensure that Reb Kalonymus would choose Piaseczno as his permanent home.

The small town of Piaseczno thus became a large center of Chasidism. The whole appearance of the town changed as it became associated with the spiritual royalty of Reb Kalonymus's court. Reb Kalonymus was concerned both with the elite of his chasidim, who were striving toward spiritual advancement, and with the great mass of people who were concerned with survival and with finding a modicum of happiness and fulfillment. To those who were seeking, he provided a ladder of ascent; to those who were hurting, he offered a helping hand, great spiritual comfort, and material assistance.

On Shabbat and on the various holidays, Piaseczno was crowded with people who came to see and hear Reb Kalonymus. His prayers, which were uttered with tremendous feeling, elevated everyone who was present. At his Shabbat and holiday tables, he discoursed on the Torah. His words were profound and inspiring, and he wove together many different levels of meaning—the revealed and the hidden, the simple and the complex. His sermons were described as being like fire mingled with water, and the sharpest minds among his disciples found stimulation and delight in his deep insights into Torah and Chasidism. His table was famous too for the songs of praise (*zemirot*) that were sung by the Rebbe and his chasidim with great passion, longing, and fervor.

Reb Kalonymus had a gift for creating and maintaining personal connections with each of his chasidim. An elderly chasid by the name of Reb Vovve Vorker, who used to travel to the rebbes of Radoshitz, Shedlovtze, and Byalovzig, once found himself in Piaseczno for the night. He fell asleep in the midst of contemplating whether to visit Reb Kalonymus or whether it was inappropriate for him to visit a rebbe who was so young. Just then there was a knock on the door—an emissary from Reb Kalonymus was there inviting him to the Rebbe's home. "I just took account of my chasidim," Reb Kalonymus told him, "and didn't find you listed among them." From then on Reb Vovve Vorker became greatly attached to Reb Kalonymus.

The attachment the older chasidim felt for Reb Kalonymus was nothing, however, compared to the attachment that the young people felt toward him. They were as devoted to him as children are to their parents, and they were always eager to see him, be close to him, hear his voice. And Reb Kalonymus reciprocated and gave each child individual attention. Reb Kalonymus once said that from the age of 4 or 5 a child must have a rebbe—a true spiritual master— as a guide. He counseled each child about his or her particular problems or concerns. This child-centeredness, this deep interest in the spiritual lives of children, is, of course, one of the hallmarks of Piaseczno Chasidism, and is reflected in Reb Kalonymus's *Chovat HaTalmidim.*

Reb Kalonymus worked both with the faithful and with those children and adults who had already begun to stray from the Jewish tradition. He had an instinctive understanding of what was profound and what was superficial in spiritual life, what was valuable and essential and what was of secondary importance. He was thus able to appeal to a range of different kinds of personalities and help them all find their place within Chasidism. He succeeded in educating a large army of young chasidim—a new generation that was in every way the equal of preceding generations. Many are the wonders worked by Reb Kalonymus, according to the testimony of his chasidim. But the greatest of his wonders was his captivating presence, through which he reproduced the miracle performed by Elijah the prophet, of blessed memory: "A man whose people followed after him and repeated 'The Lord is God.' "

Rabbi in Piaseczno

Reb Kalonymus's fame extended throughout Poland, but his closest ties were to the town of Piaseczno, where he was especially loved and appreciated. In 1913, the Rabbi of Piaseczno, Reb Noach, who had been instrumental in bringing Reb Kalonymus to the town, passed away. The townspeople wished to appoint Reb Kalonymus as the official Chief Rabbi of the town. Reb Kalonymus refused, reasoning that this position should logically be conferred upon Reb Noach's heir, his son-in-law Reb Henoch. The townspeople were insistent. Eventually Reb Kalonymus agreed to the appointment, provided that his salary be paid to Reb Noach's widow instead of him and that Reb Henoch be appointed to the position of Dayan— Chief Judge—of the town.

As Rabbi of Piaseczno, Reb Kalonymus had to work with all members of the Jewish community there, not only his own chasidic followers. Reb Kalonymus was strict and uncompromising when it came to upholding Jewish law, but he was pleasant and peaceful in his manner and in his approach to conflict. After the first World War Reb Kalonymus moved to Warsaw with his family, yet Piaseczno refused to accept his absence as permanent; they asked him to guide them from his residence in Warsaw, which he did. Nothing of importance was decided in the communal life of the town of Piaseczno without consulting Reb Kalonymus.

Reb Kalonymus would come to Piaseczno for an extended stay during the nine weeks from Shabbat Nachamu to Shabbat Bereishit (usually mid-August until October). Occasionally he would visit Piaseczno for a special occasion. When a question was considered especially complex, or a situation extremely difficult, Reb Kalonymus was contacted in Warsaw for his advice.

During the weeks that Reb Kalonymus was in Piaseczno, the city bustled with life. Many chasidim came from far and wide to spend this time with Reb Kalonymus in the intimate setting of Piaseczno. During this period he fulfilled both his duties—as chasidic rebbe and as town rabbi. On Shabbat Shuvah—the Shabbat before Yom Kippur, when it is customary for the town rabbi to speak in public—he would conduct a chasidic *tish* and then adjourn to the synagogue where he would present his Shabbat Shuvah sermon (*drashah*). These sermons were memorable for their insight, passion, and erudition.

One particularly memorable Shabbat Shuvah *drashah* impressed on the town Reb Kalonymus's willingness to sacrifice his personal well-being for the cause of Torah and the Jewish people. It happened as follows:

Reb Kalonymus's custom was to travel to Kozhnitz for the anniversary of his father-in-law's passing, the 13th of Elul. Before and after visiting the grave he would immerse himself in a mikvah (ritual bath), and on the way back to Piaseczno he would stop off in Radom and immerse himself in a cold mikvah that was said to have been used by the Baal Shem Tov.

In Kozhnitz that year he had a cold, which had developed into a fever by the time he reached Radom. His close disciples tried to persuade him not to immerse in the cold mikvah; his son, Reb Elimelech, threatened to fast if he insisted on immersing. Reb Kalonymus went ahead with his customary immersion, and his illness grew more severe. Two weeks later, as Rosh Hashanah approached, he had developed pneumonia, and doctors were considering inserting a bronchial tube into his chest. He still insisted on immersing in the mikvah and blowing the shofar, as he always did on Rosh Hashanah. Everyone assumed that Reb Kalonymus would not be able to speak on the following Shabbat, Shabbat Shuvah, and indeed his doctors forbade him to speak. But a special concern prompted him to risk his already failing health and speak anyway.

A certain Jewish merchant in town, one of the wealthier members of the community, in a flagrant manner had begun to commit a breach in the observance of Shabbat—something unheard of until then in this small Polish community. Reb Kalonymus had tried very hard to persuade him to change his behavior, but to no avail. Instead, the merchant threatened to slander Reb Kalonymus to the Polish authorities, who required all town rabbis to have a working knowledge of Polish, which Reb Kalonymus did not. Reb Kalonymus therefore felt compelled to speak.

Reb Kalonymus's speech was a beautiful and inspiring depiction of the spiritual significance of the Shabbat. Delivered in a thundering voice despite his condition, it emphasized the holiness of Shabbat and succeeded in uniting everyone present in an effort to strengthen the town's Shabbat observance. "When I began to attempt to strengthen the observance of Shabbat," Reb Kalonymus said, "I was threatened with the loss of my rabbinical position. How foolish is anyone who tries to frighten me away from pursuing my efforts to enhance the observance of Torah! I am prepared to lose not only my rabbinical position, but also my life for God. Are people not aware that any person who recites *Shma Yisrael* (Hear, O Israel, the Lord our God, the Lord is One) is prepared to be killed in order to sanctify God's name? I ask, however, that no one should speak about this further and no one should attempt to do anything to restore my honor in this particular case."

In these lines we can see the extent of Reb Kalonymus's self-sacrifice, and a foreshadowing of the great suffering and sacrifice he would submit to in the service of his people in the terrible times to come. For it was not only for religious principles that he was so ready to sacrifice himself, but, like all great leaders in the spirit of Torah, for the smallest of his flock. Reb Kalonymus's father wrote, in his book *Imrei Elimelech*, that one who sacrifices his soul for a fellow Jew is even greater than one who sacrifices himself for God, because he is akin to a subject who sacrifices himself for the benefit of his king's children. "How beloved is such a servant! Not only for his king, but for his king's child does he give his life."

Reb Kalonymus's efforts on behalf of his flock took him into every realm of life. If he was told about a Jew who was critically ill, he would spare neither material nor spiritual efforts in his battle to aid that person. And if it was a question of a young person who had strayed from the right path, nothing could deter him—certainly not concern for his own well-being—in his attempt to offer guidance back to the house of God.

Those who were close to him heard him say many times that whenever he spoke, he directed his words toward one person in particular. He aimed an attack right at the spiritual enemy of that person and did away with his hardness of heart. Many times after he had spoken, someone from the audience would approach him afterward and say, "I know you were talking right to me. You certainly must have read my thoughts! Please help me fix my soul and find my way back to God."

His daily schedule was most exhausting—he taught and studied with many different groups and attended to all sorts of communal matters. His day started at dawn and ended after midnight. But despite all his various concerns, he tore himself away from everything for a few hours each day to receive visitors who came to him with their problems.

Before they entered the Rebbe's study, each person would write his name and the name of his mother, along with the problem that he wished to discuss with the Rebbe, on a slip of paper, called in Yiddish a *kvittel*. This would be handed to the Rebbe upon entering. Reb Kalonymus would read the *kvittel* and then listen with complete attentiveness and an open heart to the person's verbal account of what was troubling him. All kinds of people approached him with problems of every kind—physical, financial, psychological, familial, and spiritual. He seemed to take on the problems of the brokenhearted people who poured out their hearts to him. They would leave feeling that their burdens had been relieved, now that the Rebbe was carrying them on his broad shoulders.

The sessions in which he received visitors were characterized by one extraordinary phenomenon: the Rebbe's ability to step back and forth from the most mundane matters to the most sublime, from mystical contemplation to the day-to-day problems of whomever he was speaking to. After each session, before the next person was ushered in to speak to him, he would pause briefly and write down notes containing the thoughts that had occurred to him while he was reading the *kvittel* of the previous visitor. These notes usually concerned the esoteric wisdom of the Kabbalah. The extraordinary state of consciousness that allowed the Rebbe to be aware of both heaven and earth at the same time was evident for all to see.

Reb Yisroel, the Rebbe of Kuzmir, once spent Shavuot with Reb Kalonymus. After Shavuot, when he was ready to return home, he tried to approach Reb Kalonymus to say good-bye, but he was unable to make it through the large crowds that were gathered around the Rebbe's door. Reb Yisroel wondered out loud whether there wasn't anything that could be done to prevent these throngs of people from constantly interfering with Reb Kalonymus's spiritual work—his prayer and his study. Reb Kalonymus's attendants reported Reb Yisroel's remarks to the Rebbe, who immediately requested that Reb Yisroel be ushered in. Reb Kalonymus showed him a sheet of paper that he had been writing on, filled with revelations about wondrous secrets of the Torah. Despite Reb Yisroel's extensive knowledge of Kabbalah, the concepts Reb Kalonymus was working on were far beyond his comprehension. "I wrote down these thoughts while I was receiving *kvitlach,*" Reb Kalonymus told him. "Now wait until I finish speaking to the crowd, which you find so disturbing, and together with Reb Eliezer of Tertchin, we'll study these matters."

Reb Kalonymus would exert all his strength in order to free any of his chasidim who had been drafted into the Polish army. He would spend large sums of money in bribing the draft authorities, and he would employ all kinds of strategies and tactics until he had secured the release of the young man in question.

A chasid who was not among his followers once asked him why he went to such great lengths and expended so much effort in these battles, as if his very life depended on it. Reb Kalonymus answered, "When Moshe asked God to choose a leader to succeed him, he said, 'Let God appoint a leader for the people who will go out with them and return with them.' The chasidic masters have interpreted this to mean 'someone whose soul will go out for every Jew.'" This attribute characterized the greatest shepherds of Israel—such as Reb Kalonymus Kalman of Piaseczno.

Flames

Reb Kalonymus's every action was filled with the holy fire of his spiritual energy. With its flames he ignited and inspired all those around him. This fire preceded him and enveloped his whole being. Whether he was praying, studying, or opening his heart to another person's pain, he was full of superhuman energy, and his face shone with pure devotion and concentration.

On Shabbat his face was radiant with light from another world. He sang the Shabbat hymns with a heavenly longing that was enough to cause a revolution to occur within the soul of anyone who heard him. Anyone who served God with indifference would find his or her heart warmed and transformed by even the slightest contact with Reb Kalonymus.

His daily schedule began with the study of the Talmud in depth, according to the tradition of the house of Karlin that "learning before davening is like a taste of the world-to-come." He would then begin to pray with freshness and enthusiasm, and with such joy that it seemed as if he were a person praying for the first time in his life. Even when he had begun to suffer from a heart condition that caused him great physical pain, he braced himself and set about praying with the strength of a lion. As he prayed, his limbs would begin to tremble and beads of sweat would pour from his forehead.

His voice was pleasant, and he pronounced each word of prayer out loud, in a clear, strong tone—with a sweetness that captured the hearts of the listeners. He would encourage young children to sing, too. He would search for children whose voices indicated intense spiritual concentration and an awakening of the soul. On Shabbat, he would surround himself with a semicircle of children who would pray very loudly. Sometimes people would complain about the noise; the Rebbe would tell them to let the children pray as loudly as they wanted to.

One of his major concerns as a teacher was to guide his disciples in learning to concentrate and direct their inner thoughts and intentions as they prayed. He suggested paths for contemplation and special meditations to be associated with specific prayers. Most of all, he emphasized that prayer must not be something done habitually, without feeling. Prayer, he taught, meant pouring out one's heart before God.

In Piaseczno once, during the ten days of penitence between Rosh Hashanah and Yom Kippur, the Rebbe sent a message from his room to the prayer-study hall downstairs: "Pray in such a way," he told his flock, "that even the floor should sense that there is a great King of the World."

When he was not in the midst of prayer, his actions were calm and his manner peaceful. He spoke calmly and quietly and moved slowly, with a grace that created a delightful atmosphere around him.

His nights were filled with the service of God. There was a group of young boys, his close disciples, who attended him in various ways. They slept in a room near his room. After he was sure they were asleep, he would begin his nightly devotions. Sometimes one of them would only pretend to be asleep and would stay awake and listen to the sound of the Rebbe's voice as it emanated from the room. "Once," a pupil of his reported, "I slept near his room, and heard him saying, as if talking in his sleep: 'HaShem [Lord], I desire to be close to You.' This he repeated many times, and then he began to say, 'There is no one like You, and no one other than You, and the whole world is only a reflection of Your holy radiance. . . .' And then he repeated this phrase over and over again."

Each of his motions was a prayer in a most silent, hidden form. His service of God was a service of the heart and mind, more hidden than revealed. Only a keen eye could see the intense flames in his soul and the feeling that poured out from within him. A deep longing and great thirst to be close to God was hidden beneath the cover of calmness that he wore on his face. Fortunate was the eye that saw him when this mask of calmness was removed.

In the Path of Kozhnitz

Reb Kalonymus led his congregation in the best tradition of Chasidism—in the spirit of the Baal Shem Tov, who said, "Not only the fear of punishment and remembrance of the day of death arouses a person's heart to penitence, but also the desire to cling to the source of life and righteousness." Therefore, Reb Kalonymus strove to cultivate in the souls of his chasidim the sense and feeling that God's glory fills every corner of the word.

One of Reb Kalonymus's outstanding traits of character was his sincere and amazing humility. His chasidim testified that "whoever has not heard Reb Kalonymus's prayers on Rosh Hashanah and Yom Kippur has never heard a broken heart in his lifetime." Reb Kalonymus's great-grandfather, the Maggid of Kozhnitz, once made a play on words on a phrase in the Yom Kippur service, "When there is no advocate." He said, "When one makes himself into nothing, that in itself is an advocate on your behalf." Reb Kalonymus truly made himself into nothing. Despite the fact that he devoted all his energy to the service of God, he felt that he was on a lower rung than anybody else. His chasidim felt that the story told about Reb Elimelech of Lyzhensk, one of the great leaders of Chasidism in the second generation after the Baal Shem Tov, described their Rebbe's personality as well. Reb Elimelech was once visiting a small town when he heard an old woman say that the Maggid of Zlotchov, who had the power to see another person's sins, was coming to town. He quickly fled, frightened that the Maggid would see him and reveal all of Reb Elimelech's great sins and describe how all the fires of Gehenna would not be sufficient for his punishment.

On his fortieth birthday, the 19th of Iyar 5689, he wrote the following lines, which some of his chasidim later discovered:

> What can I take upon myself to learn? It seems to me that I use my time to the utmost and that I am quite removed from forbidden desires. If my evil inclination is not fooling me, I can say that I am not addicted to desires. What I'm lacking, plainly, is to be a Jew. I see myself as a person who has all the right colors and forms, who has everything, and is lacking only a soul. I confess before You, who sees every hidden thing, I plead before You . . . I am very far from You and Your chambers. I simply want to convert and to be a Jew from now on. Help me not to waste the rest of my years, draw me near and bring me into Your secret, hidden chambers. Bind me to You forever in an expanse of pleasure.

There are some tzaddikim, Reb Levi Yitzchak of Berditchev has said, who are accomplished and complete within themselves, and there are other tzaddikim who are not complete. The latter, he believed, are the true tzaddikim because they constantly repent. About these it has been said, "Where penitents stand, complete tzaddikim cannot stand."

Reb Kalonymus was truly among those great, true tzaddikim who were constantly in the midst of penitence.

Love of Israel

Reb Kalonymus gained a reputation as a wonder-worker, a righteous man whose power stemmed from the spiritual law articulated by the Talmud: "The righteous decree and God fulfills." Modest by nature, it was only because his love for his people overpowered his hesitations and stirred him to attempt to help every

Jew who came to him for counsel, that he became known for his supernatural—as well as natural—interventions. He took a special interest in medical problems—psychological and physical—and learned as much as he could about the science of medicine and the details of every illness or injury he was confronted with. After he was satisfied that he understood the nature of the illness, he expressed his views with great confidence and with specific instructions. There are stories about people whose doctors were unsure whether or not to attempt a potentially risky surgery; Reb Kalonymus strongly encouraged the surgeons to go ahead with the procedure, taking personal responsibility for the outcome.

His fame as a counselor on medical problems spread until it became a regular practice in the Jewish community of Warsaw—a city of millions of Jews—to ask his advice in particularly dangerous or complex situations. The great talmudic scholar Rabbi Shimon Shkop, who had traveled from Lithuania for medical treatment in Warsaw, refused to take any medication without consulting Reb Kalonymus first. The Rebbe's reputation spread to far-off lands as well. Once, one of the elders of a community in Morocco who had heard of Reb Kalonymus through his book, *Chovat HaTalmidim*, sent him a *kvittel* because someone in his family was gravely ill. The person recovered miraculously. After this incident, a large scroll of parchment arrived from Morocco with the names of all the sick in that particular community who wanted Reb Kalonymus to keep them in mind during his prayers. And yet, despite the fact that he prayed for the sick, he would constantly emphasize that the greatest cure came from the faith that the sick person himself had in the Creator: "There is no greater cure than faith in *HaShem* and trusting in Him."

Large sums of money were brought to him every day. People who came for help sometimes left treasures of money on his table. Yet according to the testimony of his disciples, not a penny remained in his possession overnight. Either the money went toward the upkeep and expenses of the yeshivah, where hundreds of young boys had to be housed and fed, or he donated the money to another charity that very same day.

Once his son Elimelech was very sick and lay in bed in one of the Warsaw hospitals; a fortune of money was needed to provide the treatment that would save his life. While visiting him, Reb

Kalonymus was approached by a stranger, a Jew, who offered to give him all the money that was needed for his son's treatment. Reb Kalonymus asked the man for his name and the name of his mother. The man did not wish to disclose this information. Reb Kalonymus refused to take the money and explained that he never takes money from anyone unless he knows the origin of the person's soul.

Reb Kalonymus's wife, like him, was also famous for her charitable nature. Their charity knew no limits and no bounds; therefore, despite the great sums of money that passed through their hands, they were always lacking in basic necessities, were constantly in debt, and had no money with which to pay their household expenses. Reb Kalonymus's chasidim tried in various ways to ease his financial situation. They even brought him money with the stipulation that it was being given only under the condition that he use it for household expenses. Yet nothing seemed to help. Reb Kalonymus's basic belief was that charity must be given until the giver felt it, until the heart itself was pressed and squeezed by the act of giving.

Just as Reb Kalonymus loved the people of Israel, he also had a tremendous love and longing for the land of Israel. Many times he tried to move to the Holy Land but was unable to leave Poland because of his many commitments and attachments to his disciples and followers. His younger brother Reb Yeshayahu, who came to be known affectionately as HaAdmor HeChalutz (the pioneering rebbe), moved to Israel as a young man and became one of the leaders of religious Zionism. When Reb Yeshayahu once came back to Poland from the Holy Land, Reb Kalonymus was struck by a desire to move there immediately. He sold all his possessions, including some land that he owned in Piaseczno, and bought a plot of land on the outskirts of Jerusalem. Some of his chasidim offered to help him financially with this purchase. He answered them, "It's no great feat to buy with someone else's money."

Reb Kalonymus was always in the land of Israel in his heart and soul, even if the generation did not merit his actual physical presence in the land. All of his life he lived with a painful longing for the land, and thus the "air of the land of Israel" surrounded him completely wherever he was.

Rebuke

What was the secret quality that drew so many to Reb Kalonymus, that attached so many hearts to him with bonds of love? For Reb Kalonymus was loved not only by his disciples and close followers, but by the masses of simple Jews and by his peers as well—the great rabbis, chasidic and otherwise, of his generation. Perhaps this secret quality was simply what kabbalists would call *or chozer*—returning light—the result and the reflection of the love for people that emanated from his heart.

His customary mien was one of serenity and pleasantness. When he felt the need to rebuke someone, often a single piercing glance was enough to melt the heart of whoever had offended him or his principles. The hidden intent of his rebukes was always to draw people near, never to create enmity or push people away.

On the Saturday night before Rosh Hashanah, when *Slichos* (penitential prayers) are recited, Reb Kalonymus would often deliver a sharp sermon of ethical rebuke in order to stimulate his congregants to turn back to God before the day of judgment. One particular year, Reb Kalonymus sensed that a certain segment of the audience had come to hear him more for the entertainment value, the excitement of the event, than out of real spiritual intent. Instead of delivering a sermon, he turned toward the audience and said, "People are drawn by nature to hear words that will excite them, disturb them, frighten them, and make their hearts beat faster. This is similar to the longing people have for beer, which affects the whole body with its power to intoxicate. If you want to drink beer, do I have to serve as your glass?" With these words, he turned back to his prayers. His remarks penetrated deeply into everyone's heart and left a deeper impression than any sermon could have.

Another famous incident in which Reb Kalonymus rebuked one of his disciples is remembered as follows: One of Reb Kalonymus's students changed his traditional garments and arrived at the Rebbe's lecture wearing a tie. Ties are frowned upon in the chasidic world because they symbolically separate the head from the heart, which, according to Kabbalah, are "two friends who should never part from one another." The student was sitting in the back row of a large hall that was filled to capacity. Before starting the lecture, Reb Kalonymus, as if through a sixth sense, walked down the aisle to where the student was sitting and tore the tie off his neck. "My grandfather, the Maggid of Kozhnitz," he said, "classified this as *kesher reshoim*—knot of the wicked."

Whoever received rebuke from Reb Kalonymus became attached to him with a love even greater than before and accepted his authority wholeheartedly. The words of the wisest of men, King Solomon—"Faithful are the words of a friend"—were fulfilled in him.

The Yeshivah

In 1923, Reb Kalonymus founded a yeshivah that he called Daas Moshe after his father-in-law, Rav Yerachmiel Moshe of Kozhnitz. Up until the war years, the yeshivah remained at the center of his life and his ambitions. He often said that the reason he kept on going as Rebbe was to sustain the yeshivah. The reason he poured so much energy into the yeshivah was for the ten *Bnai Aliyah* (spiritually gifted young people headed for great achievement in serving God) that he hoped the yeshivah would produce.

The yeshivah started out small. At first it had only two classes, and they were filled largely with the children of his own chasidim. But the yeshivah's reputation grew quickly, and, before long, hundreds of young people from all over Poland were studying there. During the two decades of its existence, the yeshivah trained thousands of students, some of whom grew into great Torah scholars and chasidic leaders all over Poland. Reb Kalonymus instituted a *Smichah* course, in which all facets of Jewish law were studied, with a special emphasis on the kinds of problems that might actually be encountered in the daily life of a community. In 1927 the first class of rabbinical students graduated from the course and were awarded their certificates of ordination at a celebration attended by many of the great rabbis and sages of Poland.

Reb Kalonymus took a personal interest in every aspect of the yeshivah's life. He supervised all the courses, tested the students from time to time, and shared with them his insights into the matters they were studying. From time to time he also invited groups of boys to his house to speak to them personally, in a more intimate setting, about Torah, Chasidism, and matters of the spirit. He tried to attend to each student's individual needs, problems, and desires, to as great a degree as time would allow.

He kept a sharp eye out for promising students, students who might be spiritually sensitive. He would attempt to fan the holy spark within them until it grew into a self-sustaining fire. His desire was to help develop great spiritual personalities who could turn on the world to God the way the disciples of the Baal Shem Tov did in the first few generations of the chasidic movement.

He supported the yeshivah financially at great personal cost. As mentioned earlier, almost all the money that came his way was immediately consigned to the yeshivah. While he and his family lived a life of poverty and debt, he poured lavish sums into the yeshivah. The more the yeshivah grew, the more his debts grew. He ignored his physical and financial health in deference to the yeshivah. He began to suffer acutely from arthritis and was ordered by his doctors to travel to a health spa, such as Marienbad and Karlsbad, with their warm springs, to convalesce and recover. He refused to go. "What will happen to the yeshivah in my absence?" he asked.

For the sake of the yeshivah, Reb Kalonymus was even prepared to work wonders. One of his chasidim had settled in London and had become very successful in business. At a certain point his luck turned; it seemed as if his competitors had found a way to ruin him and drive him out of business. He wrote to Reb Kalonymus with an urgent request for help. Reb Kalonymus sent him a reply: If you donate 14 × 14 pounds sterling for the sake of the yeshivah, you will gain the upper hand over your opponents. The chasid followed Reb Kalonymus's instructions, and immediately his luck changed: his competitors were foiled and he remained successful.

The efforts he made were not only for the yeshivah as a whole, but for every individual student who was in need. If one of his many students became ill, the Rebbe would take him back to his own home and nurse him there until he had returned to full strength. If a student was drafted into the Polish army despite the Rebbe's efforts to prevent it, he used every possible tactic to free him. He would pray for him, ask others to recite psalms for him, and even give him a *segulah*—an amulet or other sacred object, or an act to be performed—that would have the miraculous effect of guaranteeing an exemption for the pupil.

One extraordinary story about Reb Kalonymus revolves around just such an incident. One of the pupils at the yeshivah was drafted. Because he was healthy and of an exceptionally powerful build, he had virtually no chance of obtaining an exemption. Reb Kalonymus called him into his office before he was to appear before the draft board, dipped his own fingers in ashes from the stove that was burning there, and wrote something on the boy's forehead. He then took a piece of paper and with it he erased what he had written. He instructed the boy not to look directly into the face of anyone in the army office, or anyone on the street, until he returned to the yeshivah. The doctors at the draft board were shocked when they looked at the young man. He appeared deformed and monstrous to them, and they immediately sent him home with an exemption certificate. When the boy returned to the yeshivah he went to tell Reb Kalonymus the good news. "What did you do to my forehead?" he asked. "I wrote on it with a kind of writing that is used by the angels," Reb Kalonymus answered.

Reb Kalonymus also took an active role in assuring that all his students were happily married when their time for marriage came around. If a student was poor, Reb Kalonymus would assume all the expenses of the wedding. Reb Kalonymus saw himself as his students' father. If a student from an ordinary background had his heart set on marrying a certain girl whose family came from a distinguished line of scholars, and her parents were hesitating, Reb Kalonymus would say, "What? You don't want to be *mechutanim* (in-laws) with me?" Thus he lent his own prestigious lineage to all his students.

Education of the Spirit

Many great chasidic leaders had their own special areas of excellence. Some focused their energies on blazing new paths in Torah; others concentrated their efforts mainly on trying to help the stricken or impoverished among the Jewish people. Reb Kalonymus, accomplished as he was in both these spheres, was a specialist in spiritual education—in training the young generation in the path of Chasidism, the path that, as Reb Kalonymus often said, "leads upward toward God."

Reb Kalonymus's educational touch was transformative. This is what attracted so many chasidim, young and old, to his doorstep. When one chasidic rebbe was told about the miracles that another rebbe had performed, he exclaimed, "But the greatest of wonders is to turn people into chasidim!" At this kind of wonder Reb Kalonymus was exceptionally adept. With consummate skill and great compassion, he performed "surgery" of the heart and brain on his students. It was as if he took their souls into his hands and returned them cleansed and purified.

Chasidim tell that when Reb Avraham of Kalish, one of the disciples of the great Maggid of Mezeritch, was appointed rabbi in a certain town, he began his first sermon as follows: "Your last rabbi taught you the tactics of waging war against the evil inclination. He taught you how to shoot, but forgot to teach you how to aim the rifle in the right direction. You were left with the possibility that you might aim wrong, and the bullets might hit your own soul. Let me show you the right path, the way of aiming the rifle in the proper direction."

Reb Kalonymus Kalman's educational method focused similarly on guiding every person in the way that would be most effective for him, based on the particular needs and nature of his individual soul. And just as each person is different, so every generation is different and must be educated with an approach attentive to the nuances of its special characteristics. Otherwise, the teacher might find himself injuring—or alienating—the very audience he intended to help or heal.

The basic principles of Reb Kalonymus's educational method are expressed in *Chovat HaTalmidim—A Student's Obligation*—in both his introduction to parents and educators and in the book itself. This original volume quickly gained a wide audience. It is addressed to young Torah students, but the principles it outlines are of great benefit to every person, no matter what their age or stage in life. Reb Kalonymus once said that when he sat down to work on *Chovat HaTalmidim*, he would not begin to write until he had the image of a young student fixed in his mind, as if he were standing in front of him. The book itself is vivid and incisive at once, filled with the fruits of the imagination as well as the penetrating insights of the intellect. Essentially, this book is a call for a renewed intensity of spiritual life, of prayer and meditation and longing for God, and an exhortation to combat the various seductive ideologies as well as the exigencies of survival that were leading young Jews away from the path of Torah. The warmth of Reb Kalonymus's personality, as well as the Rebbe's deep concern for the future of the Jewish people, can be felt on every page. The fact that the generation Reb Kalonymus addressed with so much love and such concern was destined, for the most part, for the concentration camps and gas chambers adds another dimension of poignancy to his writing.

Reb Kalonymus himself thought very highly of *Chovat Ha-Talmidim*. Once, speaking to Reb Eliyahu Lipshitz of Gritza, he remarked, "If I didn't know that I was the author, I would never believe that it was within my capacity to write such a book." On Simchat Torah it was customary for his chasidim to recount, during one of the *hakafot*, their rebbe's family tree, which led back to King David. Reb Kalonymus asked to be mentioned, on one occasion, as the author of *Chovat HaTalmidim*.

This was the only book Reb Kalonymus wrote that was published during his lifetime. As we shall mention later, several volumes of his unpublished writings were found after the war under a stone in the rubble of Warsaw, where he had hidden them before he was taken to die. Reb Kalonymus also published several articles, called *Bnai Machshavot Tovot* (People of Good Thoughts). These pamphlets reflected his belief that it was not only what people said or did that was important, but what people thought. Reb Kalonymus tried to organize groups that would meet together and work on their thoughts and on drawing close to God through intensive spiritual work and meditation.

The Second World War

One bright day toward the end of the Jewish calendar year of 5699, World War II broke out. With great ferocity the Nazi army began a total war against Poland, a war of great cruelty and destruction. Their aim was to conquer all of Poland as quickly as possible, so they set out toward the capital city of Warsaw. Reb Kalonymus was in Piaseczno when the war broke out. He immediately headed back to Warsaw, which was being bombarded by the Nazi air force. Death and destruction filled the entire city.

All roads led to Warsaw for Polish Jewry during those dark times. From the cities and towns surrounding Warsaw, thousands and thousands of Jewish refugees poured into the capital. Among them were Piaseczno chasidim, who streamed toward the Rebbe's home, hoping to find comfort there in the midst of the terrible storm. They did indeed find both material and spiritual comfort there. The Rebbe did not allow the battle raging outside to disturb the spiritual devotions of the Days of Awe. While bombs exploded outside the window of the synagogue, he continued to pray in his customary place—by the window, in the corner. He prayed that year with wondrous concentration and attachment to God, as if he were not in this world at all, and so did his chasidim. It was later said that the chasidim of Piaseczno never prayed with such feeling, with such broken hearts filled with longing, as they did then, as they stood at the brink of the abyss.

Reb Kalonymus's chasidim felt a ray of divine comfort simply in the fact that they merited to be in his presence during these terrible times. One chasid later remembered those times as follows: "The night of Yom Kippur, bombs were falling everywhere; explosions punctuated every passing moment with their exclamations. I was with a small group of friends that night, and we decided not to move from the Rebbe's doorstep the whole night. We just wanted to be near him. As the first light of morning streamed over the horizon we heard the Rebbe recite the morning blessings. When he got to the words 'Train us in your Torah, and make us cleave to your mitzvot,' the Rebbe stopped and began to repeat these words over and over again for about twenty minutes, with a voice filled with such incredible attachment to God and such longing that it seemed as if his soul might expire from passion. The sound of his voice filled us with a feeling of sweetness that melted and flowed into all our limbs."

That year, 5700, Yom Kippur was celebrated on Shabbat. The following Monday, the Nazi troops attacked Warsaw with renewed force and even greater fury. They bombarded the city from all sides. Within a few days, 30,000 Jews had died. On Tuesday a bomb fell close to the Rebbe's house. His son, Elimelech Benzion, was struck by shrapnel. He was severely injured and was taken to the nearest hospital. A few hours later, a bomb exploded outside the hospital gates. The Rebbe's daughter-in-law, Gittel, who was waiting anxiously for news of her husband, was killed instantly, along with her aunt Channa, Reb Kalonymus's sister-in-law, who had been the daughter-in-law of his teacher and father-in-law, Reb Yerachmiel Moshe.

The next day, the Polish army defending Warsaw surrendered, and the Nazis marched into the city. The city looked like a battlefield, filled with corpses, blood flowing in the streets, buildings in ruin. The condition of the Rebbe's son, meanwhile, had taken a turn for the worse. It became necessary to transport him to a better-equipped hospital. This was an extremely dangerous mission, for the occupying Nazi troops were now storming through the city, drunk with victory, killing and destroying without mercy. In addition, the Rebbe needed to find a way to bring the bodies of his daughter-in-law and sister-in-law to a Jewish burial.

Even under these exceptional circumstances, his chasidim again had the opportunity to see evidence of Reb Kalonymus's tremendous love of the Jewish people, which showed itself in his willingness to sacrifice himself for a single individual.

After Reb Kalonymus's daughter-in-law and sister-in-law had been felled by the explosion, their bodies lay by the gate of the hospital. It was the practice of chasidic women, in times of emergency, to wear all their jewelry on their persons in case they needed to flee or to bribe an official or enemy. A young Piaseczno chasid approached the bodies and stripped them of the jewelry, in order to save these heirlooms of the house of Kozhnitz from falling into enemy hands. He was arrested by the Nazis and was accused of robbing the dead, a crime that carried with it a severe punishment—made all the more severe by the fact that his captors were the Gestapo. When Reb Kalonymus heard about the incident, he dropped his other pressing concerns—his son's condition and the burial of his relatives—and endangered his life by running to the Gestapo, from whose clutches, so it was rightly said, Jews did not return alive. This he did in order to testify that the boy's intentions had been honest, and to plead for his life.

God only knows how Reb Kalonymus was saved from the talons

of the Gestapo beasts, but somehow they were convinced by his testimony, and they promised to investigate the incident further. They invited him to return the next day, which was the first day of Succot. That next morning the Rebbe set out once again for the Gestapo, as his family and followers prayed for him and waited anxiously, fearing once more for his life. A few hours later he returned, along with the boy. His eyes were filled with the joy and satisfaction of having saved a Jewish soul. In the midst of all the suffering, his family and friends let out a cry of joy as well.

The first night of Succot, Reb Kalonymus ate in a corner of the courtyard in a small succah, placed there secretly out of fear of the Nazis. The next day, in the synagogue, the Rebbe began to daven as he did on every holiday, as if the world around him were not in flames. The Rebbe prayed at great length and recited the prayer "The soul of all that is alive will bless Your name" with particular and astonishing devotion. One particular young man, who regularly served as the cantor, was afraid he would break into tears in the middle of his devotions because of all the evil that had befallen the house of the Rebbe, and he declined to serve in his usual capacity. An older chasid was chosen in his stead. He gathered up all his remaining strength and sang the prayers according to the melodies specially composed for the Succot holiday. But as the Torah was taken out, and the special Kozhnitzer melody was sung, something broke inside him; he began to weep bitterly. The Rebbe immediately called out: "Nu, Yom Tov!" (It's a holiday!). His congregation tried to fulfill his wish not to disregard the holiday, and to keep up the joyous atmosphere even in the midst of the flames.

The second day of Succot passed in the same way. As the day ended and Shabbat began, Reb Kalonymus was forced to drink the bitter cup of misfortune to the last drop. Toward evening, Reb Elimelech Benzion asked for a cup of wine to recite the Kiddush. He said the Kiddush with his last breaths, and then he died. His father was at his bedside.

Reb Kalonymus recited the blessing "Blessed is the true Judge" with great love. Because of the holiness of the holiday, he did not allow his sorrow to show. He conducted himself on Shabbat in similar fashion. His son's body was carried back to his house, as he continued to celebrate Shabbat with his chasidim—punctuating the

meal with words of Torah, even giving out *shirayim* (portions of food
from which the rebbe has taken a bit—the chasidim thus literally
break bread with their master). Only after the Shabbat was over
did he burst into tears and begin to mourn, in heartrending cries,
his terrible losses. To one of his close friends he said, "I have already
been defeated in this war. May God help the people of Israel to
emerge victorious."

The intermediate days of Succot passed, and Simchat Torah
approached amidst this atmosphere of sadness. Usually, in better
times, the celebration on Simchat Torah lasted until the middle of
the night. This year was different. Only a small number of chasidim
participated in the prayer service. The *hakafot* (encircling of the ark
while dancing with the Torahs) were accomplished quickly, and
almost everyone immediately returned home because of the evil and
dangerous presence of Nazi soldiers outside. Only a handful of
young men who were very attached to the Rebbe remained because
they sensed that his soul was filled with a gathering passion, a
turbulence that might still break forth at any moment.

One outstanding student, Reb Eliezer Bain, who survived the
war, was there that night. The following words are his:

Those moments of happiness are engraved on my heart forever.
Less than ten of us remained. We were broken-hearted and
depressed. Suddenly the Rebbe walked to the stand in front
of the holy ark and began to sing the famous Karlin melody
for *Ayshet Chayil* (Woman of Valor). He sang with deep feeling,
passion, and devotion for more than an hour. The longing and
thirst for God in his voice were remarkable. His fiery soul burst
out of all its boundaries. He was not aware that anyone else
was there—he was completely beyond this world. His eyes
streamed with tears. His voice was so beautiful! None of us
could believe that he had just lost his only son.

Slowly our fear and depression melted away. We forgot
the whole world. What did we care for the war? What did all
the tribulations have to do with us? We forgot everything—
the satanic Nazis who controlled the streets, the explosions,
the casualties. We hovered in another world. The Rebbe's
singing got stronger and stronger, and we were all swept up

into it. It seemed as if all of us and everything were ascending with the flame that was bursting from his heart. Each of us actually felt how the innocent dove, the congregation of Israel above—the woman of valor, the crown of her husband, was uniting with her beloved (may His name be blessed) on this holy night. And even in this evil hour, a time when God's face was hidden, we could hear God's voice from behind a mist of darkness and cloud and fog, beckoning us to rejoice with Him. God was not hiding! We had everything we desired—we were enjoying the radiance of the divine presence.

Disaster Follows Disaster

The situation in Warsaw continued to worsen. Every day, Jews were kidnapped and sent to forced labor camps. Whole streets were emptied. There was no mistaking the final intent of the Nazis—the total destruction of Polish Jewry. The Rebbe ordered those who were in the most immediate danger to take every opportunity to flee. His chasidim did not want to abandon him during this terrible catastrophe; moreover, they wished to remain near his comforting presence. But he ordered them in no uncertain terms to attempt escape. They scattered in every direction.

One group of chasidim, who managed to reach Vilna after many dangerous adventures, were surprised to receive a telegram toward the end of 5700 (autumn 1940). It was a message of encouragement from the Rebbe, written in German. The telegram gave them some much needed new strength. About a year later they had reached Japan, and from there they exchanged letters with the Rebbe, who stood guard at his post like a devoted soldier until his last day, encouraging and comforting his congregation in all the many corners of the world to which they had been scattered.

From the Depths

"Has an angel ever tasted of the suffering a Jews feels when he is being beaten? Or his shame when he is being chased and humiliated? Or his fear or his suffering when there is no food to be found?"

These words were said by the rebbe from Piaseczno, the last rebbe carrying the torch of Chasidism amidst the satanic kingdom of the Warsaw Ghetto. He continued to lead his chasidim, to strengthen their spirits, to sit at the Shabbat table and speak words of Torah that were filled with holiness and the sanctification of God's name, along with unceasing words of praise and advocacy for the people of Israel. The words of Torah that he said in the ghetto on Shabbat and on holidays were saved from the ashes of Warsaw and published later in the book *Aish Kodesh* (Holy Fire). His words there describe, with painful clarity, the terrible conditions in the ghetto, and they give expression to the hurt the Rebbe felt in witnessing the suffering of his people. Every line of the book is heart-rending. Its screams break through the skies. The Holocaust terror, which is the black fire in which the Rebbe wrote his words in white fire, shakes and frightens the reader.

Warsaw, in those terrible days, was totally under the administration of the Holocaust kingdom. All of Poland had been ruined, trampled underfoot—and the Warsaw Ghetto? It was hell, nothing less or more. The S.S. ruled the streets and stole Jews away for "work." The children? They were simply sent off to slaughter. The Jews wandered around in a state of shock. No one understood what was happening.

In one tiny corner of the ghetto, the Rebbe of Piaseczno continued to live surrounded by an aura of holiness. Streams of comfort flowed from him, healing wounded hearts, bloodied souls. "God's salvation can come in the blink of an eye," he told the people. "Even if the sword is on your throat, do not give up hope of God's mercy," he said. He stood guard at his post as if to prevent people from forgetting, in the midst of their suffering, the Torah's teaching that man is made in the image of God. He went to tremendous lengths to keep every letter of the *Shulchan Aruch* (Code of Jewish Law). After all the mikvahs (ritual baths) in Warsaw had been ruined, he devoted himself to ensuring that the women's mikvah in Piaseczno, where his chasidim traveled at great danger to their lives, remained open. He also risked his life to initiate infants into the covenant of Abraham—for he was a skilled mohel (surgeon for ritual circumcisions). The circumcisions had to be held under the cover of complete secrecy.

Purim 5741 (1941) arrived. No one in the Warsaw Ghetto even thought about celebrating—but the Rebbe insisted. He recalled the *Zohar*'s statement that "Purim is like Yom Kippurim" and said that just as on Yom Kippur one is commanded to fast, so on Purim one is commanded to be joyful. One *must* be joyful. This is what he argued, and he even succeeded in igniting some sparks of joy in the souls and broken bodies of the Jews. Waves of hunger passed through their bodies—but their souls were sustained by the always fresh spiritual energy flowing from the Rebbe with unceasing consistency.

Out of the 600,000 Jews of Warsaw, only a few thousand survived. The one ray of light in the city was the Shultz Shoe Factory, which was kept open by the Nazis to provide shoes for the Nazi troops. If you had a work permit that indicated you were employed by this factory, you were safe from the *aktions* and transports leading to the death camps. Many of the leading rabbis and chasidic rebbes of Warsaw had been given work permits for this factory, and among them was Reb Kalonymus Kalman. There, he was surrounded by a small group of his students and numerous others who now clung to him for support. He spoke words of Torah and Chasidism to them the whole day through. He spoke about spiritual matters that urgently weighed on him and his companions—matters such as self-sacrifice and giving one's life for God. In this fashion he encouraged everyone around him and planted faith and trust in their hearts.

Yet his turbulent soul knew no limits. He tried to storm heaven with his questions: *"How can the world go on?"* he asked in words that were published in *Aish Kodesh* after his death. "Why doesn't the world return to primordial chaos? When the ten martyrs [Rabbi Akiva and nine other great Jewish sages] were executed by the Romans, the angels protested: 'Is this the reward for devotion to the Torah?' A heavenly voice answered them: 'If one more word is uttered I will return the world to chaos.' And yet now innocent children, pure angels, and also the greatest and holiest among us, are being murdered and slaughtered just because they are Jews. Jews, who are greater than angels! And the whole atmosphere, all of space, is filled with their cries that should break every iron curtain. 'This is Torah and this is its reward?' they shout. And yet the world is not turned upside down. Everything goes on as usual."

During these final months in Warsaw, Reb Kalonymus worked

on the manuscript that would later be known as *Aish Kodesh*. His original title was *Chiddushei Torah miShnot haZaam* 5700, 5701, 5702 (*Torah Novellae from the Years of Wrath*, 1940, 1941, 1942). This manuscript, along with several others he had completed before and during the war years, was found under a rock in the destroyed Warsaw Ghetto with a letter from Reb Kalonymus containing instructions as to where they should be sent when they were discovered. At the time that he was writing *Aish Kodesh*, people around him did not understand. Who was he writing for? But the rebbe himself, it is now clear, knew that he was headed for death, and he was in constant preparation for the moment when he would give himself to God. Yet he wanted the book saved. He wanted the next generation to hear his testimony. And miraculously the book *was* saved, to be published in its original Hebrew in Jerusalem in 1960.

On the eve of Passover 5703 (1943), the few remaining Jews of Warsaw revolted against the Nazis. The Nazis decided to destroy the ghetto. They turned on the gas pipes and exploded building after building; the whole ghetto went up in flames. The handful of Jews who remained alive were then taken to the death camps—Reb Kalonymus Kalman among them. The last months of his life were spent in a Nazi concentration camp near Lublin. He retained his holiness and purity until the very end, and he prepared himself to die sanctifying God's name, a single holy flame. Reb Kalonymus was burned in the oven of the Treblinka concentration camp on the 4th of Cheshvan, 5704 (November 1943).

A STUDENT'S OBLIGATION

The purpose of this work is to penetrate into the depths of the student, to reveal his soul, to train him in Torah, divine service, the ways of *Chasidut*, and to bind the soul to God. It also contains injunctions and warnings as to how to conduct one's thought, speech, and deed.

Appended thereto are three essays that explain some of the mysteries of *Chasidut* and principles of Kabbalah that are necessary for the chasidic service of students and young scholars, each according to his level.

—from the title page of the original Hebrew edition

PART I

REVEALING THE SOUL AND TRAINING THE
STUDENT IN THE WAYS OF *CHASIDUT*

AUTHOR'S INTRODUCTION

A DISCUSSION
WITH TEACHERS AND PARENTS

King Solomon, in Proverbs, advises: "Educate (*chanoch*) a child according to his own path, and even when he grows old, he will not stray from it." The most essential task of education is to teach in such a way that the child will not stray from the path we have set for him, even when he grows older and is no longer under his father's supervision. To truly educate is not just a matter of getting a child to follow your commands, or even of accustoming a child to do good deeds. True education is a much greater and more galvanizing process. Commanding and habituating children to a certain way of life are merely tools that must be used when educating them in the path of God.

Rashi, in commenting on a passage in Deuteronomy 20:5, explains the word *chinuch* (which in the passage translates as "dedicated" but which is also the word for education) as meaning "to begin." Obviously, one would not use the word *chinuch* to mean "begin" in every context. For example, in the phrase in the Talmud (*Pesachim* 116a) describing the Haggadah of Passover ("[the Haggadah] begins with shame and ends with praise"), we would never think of using the word *chinuch* for "begin." Nor would it be appropriate to use the word *chinuch* in tractate *Sanhedrin*, where it says of the judicial procedure of the high rabbinic court: "We begin from the side."

In *Parshat Lech Lecha*, Rashi gives us a deeper insight into the word *chinuch* in commenting on the word *chanichav*. This word means, according to Rashi: "He educated him toward the fulfillment of the commandments. The root CH-N-CH implies the initial entry of a person or an object into a trade or path that is his destiny. Thus we find the root CH-N-CH referring to the education of a child, the consecration of the altar in the holy temple, and the dedication of a house."

There are strict parameters for the use of the word. One would not use it to refer to a craftsman who was beginning to work on a specific job but was already expert in his trade, or for a house that was just starting to be built. The proper usage of the word *chinuch* is for a person just beginning to teach himself a skill, or for a building that has already been built and is just beginning to be used. Rashi is precise in writing of "the initial entry of a person or object . . . which is his destiny," because the word *chinuch* refers not to a trade or skill, but to the potential, the predilection and capability that a person might possess, which makes him suited for a particular task. In a house or vessel, *chinuch* refers to the preparation that has made a house or a vessel suitable for a certain task or usage. The word *chinuch* is a special word that implies the realization of the already inherent capacity of a person or object; the actualization of a potential. This potential will remain hidden unless we bring it out. Our task is to cause the potential to emerge, to accomplish the *chinuch* that will transform the person into a skilled artisan; will cause the house or vessels to fulfill their functions, each room according to what it is best suited for, every vessel or instrument according to the task for which it was designed and prepared.

When referring to the education of children, therefore, *chinuch* means stimulating the growth and development of what each child is suited for by his very nature. This quality or potential may be found in him only in very small measure, in total hiddenness; the task of the educator is to uncover it. Since a Jewish child has the spirit of God, the breath of the Lord, hidden and concealed within him from the very moment of his birth, it is necessary to raise him and educate him to bring out and reveal this godliness and allow it to flourish. If this is done, the child will grow into a faithful Jew, a servant of God. He will have an independent desire for Torah and will not stray as he gets older. A person whose educational strategy is one of commands and even habituation cannot be so sure that the child will continue to practice as he becomes independent. This, then, is the command of King Solomon: "Educate the child"— penetrate to his inner being and reveal the holiness of Israel that is hidden there. Only then will the child not stray from the path when he grows older.

King Solomon, however, does not just inform us here of the goal of education—to reach the child in a way that will keep him on the path even after he has matured and grown independent. In the passage "Educate the child according to his way . . ." he also illuminates for us the way and the means through which this goal can be accomplished. Someone who is trying to educate through command and habituation need not pay any attention to his child or student—to his nature, to the way he thinks, or to his other distinguishing characteristics. The command itself—do this or do that—is all that is needed. Nor is it necessary to deal with each student separately. A single command can suffice for an entire age group, for it is not the student or the child that is important, but the person giving the commands: he has commanded, and that is everything.

An educator, however, who wishes to uncover the soul of the child that lies hidden and concealed within him, who wants to help it grow and to ignite it so it will burn with a heavenly fire, upwards, towards the holy, so that the student's entire being, including his physical body, will increase in holiness and will long for God's Torah, such an educator must adapt himself attentively to the student, must penetrate into the midst of his limited consciousness and small-mindedness, until he reaches the hidden soul-spark. Then he can help it emerge, blossom, and grow.

The education of each and every child must therefore be different, depending on his nature, mind, character, and all his other unique qualities. The educator must become aware of these qualities; it will not suffice for him to know himself and his own mind alone, since everything depends on the student who is being educated. It is not enough to utilize his own mind and his own strength in activating, commanding, and instructing his students; he must grasp the student's mind and the student's strength, working and acting within the parameters of each child's abilities. What he commands and instructs one child should be different from what he commands and instructs the next child, whose nature, will, and personality are completely different from the first. And this is what King Solomon is hinting to us—"educate the child according to his path"—according to the particular path of each and every child.

Our goal here is not to teach the craft of pedagogy—how to utilize the student's mind in various ways, how to broaden his understanding and knowledge of the meaning of the Torah. For what we are seeking now is not the student's intellect alone: we are interested in the whole student. We wish to connect the *Nefesh*, *Ruach*, and *Neshamah* of Jewish children to the God of Israel, so that they will emerge as Jews who revere the word of the Lord and direct all their desires toward Him.

Every father and every teacher knows that their children and students will not remain children forever, but will eventually grow; in years, and possibly in Torah knowledge and spiritual devotion. Yet there exist fathers and teachers who are concerned only with what they see right now. Since all they see right now are children, the goal of their efforts is to educate their charges to become good children. They wish to infuse them with only a child's measure of Torah and awe of God. This they consider sufficient. But a teacher or parent who does this is sinning against God and against His people. Fathers and teachers must know that their task is to educate and uncover children of the Lord and giants of Israel. They must see the children sitting in front of them as great souls still immature; their task is to get them to grow and flourish. A teacher is a gardener in the garden of God, assigned to cultivate it and guard it from harm. Even if some of the children seem rebellious, or flawed in their character, the teacher must know that the nature of soul-seeds, of unripe angels, is to taste bitter as they are ripening and to be filled with nectar in their maturity. Neither the nature, nor any particular quality of a Jewish child, is absolutely evil. This is what the holy Baal Shem Tov and his disciples have taught us. What is necessary is just to know how to use these qualities and how to help them develop and grow. For example, a particular child may be very stubborn—which is a character flaw. His teacher may suffer greatly because of the child's stubbornness. Yet if the teacher were to reflect, he would realize that when this child matures and receives as his own the yoke of Torah and of service to God, he will perform all his service of God with great stubbornness and self-sacrifice. He will not be frivolous or inclined to vacillate but will be the kind of Jew the *Midrash* described: In all matters of devotion, he will be as strong as the wall of a fortress.

Take another example—a child whose personality has an angry quality. True, the way that the child is expressing his anger at this point in time is extremely bad. But are we able to therefore decide that he is from a corrupt source, that he is inferior and base by nature? If an idiot heard the praises of the *etrog* fruit, grabbed a seed or an unripe *etrog* fruit, bit into it, and then shrieked and howled at how bitter and poisonous-tasting a fruit the *etrog* is, would we not laugh at him and consider him a great fool?

It is impossible to predict ahead of time how great a benefit may emerge, through the efforts of the principal or teacher, from the very anger of the angry child. One must penetrate into his inner life, bring him close, ignite his heart and his soul until they are dedicated to God. Then his anger will be transformed into a fire from above. All of his acts of devotion will burn like fiery coals, and all the words that he will speak to God, in prayer and in Torah, will thunder from a voice of fire. See the commentary of the Rav on the *Siddur* if you wish to confirm this. There he explains as follows: "The heat that is in anger stems from the heat of the heart. Any person that is hot-tempered by nature has a heart that is inclined to burn with fiery flames of desire (for God)." And certainly if such a person finds within himself any stain or defect, he will be filled

with tremendous rage and wrath. His good inclination will immediately rouse him to anger and indignation, and he will cast away
and even destroy his evil inclination from out of his very midst. If
he finds it necessary to chastise a friend for a spiritual failing, he
will not insult or degrade him, but will speak simply, with words
as hot as a boiling furnace that will rush from him like a stormy
sea. In this way, he will succeed in melting and uprooting all the
stains and soul-sicknesses of his friends as well.

We should be heartsick, however, and our hair should stand
on end when we see the way the younger generation has turned to
heresy and has lost all spiritual discipline. They possess neither faith,
nor fear of God, nor knowledge of Torah. They have actually come
to despise God and His servants, the people of Israel. The admin-
istrators and deans of the yeshivot, who are totally immersed in the
life of the yeshivah and its students and encounter only the elite of
our youth, are unaware of the gravity of this problem. They console
themselves, saying: "Yes, it may be true that many of our young
people have freed themselves of any commitment to Torah, but
still, Israel has not been abandoned. There are still young men, sons
of our people, outstanding in their Judaic scholarship, whose heart
is steadfast with the Lord." Poke your heads outside of the four
cubits of your yeshivah! You will see the great mass of people who
have broken from the observances of our faith, may God have mercy
on them and us. You will see houses of study where the destruction
of Jerusalem has been reenacted. Once they were filled with Torah
scholars; now they have become empty, and instead, groups and
organizations whose goals include the dissemination of heresy and
the rejection of Torah have been filled with members. In former
good days, even the laborers and merchants who were not necessarily scholars were at least faithful Jews. Now their youth have
denied Torah, have wandered and fallen into a great depth of spiritual darkness. Should we be satisfied with merely the handful of
students who attend our yeshivot? Is this the entirety of the people
of Israel?

And are we really so sure of our yeshivah students? Have we
done everything we should do concerning their education? Yes, we
can be confident that the students who have reached the upper level
of classes, and especially those who have already begun to instruct

others and render halachic judgments, and have filled themselves with Torah and acts of devotion, will remain within the holy palace of Judaism and of divine service. But will all our students reach the upper level of classes? Many of our students in the lower grades will be unable to continue their studies much longer. They will leave the yeshivah to become merchants or laborers, either of their own free will, or by force of circumstances. As the *Midrash* says: "A thousand enter to study, and only one emerges to instruct (from among the whole group)." Do we have any assurance that, a short time after having left the yeshivah, these students will not divest themselves of the commandments and, God forbid, cease to observe the Shabbat? Why should we not strategize on how to influence them while they are still in our schools? All the children that eventually throw off the yoke of Torah are in our hands during their childhood and grow up in our schools. Why should we abandon them without binding them and their souls to God and to His Torah in their childhood in a way that will last until their old age?

We tend to look at the straying of our youth as if they alone were to blame and we were completely innocent. God, however, declared the following about his relationship to Avraham: "I have made Myself known to him in order that he command his children and his household after him to guard the path of God (Genesis 18:19)." Every generation in Israel is a link in the chain of our heritage, a chain whose beginning stretches back to Avraham and whose end will reach our righteous Messiah (may he come soon). Every generation receives its faith, its Torah, and its sense of awe before God from the generation that preceded it. They take what they have received, serve the Lord with it, and pass it on to the next generation. "In order that he command his children" is the mainstay of our existence. And if this chain has been broken in our generation, and we are not succeeding in our attempt to pass the Torah on to the next generation, can we truthfully put all the blame on them? Are they not from the seed of Avraham, Isaac, and Jacob? Are they not also holy souls? Why deceive ourselves with the faulty excuse that we want to pass on the tradition, that it is their fault for refusing to receive it? For however much they are at fault and however true it is that they refuse to listen, try and imagine what would have become of these same "criminals" in earlier generations.

No matter how much they are to blame, no matter how flawed their souls are with defects that did not afflict previous generations, would they still have refused to accept their place in the chain? Would not most, if not all of them have been *tzaddikim*, or, at the very least, simple, faithful Jews? This is because their parents, and the whole generation that would have preceded them, would have taken such great care in educating the next generation, as they did in fulfilling all of God's word—much more care than we take now. They would have burned like fiery torches and would not have looked on calmly and coldly as the younger generation was spiritually drowning and as God's people were falling headlong into heretical ideologies. They would have risen and dedicated their whole soul and might to saving them and educating them, using various stratagems and pretexts.

Are we really devoid of responsibility, we, the older generation, their educators, upon whom the responsibility for passing on the awareness of God's holiness, the knowledge of His Torah, and dedication to His service rests? Can we truly say, with an untroubled soul, "Our hands have not spilled this blood," the lifeblood of the Jewish souls that are descending to spiritual darkness? What will we answer the One who dwells on high, how will we justify ourselves before He whose abode is in the heavens? He will come to count His spiritual army on earth, and among them the young generation, the sheep of His flock, whom He left for safekeeping in our hands, relying on our sense of responsibility. He will roar from on high, and shout from the place of Holiness: "Where are My children, whom I love tenderly, the children of Avraham, Isaac, and Jacob? Where are my children?"

And if we truly want to return to God and to straighten out what we have made crooked, we must acknowledge our own share of guilt. For even if they are flawed in a way that previous generations of young people were not, this does not justify our neglecting them, our failure to investigate and discover the source of their soul-sickness while they are still young, while it is still possible to know how and with what they can be healed. Can the father or guardian of a child claim to be innocent of blame when his child has lost a limb, if the infection that led to this maiming started off as a small cut that could have been easily healed, and it spread out only through neglect?

For all that the young people are to blame, for all their corruption, we cannot simply justify ourselves by sighing bitterly. We must feel pain and heartache because of our neglectfulness as well. Only then will we be able to search for a way to take action, to repair, to heal our nation's brokenness. And we must pray to God to show us His path, and to remove the heart of stone from our children so that together we can merit to serve Him in truth and with a full heart. Then we can be "Israel, in whom You are glorified," and we can say "Look at this child whom I have placed before You."

With strong principles and with hard facts—not with guesses and presumptions—we must explain, first of all, what the difference is between the generations. Why, in previous generations, did just about any kind of education seem effective? Almost every student of every teacher and every child of every father were servants of God, while now this is not the case.

The simplest and most important reason is that today's youth consider themselves grown-up before their time. This is not simply a wild guess; the whole world, actually, is lamenting about the same phenomenon. Our purpose is not to explain the reason or cause for this attitude among young people, but the fact is that it does exist. An atmosphere of foolishness has surrounded the young people of our time, in which they have come to think of themselves as grown-up and independent—in their opinions and in their desires—though their mind is still upside down and their desires unripe and bitter. Our sages have told us all along (*Sotah* 49) that in the time preceding the coming of the Messiah, arrogance would be rampant. To think of oneself as trustworthy, secure, and authoritative in one's own opinions is surely arrogant. This trait has caught fire to such an extent that one is sometimes astonished to encounter this independent spirit and false strength bursting forth in very small children who already consider themselves grown men and women.

There are two ways in which this trait results in harm. Firstly, it causes the child to see any guide, teacher, or educator as a foreign overlord who has come to rule over him with a strong hand, and to strip him of his independent mind and will. This causes a feeling of opposition or even hatred to arise within the child, directed at his teachers and his father. As a result, he does not really absorb their instruction and take it to heart, but only concentrates on plans

to escape their control. The second effect may be even more dam-
aging. In former days, when children's feelings of independence and
maturity did not develop so rapidly, before the child was ready, his
feelings, his opinions and, in general, his entire outlook and all his
aspirations also did not develop prematurely. A child was like a clean
sheet of paper, ready to receive the images and words that his
teachers and rabbis would impress upon his pure soul. And his
teachers, indeed, fed him like an ox. They put not only their words,
but their souls into the children. They chiseled their teaching onto
his soul. Then, when the child's feelings and aspirations slowly began
to blossom and grow, he found soil made fertile by the richness of
Torah and the oil of holy anointment. His newly blossoming feelings and aspirations added strength and an extra measure of soul to
quicken the growth and enlarge the scope of the Torah and dedication to God that his teachers had implanted within him. This was
the process through which he was educated, and through this atmosphere of holiness he developed and grew.

Now, however, since the child's sense of independence and
feeling of maturity becomes defined and developed before it should,
his aspirations, opinions, and his outlook also develop rapidly, when
they have not had a chance to ripen and are still bitter and poisonous.
Stimulated by these feelings, the child begins to think about and
investigate everything, including matters that are forbidden, as if
he were a completely independent person. He begins to feel and
to be moved through emotions that have not had a chance to ripen.
From opinions and feelings and actions whose source is harmful,
can we expect anything other than harmful aspirations and a harmful
outlook?

If we penetrate into the child's soul and reflect on its workings,
examining it delicately and truthfully, we will find that usually a
child does not turn away from God all at once. He does not violate
the Shabbat, nor leave the Bet Midrash for the theaters, in one fell
swoop. The Talmud, in tractate Shabbat 105, testifies: "This is the
way the evil inclination practices its craft: today it says 'do such
and such' and tomorrow it says 'do so and so.' " With our superficial
vision, we see the process of corruption only when it begins to be
manifested in action. Our children do not start off right away committing grievous transgressions; they descend level by level, in grad-

uated steps. But we must be aware that before a young person actually commits even the most insignificant sin, he has been experiencing a gradual inner crisis that began a year or more earlier. His opinions became infected slowly, almost imperceptibly. From this infection, a very delicate shift in his thinking arises, and he begins to look at Torah and devotion to God as he would at something degraded, as a waste of time. The outside world, meanwhile, in all its folly, its crassness and its wantonness, he begins to see as beautiful and good. The smallest cause can result in the initial infection; it begins as very minute, and has little effect at first on him or his actions. His teachers, and even his close friends, do not recognize any change in him. Slowly, this infection sinks deeper into his soul and expands in his mind until it reaches his flesh. All of a sudden there is shocking news: he has abandoned the house of God and fallen into a deep pit of spiritual darkness.

Mostly, this internal disease emanates from the feelings of egotistical independence and contrariness we have described. Since the child feels himself to have already become a fully independent being, feelings of opposition and even hatred, directed at his parents and teachers, spring up within him. This feeling of opposition to his parents and teachers that has been aroused does not remain confined to their personalities; it includes a resistance to everything they have tried to teach him as well. He begins to look at all their behavior and their whole path of life—the path of holiness—with contempt and hostility.

In short: in the past, every parent and teacher was well able to educate Jewish children and to instruct them in the path of God. Even if they did not carefully educate them along the lines which King Solomon alluded to—according to the inner path of each child, his way of thinking and his unique core—and all that they did was to habituate them in the performance of the mitzvot, they would still succeed. This is because a child in those generations, in his childhood and even in his youth, was an unblemished soul. Moreover, the child himself was aware of his own inner emptiness and of the darkness that was the condition of his mind, and thus had an inner thirst to hear the word of God from every guide or teacher. Even though at times he might go through periods of wildness and of refusal to listen, he himself would afterwards feel that he had done wrong and that his father or teacher, who had chastised or even hit him, was righteous and thus it was he who was the criminal. He would feel downhearted and would take it upon himself to listen to his parents and teachers from then on and to abnegate his will before theirs. Little by little, he would absorb God's Torah and would become a faithful Jew. Some of these children might wind up being greater scholars than others, but all would definitely grow up and remain real Jews, servants of God.

This is not the case in our times, when children prematurely develop a well-defined sense of independence and ego; and feelings, aspirations, and a general outlook emerge while yet unripe. This causes alienation and hostility between children and their parents. Children of our generation who had the potential and capability that would enable them to be faithful Jews have grown up and disappeared; they have been transformed into enemies; they laugh at us and scorn us and our faith. King Solomon foresaw this in his divine wisdom, and admonished us: "Educate the child according to his path," not merely by giving him orders but with true education, education that conforms to the path of each individual child.

Earlier we said that each Jewish soul is a storehouse of holiness; the question is only how to activate this holiness. Concerning this matter as well, it is true that the Jewish child has been moved by the spirit of the times, which has swept through all of the world's youth and results in the premature emergence and definition of the young personality. Yet this emergent personality is still a Jewish personality! It is up to us to bring our minds down toward him, toward his personality, in order to be able to grasp hold of him and influence him toward holiness before he is transformed into our enemy. Moshe, our teacher, the prophets, and all the *tzaddikim* similarly adapted themselves, descending from their high spiritual levels to concern themselves with even our physical needs. Would we not be sinning were we to abandon these children without adapting ourselves to each and every child, in order to educate them according to their own path while they are still at the critical point when it will be determined whether they become faithful servants of God or, God forbid, sinners? We must adapt ourselves and speak their language, practically turning ourselves into children in order to speak to them according to the way they think and the level they are on.

It is not sufficient to simply teach the child that it is his duty to listen to his teachers and that's all, for this alone will not have any effect. In the end he will see his teacher as an opponent, a foreign despot, as we have already said. The most important thing is to make him understand the following: he must know that he himself is his own most basic and important educator. He is not a mere child or youth, but a shoot planted by God in the vineyard of Israel. God has placed upon him the duty of causing this shoot to grow, of cultivating it—himself—until it becomes a great tree, a tree of life. He must make of it—of himself—a servant of God, a righteous person, great in Torah knowledge. Meanwhile, since his mind and spirit are still small, since there is much Torah he has not yet learned, and his evil inclination is already dancing within him—out of fear of God, fear of sin, fear of causing the destruction of the vineyard of the Lord of Hosts—he must listen to God's Torah and to His ways, as taught by his father and his teachers, both in regard to those matters mentioned specifically in the Torah or the *Shulchan Aruch*, and in regard to those that are not. The Torah admonishes us so many times to listen to our parents and teachers! "Ask your father and he will tell you, your elders and they will say it to you," "Do not turn aside from all that they will instruct you," "Listen, my child, to the admonitions of your father." The rebellious son mentioned in Deuteronomy has not necessarily committed any sin proscribed by the written or oral Torah, yet the Torah deals with him extremely stringently because his father and mother have testified that he does not listen to them. He is not referred to by his other actions—by his gluttony, for example—but is designated as "rebellious" because of his disobedience to his parents and educators.

The child must be told over and over again and made to understand the duty that he carries: to raise and educate himself as a Jew, a tree in the garden of God, in Eden. His father and teacher are there only to instruct him as to how to do this, how he is to educate himself and to know what God has spoken. This can be compared to someone who comes to a rabbi to ask him a question on the laws of *Kashrut*. The rabbi instructs him as to whether the food is kosher or not, but the main party in the whole matter is the householder in the privacy of his own home. It is up to him to keep his house kosher and to throw away the food that has been declared unfit. There is much to be gained by this approach. First of all, if he grows up with this awareness he will not see his father or teachers as despots, foreign tyrants who want to control him, for it is his own duty, and it is he himself, with his own sense of independence and self-esteem, which have developed so quickly, who must rule and educate himself. He will therefore understand that he must have a sense of gratitude toward his father and teachers, for helping him and making his task easier.

There is another advantage in this approach. The children who are not completely alienated from us and have not become our enemies, but have simply not dedicated themselves to holiness out of laziness and neglect, will also be aroused and strengthened to serve God if we inculcate this attitude in them. For, as the Talmud (*Eruvin* 3) says: "A pot owned by partners will get neither hot nor cold." It is a principle of the human spirit that when a person has someone else to rely on, he allows himself to be neglectful and depends on the other person. The same is true of young people; even if they do not actually refuse to listen, they become neglectful because they think their father or teacher is going to do everything for them. However, when they come to realize that it is all their duty, and that they are their own guide and educator, they will exert themselves and cease to be neglectful.

But with this idea we still have not completed our task. We may succeed in penetrating to the independent existence of the child's mind and making him understand that the responsibility is all his. He himself may even begin to want to grow strong and become dedicated to holy work. Yet, as we have already said, it is not only his mind that has become prematurely independent, but his feelings as well. He feels autonomous and independent concerning what excites and what moves him, and since these feelings have emerged before he was ready for them, he is moved and excited by the illusory beauty of all the foolish things the world is full of, such as the theaters and all the folly and the licentiousness that can be found in the world. If we don't first begin to arouse his soul so that it will be moved and affected by every mitzvah, by the Torah and by the light of God, we will not accomplish anything, God forbid. For even if the child understands intellectually that he is responsible for his own education, his feelings and desires will steer him off the good path to the path that he himself knows is evil. For aren't most criminals aware at first that their actions are evil? Yet their desires are stronger than their minds and push them toward doom.

This is the main principle of chasidic teaching: That a person must not consider it sufficient that he has firmly placed his intellect into the service of God. A connection made with the intellect alone is not a lasting connection. A person can subject his whole intellect to spiritual searching and can come to know with complete clarity of mind that he must serve only God in his every single thought, word, or action. And yet his heart and his whole body may still be very far away from this reality. He must link his whole soul and the life that abides in his body to divine service and devotion. He must penetrate to his soul, in order to lift it up and awaken it to feel passionately as it performs every mitzvah, learns Torah, or prays. It should experience spiritual bliss and rejoice in this bliss. And when he connects his whole soul and the life of his body to God, he accomplishes two things: The mitzvot and the divine service he performs become spiritually more elevated and holier than they would have been otherwise. In addition, he becomes much more confident in his ability to oppose his evil inclination. He will not be torn from the source of life so quickly or cast down to spiritual destruction through the seductions of his desires.

In the past, it was always necessary to put off working with the emotions and passions of the child until he grew up. It is very difficult for a child to really become inflamed with the true passion that characterizes Chasidism. In general, when the Scripture writes about *chukim umishpatim* (laws and judgments) it always places *chukim* before *mishpatim* because *mishpatim* are laws that have a reason. This reason is not necessarily only an intellectual reason, but also a reason that is apparent to the heart. A young child, whose intelligence is as yet undeveloped, understands why he wants to kiss his father with his lips. The fact that he would be unable intellectually to articulate the reason does not make the kiss and its meaning any less clear or less known. The urge he feels in his heart to kiss his father is in fact the most basic kind of knowledge there is and is more certain than all the intellect or logic in the world. When a Jew yearns to perform a mitzvah and passionately connects himself to God with a faith that is strong and certain, this mitzvah is a *mishpat* for him because of its clarity and sureness. A mitzvah that does not move him in the least, either intellectually or emotionally— that is called a *chukah*. A Jew must first perform many mitzvot, must immerse himself in Torah and in divine service, must devote himself, mind and soul, to God. Then, according to the degree that he immerses himself in devotion and in holiness, he will find that at propitious moments his soul will emerge and draw closer to holiness and to the divine light. His *Neshamah* will cleave to God, and even his body will feel passion and awe, will rejoice, yearn, and dissolve in God's embrace.

First come *chukim*, which must be done without knowing or feeling their sense or reason, and afterward *mishpatim*, whose sense can be tasted and which are performed with passion. That is why it is natural that young people first engage in the performance of *chukim*, immersing themselves in their performance without immediately feeling moved and excited. But what choice do we have in our generation, when feelings and sense of self develop so precociously? And if we do not hasten to lay hold of their passion, and harness it and activate it through the excitement whose source is holiness, our young people will instead be moved and excited by foolish stimulants, by the base beauty that is found in the world. They will be amazed by the ways of the world and envious of all kinds of vile caprices.

For the young people of our generation, whose feelings and capacity for excitement have already matured and been delineated, it is very difficult to become attached to *chukim*, which are missing the dimension of feeling. It is even difficult to become attached to intellectual material, if it is merely dry intellect. We must pierce through to their soul, to arouse and inflame it, so that it will be able to feel at least a little of the sweetness of the illumination emanating from the glow of the divine. In that way, they will be filled with yearning and with a feeling of connection to the Torah and the mitzvot. Thus, if we wish to bind the child to God and the

Jewish people, and to educate him in a way that will keep him on the path even as he grows old, not because he is being commanded to, but because he is being pushed internally by his soul, then we must not wait; we must educate him in the true path of Chasidism even when he is still very small. "Educate the child along his path": The path that our youth needs is the true path of Chasidism of the heart and soul. Even if we can't expect the child to reach the true passion of Chasidism so early in life, still, we can help him touch the surface and connect to it. To the extent that the child grows in the chasidic path and works at it, he will rise and merit to be a true chasid.

To explain this further, let us look at the following quotation from the *Pardes*:

> The color and appearance of physical forms have an effect on high. Thus, when one wishes to stimulate *Chesed* (loving kindness) above, one should dress in white; if it is *Gevurah* (strength, rigor) one wishes to activate, then red clothes should be worn, and so on. If a person stares at coursing water, he will stimulate within himself the white humor . . . because through the colors that one sees with one's eyes or that one imagines physically in one's mind, the spirit is activated. The *Nefesh* then arouses the *Ruach*, the *Ruach* arouses the *Neshamah*, and the *Neshamah* travels upward from one reality to the next until it reaches the place from which it draws its sustenance, which is then aroused according to the reality of the image. [*Shaar* 10:1]

This is the foundation of Chasidism: to induce in oneself states of passion and excitement. One begins with matters that are of little spiritual significance, and with physical sensations, and uses them in a way that makes them suitable tools for awakening to holiness. Even if the awakening is only of the body, the *Nefesh* will then arouse the *Ruach*, and the *Ruach* will in turn arouse the *Neshamah*. And this is the difference between a child and an adult. A mature chasid may begin by being moved, aroused, and excited by physical matters, or even by bodily activities such as drinking whiskey with his chasidic brethren. He may also use various sorts of mental imagery techniques of the kind we will describe later in the book. But even if that is how he begins, he will not remain confined to the body in his process of arousal. Immediately, he will awaken his *Nefesh* and *Ruach* and so on, until his *Neshamah* also has become aroused and reveals itself within him, according to his level of spiritual advancement and his situation at that particular moment in time. The menorah in the Holy Temple was also lit with a flame that came from somewhere else, but the Kohen wouldn't leave until the flames were rising of their own accord. A child, however, may remain in a state of merely bodily arousal and sensation. Yet even so, some sort of glow, and a very weak and delicate ray of light shining at a distance from the *Nefesh*, will reach him, and this, too, is good, for it connects his little body to his *Nefesh*. When a young person is moved on the night of Pesach by the sparkling cleanness of the room, by the multitude of candles and the table, which is arranged so beautifully, this, too, is beneficial. His body feels the changes in the environment, and then his *Nefesh* emerges within him, and he recites the Haggadah with a little more passion towards God, even if he doesn't know exactly what he is saying or why.

The kind of individualized path—the path of Chasidism—to which this book hopes it will help accustom our children, is an urgent necessity for them. This urgency stems from their precocity and the premature emergence of their feelings. Even if they are unable, because of their youth, to really connect with the essence of their *Neshamah*, even if their excitement and their passion is more physical than really spiritual, there is still much benefit to these practices, because it is through holiness that their feelings are being aroused. Through their physical sensations they become connected to holiness, and this will make it easier for them to become true chasidim as they grow up. For does a child really understand the Talmud and its commentaries in the same way as an adult does? And yet his studying is still beneficial, and even this simple level of learning and of understanding connects him to the Torah.

We did not intend in this introduction to discuss the specifics of all the various aspects of education. We just wished to point out the main reason that the educational process has been deteriorating in recent years. We also wished to indicate that we must be much more careful in our methods than previous generations have been. Also, we have mapped out a way in which teachers and parents can use the potentially poisonous quality of children's precocious sense of self to good advantage. All the other specifics necessary for good educational practice can be found in our holy Torah; the parents and teachers must simply search for them. Nothing that we have said is original; our Torah is eternal and will always direct us in how we are to ascend to God and how we are to comport ourselves in all our actions and in every particular of our existence. The Talmud (*Shabbat* 30:2), for example, relates: "Rabbah, before he began teaching the rabbis, would tell a joke. The rabbis would laugh. Then he would sit down and in a state of awe would begin the day's lesson." The reason for the joke was to create joy, for the presence of God can dwell only where there is joy, as the Talmud states (*Shabbat* 30:2). The Torah, however, "like a hammer smashing a rock," explodes into many sparks, many reasons. The Talmud is here hinting at something about the relationship between a teacher and his students that is particularly pertinent in our generation. In order to heal the wound of alienation that has come between the student and his teacher, the teacher must make an effort to capture the student's heart and to re-create the closeness that has been lost. Joy is one of the fundamental means through which young hearts can be captured: children and young people have no toleration for sadness. Their teacher must not appear to them to be an angry or contentious person. This is not to say that he should become frivolous or should sacrifice his dignity when appearing before his students; on the contrary, a teacher must present himself as an elevated person—but also as pleasant and good. The students should still tremble before their teacher even while he is joking with them; and likewise, even when he is trying to instill in them fear and respect, the awe should be laced with joy. "And rejoice with trembling": not the trembling an angry or violent person might induce, but the kind of awe that a person of great spiritual achievement inspires. The Talmud (*Moed Katan* 17a) says: "If your teacher resembles one of God's angelic hosts, you can learn from him." A teacher should appear to his students to be an angel in a body, or at least an exalted person. Then, even when the teacher gets angry, the student will not hate him for it. And when the teacher smiles at him, the student will rejoice, and his feelings of love and awe for the teacher will grow.

How illuminating are the words of the Shalah (Rabbi Isaiah Levi Horowitz), may his memory be a blessing, concerning the path our generation must take in educating our young. There is a passage in Proverbs 9:8 which reads: "Do not chastise a fool, lest he hate you; chastise a wise man and he will love you." The Shalah comments as follows: "When you approach one of your peers to rebuke him, do not shame or insult him, saying 'you fool,' for this will cause him to hate you and he won't listen to you. Rather, chastise a wise person—say to him 'You are so intelligent. Why do you wish to do such and such a thing?' Then he will love you and will listen to you." The hearts of our generation's youth are already so distant from us, independent of our chastisement; we must therefore be exceedingly careful in this matter. And besides the fact that this method of rebuke is necessary in order to close the gap that separates our hearts from the hearts of our young people, this approach is very beneficial educationally as well. It helps develop the hidden physical and mental potential of the student and strengthens and encourages his efforts in Torah and devotion to God in the same way that praising a person's generosity can give him the spiritual strength to be more generous than he might have been otherwise. The words of praise actually seduce the power latent in his soul and cause it to emerge and overcome whatever degree of miserliness he also has within him. Parents and teachers must seek out the good qualities of every student and praise him for them, giving him strength with their words. "You have so much talent and ability; you have the capacity to become great in Torah, outstanding in the service of God. The goal is set up and waiting for you—all you have to do is work and you will attain everything." You should speak such words of encouragement to your students—using your discernment and intelligence, of course, so that your praise does not foster laziness or arrogant pride.

We have not undertaken a bibliography of all the sources in the Torah or the *Shulchan Aruch* that instruct us in educational methodology. Our generation has a special need to invest extra effort in studying these sources and clarifying their every detail. The more energy we spend in seeking out and studying these sources, the more will our efforts be rewarded.

Midrash and *Ein Yaakov* should be taught several times a week;

as our sages have already told us (*Sifri Ekev* 49), "If it is your desire to know the One who spoke and brought the world into being, study *Aggadab*." Older students should regularly learn these subjects on their own. When a teacher wishes to teach his students some of the concepts to be found in the ethical–pietistic literature (*Musar*), he should not speak only about the punishing consequences of sin that are described there. He should focus as well on the greatness of Jewish souls, on their closeness to God and the possibility of their spiritual ascent beyond even what angels are capable of. While it is true that teachings about the destructiveness and punishment of sin can make a child submissive, it is more likely that such discussions would fail to bring children closer to us and may even help cause the appearance of the blight of alienation. But when combined with much emphasis on the greatness of Israel, even the ethical admonishments will help bring the desired effect, and the child's soul will be aroused and inflamed.

Teachers and parents should also not neglect the use of the parable in instructing their students and children. Our sages have already warned us (*Midrash Song of Songs* 1) "Do not view the parable as insignificant, for through the parable, a person can come to really understand the meaning of the words of Torah." It is especially necessary to use parables when teaching young people, not only in illuminating an intellectual concept, but also in demonstrating an ethical truth. One must relate the parable with precision and in detail, as if the events had actually occurred. Young people, even if they are aware that what they are hearing is only a parable, see it in their imagination as if it had all really happened. This moves and arouses them more than the abstract message the parable is pointing out. That is why, in Chapter 4, we wrote out the parable at greater length than is actually needed for making the point. We described the way the shoemaker prayed in a way we hope will move young people, will awaken them a little bit to the importance of not being terribly desirous of the things of this world, and will encourage them to draw closer to God through Torah and true devotion.

CHAPTER 1

A CALL TO THE STUDENT

Child of Israel, you are fortunate and blessed. You have merited to study Torah, which shines with divine radiance. You are God's delight; He tenderly loves you. The angelic beings who inhabit the higher spiritual dimensions envy you and recognize your preciousness. Your existence is a source of wonderment for divine seraphim: they honor you. The heavens and all the celestial beings, the earth and everything that fills it, rejoice in you and are ready to bend according to your will. The whole universe resounds with the question: Who is this child from whose mouth pillars of fire shoot forth, whom the most high and exalted God, Who is constantly surrounded by multitudes of His host, looks at as His pride and joy?

You too should be filled with joy and exultation at your great good fortune. You are like someone privileged to be in the intimate circle of the King: the Holy One, blessed be He, whispers His secrets in your ears in teaching you Torah; not to rejoice would be a sin.

If you were aware of all this, if you could experience the state of great purity of mind and heart that exists as you learn Torah, if you could inwardly feel the closeness of God who places Himself, as it were, directly in front of you and learns with you as you learn, if you realized that everything you ask of God, concerning your life or the needs of your parents and family, are like the sweet requests a child makes of a parent, so close is God to you, and if you really knew that God answers you and wishes to please you like a father does a beloved child, you would be filled with happiness and your whole being would rejoice.

Since you don't really feel all this inside, and instead, know yourself only as a child, one among many children, you are unable to rejoice in the happiness that is rightfully yours. Not only that: at times you lose the will to go on learning Torah altogether.

All of this is what prompts us to approach you in this book. We want to offer you the following vision of what you can become: Your face will shine with the radiant grace of the divine presence. Your mind and heart and all your limbs will open to the Torah and to serving God. Your heart and soul will feel a closeness to God that will not waver. Like a child you will express before God all your desires; like a loving parent, He will hasten to respond.

Perhaps this description arouses in you the following unsettling thought: You love to play with your friends, to be wild and mischievous sometimes. Along we come and approach you with the intent of depriving you of your childhood, making you silent, sedentary, and old before your time. This is absolutely not so. You will remain young. You will go on playing with your friends. And you will still reach the spiritual goal we've portrayed. You just have to know how to play and how to be wild, and to realize and have faith at the same time that God's kingship extends everywhere, and that He sees everything, even your play. No matter how spiritually developed a human being may become, he must still continue to eat and drink and attend to his physical needs. Similarly, a child must play. But at the same time, during all these physical activities, one must remember that God is the Lord of the world, the Creator who guides and guards over everything. Everything belongs to God, including us.

To try and force you to observe the Torah or to follow the path of God would run counter to our primary objective. We are interested only in what you do of your own free will. We would not be satisfied if we succeeded in getting you to perform good deeds if you were not doing them of your own free will and desire because we want your very self and essence, not just your actions, to become good.

Since this is our intention, we have to explore every corner of your mind and heart. Your thoughts and desires must be uplifted and straightened out, and whatever is undesirable must be swept away.

We are aware that you must be wondering how any of this applies to you: "How is it possible," you must be thinking, "for a simple child like me to become the kind of person just described— the special, beloved delight of God? And for this to happen while I'm still so young? Neither my father nor his father were such exalted personalities as the kind that you describe, and I, too, am only a simple child." This thought is itself one of the distorted notions that we must challenge. We must not let this kind of thought remain within you.

Child of Israel! Listen attentively to the word of God, as expressed through His prophets and His sages. Everything we are about to tell you is collected from these sources. We place His words, which are like fire, before you, in order to strengthen you, so that you may become one of the mighty cedars in the forest planted by God.

If you are discouraged because your immediate ancestry is undistinguished, lift yourself up and gaze beyond, deeper into your past. You are descended from holy men and women, from prophets, from the sages of the Mishnah and Talmud, from great rabbinic masters and *tzaddikim*. The Talmud states (*Pesachim* 66a) that the people of Israel, if they are not prophets themselves, are at least the children of prophets. It is clear from the context that the Talmud is not referring to the distant past, but means to suggest that even now a spark of the prophetic power of his ancestors is to be found within every Jewish child. All you have to do is dig for it and you will discover it within you.

The fact that you may not feel that you are any greater than all the other children you know does not prove that you don't have the capacity to rise to staggering heights of greatness and of sanctity. Do you really know the inner essence of the children you know? Do you know what a Jewish child really is, deep inside? Listen to the amazing words of the following midrash (Lamentations *Rabbah*): "Rabbi Yehuda said, 'Come and see how beloved are children to the Holy One, Blessed be He. The Sanhedrin was exiled from Jerusalem, but the *Shechinah* (God's presence) did not go into exile with them. The Kohanim and Leviim were exiled, but the *Shechinah* did not accompany them into exile. When the children were exiled, only then did the *Shechinah* go into exile along with them.' "

Children who learn Torah are so very precious to God. When the children went into exile, the *Shechinah* exclaimed: "I am so attached to these children that I am unable to be without them. Together with them I will bear the suffering and the burden of exile."

The prophet Isaiah proclaimed: "The house of Israel is the vineyard of the Lord of Hosts, and every person of Judah is one of His delightful plantings." The House of Israel as a whole is God's vineyard, and each individual Jew is a precious tree in whom God especially delights, if he walks in the path of God, the path of Torah. You, as a Jewish child, are like a young vine in this vineyard. We have no idea yet to whom we are speaking when we address you, what you may become—and you, too, have no conception yet of how far you may reach as you grow in Torah learning and in serving God. You may become a great *tzaddik* and genius whose fame will extend from one end of the world to the other. You may become a wealthy man, dedicated to serving God, outstanding in Torah knowledge, a generous benefactor to the needy, good to both God and all of His creations—the kind of person whom every parent blesses his child to become. Many of the greatest sages and *tzaddikim* of Israel were not recognized as being in any way different or better than their companions during their childhood years. Only after they began to dedicate themselves to serving God did they begin to succeed until they became so great that they became etched forever into the annals of our history. These kind of people, many of whom remained completely unrecognized as children, remain our inspiration, protection, and light until Moshiach comes.

We are not saying that all children are equal in their potential and in their abilities. What we are claiming is that it is impossible to predict what a child will be like when he grows up, what potential may be hidden within him. There have been children whose abilities remained so deeply closed and concealed—even from themselves— that no one would have believed that they would rise to greatness. To the amazement of all who knew them as children, they became so great that everyone stood in awe of them and their accomplishments. And the opposite has also unfortunately occurred. There have been great souls who were gifted with the potential and ability to be a light for all of Israel, but because they neglected to develop their potential in their youth, their light was lost.

And here we have to say the same thing to you, precious child. If you neglect the abilities that are locked up inside you, hidden so well that even you are unaware of them, it is not only you, yourself, that you hurt. You may be injuring the Jewish people as a whole— and the Holy One of Israel—by depriving them and Him of a great sage, a *tzaddik* of a high spiritual level.

This is the lament of the *Shechinah*, God's presence, as she mourns for the lost potential of a Jewish soul: "Heavens and all your angelic beings, earth in all your fullness, cry bitterly for Me. I created the world and hoped to dwell in it. The great leaders of Israel and all My servants, the *tzaddikim*, draw My presence into the world and make My great Name holy in its midst. I waited so long for this soul, who was to have developed into a great and righteous man, a servant who would sanctify Me and draw Me into the world— and all this has been lost. My presence on earth has been diminished; one of the legs of My throne of glory, which rests on the earth, has been smashed and broken."

Children, your responsibility is great, greater than you know. You must raise up and establish the whole house of Israel. From

among you must emerge *tzaddikim* and righteous people, sages and
leaders. Even the process of revealing God's presence in the world
and bringing close the coming of the Messiah has been placed in
your hands. Do you wish the world to remain in a state of exile,
without prophets or visionaries? Do you wish the Jewish people to
be diminished even further, that the coming generation be empty
of sages and *tzaddikim*? Will God be able to stand it if this occurs?

If you rely on your friends, and assume that they will provide
Israel with great leaders and sages, you will find that they in turn
will have relied on you. What will then become of Israel, the holy
people? What will become of the *Shechinah*, God's presence on earth?
Each and every Jewish young person who learns Torah and seeks
God has a duty: to discover and reveal from within himself the inner
soul of Israel. You must make of yourself a pillar that will support
the house of Israel. Not a single one of you may excuse yourself
from this great responsibility.

CHAPTER 2

FIRST STEPS
IN THE STUDENT'S DEVELOPMENT

We share your great burden with you. The purpose of this book is to ease your load. If you listen carefully and if you wish it, you will grow into a great person. Living wellsprings of Torah will emerge from you. Your light will shine out in all directions in a way that neither you nor your parents ever imagined.

Do not become depressed, do not let your heart sink, at the thought of your great responsibility. Depression is an evil trait; it has a pernicious effect on the mind and heart and leads to discouragement and neglectfulness. Instead, this is what you should do: In the morning, upon awakening, think over the essence of what we have written here; think about the great responsibility that is yours. Be concerned, but do not be depressed. The difference is as follows: Someone who had a great fortune and then lost it all might fall into despair and depression. Someone who knows where a great fortune is buried, deep in the ground, will worry and be concerned about the enormous amount of labor necessary to reach the treasure. The more concerned and worried he is about his task, the more resolved and determined he becomes to succeed and to work with great joy until he does succeed.

Be concerned and worried about the greatness of the responsibility that has been placed on your shoulders, and start the blessing before learning Torah in this mood of concern. Pray from the depths of your heart, concentrating on each phrase with new intensity. When the blessing says: "And let the words of Your Torah be pleasant in our mouths," ask for God's aid so that you too will feel the pleasant sweetness of Torah, for the Torah is, in reality, sweet and pleasant. When the blessing continues: "Let us all know Your Name and learn the Torah for its own sake," ask God to have mercy on you and allow you to develop your natural potential as a Jewish child, and to reach the level of learning Torah for its own sake and of knowing the Name of God. This is the highest level that can be achieved, and it brings the greatest bliss and satisfaction possible, both in this world and the next.

After the blessing, trust that God has accepted your prayer and will fulfill the longings of your heart. He will increase your desire for Torah and your yearning for the sweet purity of the higher levels of existence and for the holiness of your Father in heaven. Be strong and joyous in your holy task, and each day allow your concern and worry about accomplishing it to diminish (for continuous worry and concern weaken the mind and cannot be sustained for any length of time anyway). Just be sure to continually remember your purpose and your aim. Remember, but do not worry. Remember in the same way that a traveler must continuously remember his destination in order not to lose his way and must often remind himself of the purpose of his journey in order to hurry himself along and not become distracted.

Pray and learn Torah, being joyful over having merited to be a Jewish child who is so close to God. Learn with precision and depth and with the full power of your intellect. Do not deceive yourself into thinking you understand what you are learning until it is really clear to you. It is especially important to try as hard as possible not to let your mind wander while you are learning, for to do so is disrespectful to God. It leaves the impression, God forbid, that you think it is not worth the effort to concentrate deeply on these words of fire from above.

Concentrate during prayer as much as you are able. If it is difficult to concentrate on the meaning of the words during the entire prayer, keep in mind at least, as you are praying, that you are standing before your divine Father, who is full of mercy, and is at the same time awesome, exalted, and holy. Eat, drink, sleep— fulfill all your physical needs. Be happy and have fun with your friends, friends who learn Torah and have embarked, together with you, on the path of God.

Now, if you have absorbed what we have written so far into your heart and still wish to hear more about how to continue along this path that rises to God, this news fills us with hope. We will continue to explain the means through which you can bind your soul to the Torah and to the service of God. We can now certainly be confident that you will eventually reach the state which God spoke about to His prophet with you in mind: "You are My beloved child, My delightful child. As I speak to you, I remember you and will have mercy upon you."

CHAPTER 3

PRINCIPAL ILLS OF THE SOUL AND THEIR CURES

ince our purpose is to draw you closer to God's Torah and His path, we must follow the Torah's own recipe: "Turn away from evil and do good." It is forbidden to bring the King into a chamber until it has been cleansed and prepared; one cannot become holy until the evil qualities which infect the human heart have been done away with. We must search for any impurities that may be preventing you from studying Torah or establishing your bond with God and then remove these blemishes from your heart.

But this search can only take place if we search together. You are the only person who can really look for the crumbs of leaven or of decay that are within you, who can find them and destroy them. You must be your own teacher; you must educate yourself. It is you who has the primary responsibility and task of educating and nurturing the mighty cedar inside, the great person you have the potential to become. No one but you can really know what your shortcomings are, or understand the flaws within you that must be mended. Only you, yourself, are really in a position to know the unique distortions of your psyche, which are completely different for each person. It is only you, therefore, who can make what is crooked within you straight.

All we can do is try to help you, to prepare the way for you and warn you about the paths that will lead you only into the depths of misery and evil, and point out the paths that lead to the embrace of God, to His beauty and the splendor of His holiness. Parents, teachers, and advisers can tell you what to do or counsel you, but it is completely up to you whether you wish to listen to their advice and take their words to heart, in order to train yourself in the ways of God and His commandments so that every one of His words penetrates to the core of your being. If you refuse to listen, there is no one who will be able to reach and rescue you.

You alone can search into every nook and cranny, every crack and fissure of your heart and soul in order to find and repair your blemishes and failings. We can describe the symptoms of certain faults and recommend specific remedies, but it is up to you to adapt our general advice to the specific necessities and problems of your own unique soul.

There are certain people who do not recognize any faults or flaws within themself. Even when they read a description of a certain undesirable quality, they fail to realize that they possess this trait and need to work at correcting this part of their being. They don't even feel any anxiety or heartache concerning their character; they are completely oblivious. This is not a good sign. People who are very seriously ill sometimes lose even the awareness that they are sick (see Maimonides' *The Eight Chapters*, Chapter 3). There are others, however, who begin to feel anxious deep in their hearts because they are aware on some level that they have the shortcoming that is being discussed. Immediately, their defenses spring up and their mind begins a series of denials: "I certainly don't have this flaw to the extent that the book describes. No one, after all, is perfect— the small degree to which I possess this trait is perfectly natural." This kind of denial is also destructive.

Both of these responses are founded in a failure to demand spiritual greatness from oneself. It seems to such people that only the great *tzaddikim* are expected to work on themselves and improve themselves. They see themselves spiritually as comparable to a foolish child whose father is satisfied with whatever small progress he makes and is forgiving of all his errors.

This attitude is itself a terrible error. We have already discussed the responsibility each Jew has to work on himself in order to help establish and uncover from the midst of the people of Israel her *tzaddikim*, creative geniuses, and great leaders. The very presence of God wails in distress when this responsibility is neglected and potential is wasted. But even if one only wants to be a simple Jew, let us not forget what a simple Jew is. Right before the Torah was given, God made a covenant with the entire Jewish people, from the woodchoppers to the water carriers: "And now, if you listen to My voice and keep My covenant, you will be a special treasure unto Me from all the peoples . . . you will be unto Me a kingdom of priests and a holy nation." The covenant is conditional: *If* you are a kingdom of priests and a holy people, *then* you are Israelites, and if not, God forbid. . . .

Who among you would wish to turn away from being a Jew? All of you wish to be able to declare proudly: I am a member of the Jewish people. Even if being a Jew means serving God with all your might and with the full power of your mind, even if every fiber of your being must be devoted to achieving the distinction of being a Jew, not one of you would refuse to make the attempt. None of you, therefore, will turn away from the task of identifying and healing your shortcomings and flaws. You will feel heartsick inside and not justify all your character traits in a defensive manner. You will fill yourself with strength and attempt with all your might to correct and straighten what needs fixing inside.

CHAPTER 4

LAZINESS AND ITS CURE

Laziness is the most common and the most destructive of the ailments of character that afflict young people. Even laziness, however, is different in each person. There is a kind of laziness so severe that the person afflicted by it loves to sleep as much as possible, enjoys inactivity, and experiences any form of work as a burden. He is always filled with excuses and justifies himself constantly, as Scripture relates (Proverbs 26:13): "The lazy man says: 'There is a lion in the way, yes, a lion is in the streets.' " At the same time, he denigrates anyone whose achievements are greater than his own, in order to protect himself from feelings of shame and jealousy of anyone else's accomplishments.

At times he may gain the strength to work hard at his studies for the first week or two of each semester, but his determination quickly peters out. If you possess this character trait, you must quickly attempt to eradicate it at its very root. It is a ruinous trait, potentially destructive of one's entire life.

Everything in the world is constantly fulfilling a task. The sun and the moon never cease their work. The earth itself is plowed and seeded and then gives of its strength and vigor to complete the work that God assigned it, bringing forth all kinds of growing things. Oxen and horses and all the domesticated animals work with all their strength. Only the dangerous carnivorous animals, who wait to pounce and tear apart whatever they can reach, spend much of their time idle. Do you wish to resemble these beasts, in your idleness?

Our sages, who themselves were filled with dedication and self-sacrifice, always looked for inspiration from everyone and everything around them. Rabbi Eliezer, who was always the first to arrive at the house of study in the morning and the last to leave at night, noticed one morning that the garbage collectors and farm laborers had risen before him. He chastised himself: "They are getting up to work for their own personal reasons, while I rise ostensibly to serve God—yet they precede me" (*Midrash Shir HaShirim* 1). Examine yourself in this same light. Construction workers risk their lives putting up buildings. Farmers sweat over their crops. Your father works hard, sweats, and exhausts himself in order to provide for you. Everyone works, whether with their body or their mind, many at backbreaking labor. Why should you alone be idle? Why should the heavens and the earth curse you, saying "We and all that comes from us, are fulfilling the tasks that God created us for. We are all working. Why does this young person consider himself better than all the rest of creation by giving himself permission to be idle?"

Even if one has not been stricken with the plague of such extreme laziness, one must still cleanse oneself of the residue of this destructive quality: a kind of torpidity that manifests itself as a lack of willingness to give of oneself completely, a weakness of will and effort. Although not as dangerous to one's soul as excessive laziness, this weakness is a definite obstacle to self-fulfillment and spiritual ascent. The Torah was given from the heavens, and to become a Jew who really learns Torah and serves God one must rise toward God's holy presence. This can be accomplished only through labor that utilizes the combined strength and efforts of all the powers of one's body and soul.

The amount of labor necessary to acquire an object should be equal to the value of that which is being obtained. Objects that have little worth may be acquired without much labor, while one must work hard in order to obtain something that is very precious. Strenuous labor is needed to be really able to learn Torah and to dwell in the holy presence of God. The labor is difficult, but not beyond human capacity, for God never gives us tasks that transcend our powers and abilities. It is necessary, however, that we make an effort to work and serve God not only when we are faced with specific tasks. Our identity as a worker must become part of our essential self. The difference between a lazy person and one who is weak-willed and halfhearted in his efforts is that while a lazy person refuses to work altogether, a weak-willed person will work when confronted with a task, but is not, in his self-identity, a worker. As a result, even when he is working, he does not concentrate sufficiently, he is inefficient and is satisfied with the surface appearance of results. A diligent person, in contrast, who is a worker at his very core, cannot live without work. When circumstances force him to remain idle for a period of time, he becomes dissatisfied with himself. Work brings him life-energy and pleasure. Light work, surface work are not enough to satisfy his longing. He works quickly and joyfully, he reaches to the depths of each task, and like a stream of water that becomes more forceful when its path is obstructed until it finally breaks through every barrier, each obstacle to his work only strengthens his desire to push forward in his labor.

Though extreme laziness is a more serious fault than halfheartedness and weakness of will, it is also easier to overcome laziness. A child or young person has more means available to combat real laziness than to root out from himself its milder form. If he is still in school, his father and his teachers demand that he complete certain tasks. The structure of school forces him to wake up early and to accomplish at least a minimal amount of studying each and every day. In this way, the student gets used to working and will be able to continue working as he matures.

Someone who is not extremely lazy, but simply halfhearted in his efforts may have a much more difficult time in purifying himself of this trait. He may get up for school and do his work, but make only enough effort to serve appearances; he studies in a superficial manner, indeed he does everything in a superficial way. Even in his inner work, when he attempts to rid himself of an undesirable character quality, he will not reach the roots of the trait in his efforts and mend his character completely. He won't make the effort to really focus on the meaning of the words during prayer because he is more interested in surfaces and in things that are easily accomplished; it is easier for him to fantasize than to concentrate with his heart and mind on the words he is speaking before the Master of the world.

Therefore, youth of Israel, if you have compassion on yourself and wish to establish a foundation within you that will serve you well until you reach the wisdom of old age and beyond, excise the trait of laziness from yourself and search and destroy its hidden remnants: the negative attitude toward work that causes negligence and halfheartedness. Become diligent and efficient in your work, but do not become speedy. For the most part, people who work very quickly do a second-rate, superficial job, and do not work with the deep attentiveness that involves the entire body and soul. Keep your balance as you work, but put all your effort into what you are doing, and work as efficiently as possible.

As we have already emphasized, you yourself must be, to a very great extent, your own teacher. Since this is the case, it is necessary to elaborate a little more on the physical and mental differences that separate a diligent person from someone who is not diligent. This will help you understand how, in every specific situation, one can eliminate laziness and transform oneself completely into a person who loves work.

The soul is really the active force in man. All of man's activities, whether physical or mental, are affected by the soul. The mind and the body are vessels through which the soul manifests itself; the soul enclothes itself in the consciousness and physical being of man. There are many parts to the brain, and when the soul enclothes itself in these various parts, they all awaken and begin to function fully and harmoniously, working together toward the unified goal of understanding, as deeply as possible, that which the soul is focused on. Similarly, on the physical plans, the soul stirs the entire body to work together to accomplish its desired end.

A person who is still in the grip of laziness, even in its milder form, is one whose soul has not awakened completely, but is in a state of semi-slumber. Just as the mind of a sleeping person is not completely inactive, for it must assimilate the dream visions perceived by the soul and must also give symbolic dream-form to the thoughts and feelings experienced during waking hours, so, too, the soul of a lazy person is not completely dormant. Our sages have said of an idle person that he may be compared to one who is sleeping. It is not a strict comparison, for he is certainly more awake than if he were really asleep. Still, he exists in a state that is somewhere between sleep and true wakefulness. The various parts of his mind and body are not fully activated and are not working together harmoniously towards a common goal. His soul has not enclothed itself in the various organs, infusing them with a powerful surging of life and living the life of a man of power who strengthens himself and is victorious over all obstacles. The vigor and powerful life-force are missing. A weakness of the soul, not the body, is the source of laziness and halfheartedness. The soul has failed to seize hold of the mind and body and convert them into vessels that will strive with precision towards a desired end. The soul is deprived of any image or semblance of completion that might be derived from its efforts; it thus experiences neither bliss nor joy.

And yet at certain times—on the occasion of a trip, for example, that you have been anticipating with pleasure—you are transformed into a most efficient and diligent person. You wake up early and dress quickly; every movement you make is precise. Or, if Shabbat falls on the day before Pesach (when prayers and the Shabbat meal must be finished early in the morning) you manage to do everything quickly. Where have the yawning and delays of an average morning disappeared to? Enthusiasm has shaken your soul awake; in turn, it grabs hold of all the various parts of your mind and body and fills them with life. Your efforts are filled with vigor and alacrity rather than weariness and fatigue. Why does the love of divine service not awaken your soul, fill it with powerful life, cause it to stimulate your mind and body until they begin to serve God with diligence, strength, and joy?

There are many people who are devoted to God and who constantly desire to serve Him. Speaking to them leaves you with the impression that they are totally immersed in devotion to God, from their head to their toes. In reality, however, all they have is the will to serve God; they are unable to actualize their desire. Because they are constantly distracted from their resolve to serve God by all kinds of obstacles and temptations that they immediately succumb to, they remain of small spiritual stature. If they were strong, efficient, and diligent, they would be able to overcome all obstacles, great and small, and the divine spirit within them would break through every barrier. The quality of laziness, even if only in its mild form, has been part of their internal makeup since childhood, and therefore they become easily discouraged and fail to gather the heroic strength necessary to be victorious over all obstacles and hindrances. You should not, therefore, rejoice prematurely at the desire to serve God you feel inside of you. Unless you continue to absolutely uproot the quality of laziness from within you and plant in its stead diligence and efficiency, your inclination will get the better of you and you will experience spiritual failure.

We have already conveyed to you that the whole Jewish people and even God Himself wait expectantly for you. We have told you that you possess the power to sanctify the people of Israel and to bring God's presence into the world. In case this has not been sufficient to awaken your soul to a state of diligence, efficiency, and precision, listen to the following parable:

There was once a poor Jewish shoemaker in the land of Israel who lived near a crossroads. He would eke out a living from the travelers who passed his way, mending a torn boot, replacing a worn-out shoelace. Despite his poverty, his faith in God never wavered. His wife and children also had a deep faith in God, for he had taught them to understand that this ephemeral existence is insignificant. More important than this life is the eternal life in the supernal universe, where the soul will blissfully rejoice in its proximity to the precious beauty of God's kingship and will enjoy the radiance of the divine presence.

Serving God, therefore, was more important to the shoemaker than trying to become wealthy. Although he was not a scholar, he would study and pray at every opportunity he had. Sometimes, when his soul became aroused and inflamed with the desire to pray to God and pour his heart out before Him, he would leave his small one-room shack and walk into the nearby forest. Passersby who caught a glimpse of him from afar were often astounded and afraid. His face burned intensely as he praised God and thanked Him, speaking to Him as if he were actually standing before His throne and could see Him with his own eyes. His acquaintances, however, already knew about his passionate devotion, and they would respond: "Oh, that must be the righteous shoemaker." That is what the gentiles who knew him had nicknamed him.

At the beginning of the Great War, all traveling in that area ceased, and what little sustenance the shoemaker had earned was reduced to nothing. A day arrived when there was no more bread in the house, nothing to eat for the shoemaker, his wife, or his children. By the second day everyone was very hungry; the children cried out to their father: "Please find us bread, don't let us die of hunger!" By the third day the children all lay in bed; they still cried for food, but they were so weak one could hardly even hear their voices. By this time the shoemaker himself was weak, and his knees buckled beneath him because of the hunger and the heartbreak he felt over the suffering of his wife and children.

Still, he gathered strength and went outside. His wife called out after him: "Please don't leave, my husband. If we are going to die of hunger then let us at least die together." His faith in God still held firm, and he answered her: "I am not going toward my death, but toward the living God. To the forest, to pray to our Father in heaven for a miracle—that is where I am heading."

Distressed and weeping, he walked into the forest, raised his eyes toward heaven, and said: "Lord, even before You created the world, You chose us to be Your children and Your most intimate servants. Your holy presence dwelled with us in this land, You raised us up on wings of eagles, drew us up toward Your embrace. How good things were then! When we needed admonishment or rebuke,

You spoke to us. You revealed yourself from within us; through the prophets, we all heard Your voice. Other nations feared us and feared You because You dwelled with us, surrounded us, filled our bodies and souls.

"The fact that You have concealed Your face from us is so bitter. Our hearts long for the holiness You have hidden away; our souls call out for Your closeness—to no avail. Even in our moments of penitence, when we realize that our sins have driven You away and we resolve to turn toward You so that You, like a loving father, can turn again to us, we are bitterly disappointed. For ever since You hid Your face from us, we have been beset by all manner of troubles, troubles that dull our hearts and distract our minds and threaten to drive us away from You.

"Master of the world, I pray not only for myself, but for all Your children of Israel. Merciful Father, You have abandoned Your children in a sad and terrible world. How can You be silent as they bathe in the blood of their wounds?

"I am not praying only for myself and my sustenance, but also for You. I pray for the establishment of Your holy kingdom. Please come close and show Yourself, have mercy on us, redeem us, send us Your righteous Messiah now and we will serve You with awe and love, as we yearn to in our hearts."

As he continued to pray and cry, he grew exhausted and weak. Since he had nothing to refresh himself from his fasting and his tears, he fell into a faint. Then, in his unconsciousness, he smelled a fragrance of overpowering delight. Suddenly he was revived, and he saw an extraordinarily beautiful flower blossoming in the woods, exuding a delicious scent. He gathered his strength, stood up, and plucked the flower, intending to run home with it to his wife and children in the hope that the lovely fragrance would revive them somewhat.

When he was on the way back to his home, a carriage with a solitary nobleman seated within drew up next to him. The nobleman called out to him: "My good poor friend, what need have you of such a flower? Hand it over to me; in exchange, I will pay you in silver for it."

The poor shoemaker answered: "I won't sell it for silver, but if you will give me a loaf of bread to help me feed my family who are starving to death, I will certainly give you the flower, and bless you for your kindness before God." So the shoemaker exchanged the flower for a loaf of bread and ran back happily to feed his wife and children.

That night, his father appeared to him in a dream. His clothes were torn, and he was crying and weeping and beating his chest with his fist. "Know," he began, "that the prayer you uttered in the forest today caused a great uproar as it ascended to heaven. All the merciful angels were aroused. They called out to God: 'How long will You wait until You have mercy on Your ravaged flock and on Your children who remember You and are so deeply attached to You even as they are drowning in misfortune?' There is a barrier of iron that has separated the people of Israel from their Father in heaven—it seemed to break, and all the prayers that had been obstructed by this barrier poured upward, arousing God's mercy and stirring Him to reveal His redemption. A proclamation went forth: since your prayers had drawn near the time for redemption, the flower whose fragrance has the power to revive the dead was to be revealed to you. I was to have descended tonight to instruct you to take this flower to the tomb of Avraham, Isaac, and Jacob, and to the tomb of the prophets; they would have been revived and then the righteous Messiah would have come.

"Light and gladness filled the heavens and all the supernal palaces. Angels and the souls of holy *tzaddikim* rejoiced. But among Satan and his companions there was a great noise, a howling and a crying. What were they to do? They decided on a strategy: they would trick you into handing them the flower. The nobleman who bought the flower from you was an agent of Satan in disguise, sent to snatch away the flower that can revive the dead."

Sobbing in misery, the shoemaker's father continued:

"My son, you have harmed not only yourself, but all of Israel and even the Holy One of Israel. It was all in your hands: the forefathers, prophets, *tzaddikim*, even the Messiah—and you lost it all for a loaf of bread. Satan and all the angels of destruction are celebrating, laughing, and ridiculing us. We are filled with shame and weep inconsolably. Everyone asks incredulously: Who is this man that has caused so much destruction, has extinguished the light of redemption? Is it possible that this person is a Jew and can be called by the name of Israel?"

⟨ ⁓⟡⟡⁓ ⟩

You are doubtless disturbed by the fate of this poor shoemaker who lost an opportunity to revive all our holy ancestors and bring the Messiah, all for a loaf of bread. How could he have done otherwise? He didn't even know that he was being tested! Please realize that you too are being constantly put to the test, and yet you are distracted and defeated by matters of total insignificance. It is in your hands to become a great Torah scholar and a *tzaddik*. You can fill yourself with the presence of God to such an extent that other people will be sanctified by your influence and draw close to God. You will teach them the word of God, show them His way, and you and your friends will prepare the way for the coming of the Messiah.

But all your desire to be a true Jew will not bear fruit if you are lazy and do not work hard, if you are defeated by every obstacle and distracted by whatever seems attractive at the moment, if you are defeated by every test, great and small.

Our intent here is not to make you efficient like a worker whose boss is standing over him and prodding him to work faster. Nor do we want you to be like someone who must push himself and force himself to work because his work is spiritually arid and involves only his physical body. Wake up your soul! A divine spirit will carry you; there will be a great roar that will stir the waves of your soul as well as all the limbs of your body. Strengthen yourself, draw courage to serve God powerfully, passionately, in a flame of holiness and joy.

CHAPTER 5

SOME SPECIFIC ADVICE
FOR THE LAZY

The desire to become diligent in serving God is not sufficient in itself. It is necessary to explore and discover devices and strategies that will help you uproot laziness and establish diligence. The same is true in trying to transform any undesirable character trait and establish a more positive trait in its stead—each transformation needs its own devices and strategies. Undesirable qualities are a kind of disease of the soul and body; special medicines are necessary to effect a cure. You have to be your own guide in curing the disease of laziness and halfheartedness; you, yourself, must examine your illness, analyze it deeply, gain control over it, and combat it.

Before you begin your task, decide how long it should take to complete it, and commit yourself to it. Set for yourself a specific time frame—for example, "This page of *Gemara* should take me one hour; to review it should take me half an hour, and not more."

Commit yourself before every task to work without wasting time, and when you finish, check to see if you have finished on schedule. If you have, feel pleased with yourself. If you have not finished within the time period you set for yourself, not because of any unforeseen circumstance, but because you wasted time and lacked sufficient concentration, be upset with yourself and say: "What will become of me? As a result of my laziness, I am depriving myself of both worlds, and am provoking God's anger."

After a while you will have accustomed yourself to this practice, and you will automatically make specific demands of yourself. You will feel, whenever you learn, as if you had someone always supervising you and warning you constantly against slackening off or letting your mind wander while you are studying.

While you are still trying to uproot from within yourself all vestiges of laziness, it is better, when studying by yourself, to stick to the simpler levels of meaning, even if you are already capable of going deeper. You should set a time for every subject you wish to cover, for example: In one hour you should cover so much Talmud, in a half hour so much Scripture. There are two problems with exploring the deeper levels of meaning during this stage in your development. First of all, it is much more difficult to set any time limit on how long to spend on a text when you are studying in depth. Second, one is much more inclined to fantasize and let the mind wander when pondering the deep meaning of a text than when one is covering new material.

Still, it is important not to abandon deep study of the Torah either. The effort to penetrate, using all one's strength of mind, into the inner core of the Torah's holiness, is the primary goal of Torah learning. In fact, the main temptation facing a halfhearted person is to learn superficially, without effort or deep analysis. But at this beginning stage, one should learn in depth only with a teacher or a friend so that you can keep each other's mind from wandering. After one has eradicated laziness and become truly diligent and efficient, one can learn in depth even on one's own.

If you are no longer studying in yeshivah, set a schedule of learning for yourself. Don't take on too much at one time; begin moderately, and after you have managed to stick to your schedule for a number of days, add on more. For example, you may set aside two hours in the morning to complete a page of Talmud, with Rashi and *Tosafot*. After a while, if you study diligently, you may be able to finish your Talmud quota in less time and have fifteen minutes or more left in which you can study the portion of the week with Rashi's commentary. You may discover that with greater diligence and efficiency you can increase your learning even more. Little by little you will be able to fill your whole day with many courses of Torah study.

It is beneficial to write out a schedule for yourself on a sheet of paper, starting with the time you wish to get up in the morning and continuing with all your activities. Use the sheet as a reference, checking back during the day to see if you have accomplished what you set out to do.

Even someone who is still in yeshivah can add additional periods of learning to the official yeshivah schedule during lunchtime and at night. Why not steal some time to devote to God from the edges of the yeshivah schedule?

Whether you are in yeshivah or not, the schedule of study that you set for yourself should be followed to the minute. You should get to the point that if for some reason you are not able to complete a period of learning, you should feel pained, as if the day itself remained uncompleted. You should hear the pages that you were unable to study calling out to you and reprimanding you for neglecting them.

Each day, make it a practice to check yesterday's schedule. What you did not complete yesterday, you should attempt to complete today. You should only do this, however, if you were unable to finish because of laziness or lack of diligence. If you were thrown off schedule because of a particularly difficult passage, or you explored a question in depth, then you should not force yourself to complete today the pages that you missed yesterday. The whole idea of keeping to a quantitative schedule is to discipline yourself to learn crisply and without meandering. But if you are learning in depth with real diligence and are involved in trying to understand the profundity of God's Torah, so much the better. The real point of Torah learning is to learn as deeply as possible because that is the way you merit to cleave to God through your learning.

If you have reached the level where you can learn in depth

without a partner, then you should set your schedule not according to how many pages you wish to cover, but according to how many hours you want to devote. The amount of pages covered becomes insignificant.

Do not think that the more work you take on, the more you will be tempted to deceive yourself by learning only superficially, since you are trying to complete a certain quantitative schedule. On the contrary, the opposite is true. In general, the more work you take on, the more you will be stimulated to work—not just quantitatively and in a superficial way, but also in terms of depth and precision. You will grow stronger and more courageous. You will be totally transformed into an industrious person who regularly bends himself under hard labor. And the reverse is equally true. If you did not feel yourself committed to accomplishing a great deal each day, laziness would creep back into your psyche, and the little that you did study, you would learn superficially, joylessly, and without intellectual understanding.

This principle is very important. Just as it is impossible for a blind man to see, or a donkey to reason intellectually, it is impossible for a young person who does not feel himself under a yoke of obligation to rise early and work efficiently. A young person who has not made a strong commitment to himself is unable to work with diligence and precision. By now, you should be able to figure out the reason yourself. A lazy person is one whose soul-powers are slumbering. These powers must be prodded awake and forced to work. The self-imposed yoke of a rigid schedule arouses and awakens and pushes these soul-powers to work. Once they have been aroused, and are already making an effort to work, the next step—that of deepening one's learning—occurs naturally. However, without the yoke or obligation of a certain amount of work that must be completed each day, there is nothing to shake the soul awake; it remains sleeping and makes no effort. Your learning remains small in quantity and inferior in quality, without any depth whatsoever.

CHAPTER 6

THE ILL OF EGOTISM

We don't intend to catalogue in this book all the various kinds of diseases of the soul which might afflict young people, along with their remedies, as a pharmacist would. We will mention only the most fundamental. Just as we discussed laziness, which is so severe an affliction that one cannot take even the first step towards serving God until one has shaken its influence, so, too, must we discuss egotism, which is such a desperate disease that those who suffer from it, God forbid, are in grave danger of spiritual descent. To our distress, many of our young people are afflicted with this illness, the symptoms of which are a lack of understanding and a heart of stone.

An egotistical young person is one who considers himself completely independent of all others. He has formed his own opinions, which, in his estimation, are also completely independent. He is certain that he knows exactly how to behave and what is good for him and bad for him in every situation. If one of his parents or teachers tries to advise him or guide him, he is certain that his understanding is greater than theirs is, and he therefore experiences their intercessions as the arbitrary commands of tyrants who enjoy imposing their will on others.

This kind of student begins to feel increasingly distant from his teacher, until he is unwilling to accept any of his words of Torah or wisdom.

If the student himself does not hurriedly try to heal this breach and drive these feelings of alienation from his heart, he will come to a bitter end. There is nothing to hope for from such a young person; he will not develop any good qualities, and those good qualities that are inherent in every Jewish heart will become distorted and spoiled within him. They will become totally negative. He will lose all sense of right and wrong; he will hate those things that one should love and will love those things that are best avoided. The prophet Isaiah had him also in mind when he lamented on behalf of God, "I had hoped for delicious grapes, but they have grown bitter" (Isaiah 5:2). A Jewish mind and many positive qualities were planted within him. God had hoped for sweet fruits to emerge. Instead, everything has gone to waste, has turned into poison grapes and bitter clusters.

This disease is a form of pride. Our sages long ago predicted that in the era preceding the coming of the Messiah, arrogance would be increasingly prevalent. In previous generations, students felt submissive before their parents, teachers, and counselors. The students themselves recognized how limited their knowledge and experience was in the face of the awesome task they confronted: guiding and educating themselves to become great leaders in Israel. They looked on their teacher as one lost in a dark forest at night might look at a man who has suddenly arrived to lead him from terrible darkness to civilization. They loved him and constantly blessed him; every sound that came out of his mouth was sacred to them. They devoured everything he said and caused it to penetrate their heart and soul. The young people of today who are afflicted with the disease of egotism are unwilling to let the words in; instead, they pridefully believe themselves self-sufficient—"The way I understand things is the best and truest; I rely on myself and I travel my own path."

Judge for yourselves, dear readers, those among you who have absorbed what we have previously discussed: the specialness of Jewish children, their closeness to God, and the charge they have been given to make the Jewish people great. Is there any illness as great as their illness; is there any affliction as terrible? You, those of you who have attached yourselves to God, there is no need to convince you. The words of God, "Honor thy father and mother" and "Let the awe in which you hold your teacher be like the awe of heaven," are engraved on your hearts. You realize well that it is God who teaches you Torah, that His voice and words become manifest through the voice and words of your teacher. Sitting in yeshivah, you feel some of what was felt at Mount Sinai—the overwhelming awe and joy of Israel as they heard God's voice from the flames. When you remind yourself that the room you are sitting in is filled with angelic and seraphic beings, that God's voice is emerging from their midst and is transmitted through your rebbe to your ears and heart, fear, joy, awe, and love make your body shudder and your heart tremble. Your whole self submits to God's Torah as you hear it through your teacher's words.

It is not necessary to warn you of the destructive nature of haughty pride and egotism. However, the Mishnah (*Avot* 4), tells us "be exceedingly humble-spirited." More than with any of the other undesirable character traits, one must distance oneself from haughty pride. Not even a trace of this trait should remain within you. There may be students among you who are not so prideful as to directly challenge their teachers and parents, yet they still retain a vestige of haughtiness within. They don't really respect and value their person or their teaching; they don't feel a need or desire to submit to their influence. Even though this kind of student may attempt to overcome his inner pridefulness and make an effort to listen to the practical instructions of his parents and teachers, at the center his heart will still be rock hard, because of his egotistical feelings of superiority and independence. Such a person must also undergo a cleansing until his heart and soul are completely purified of all traces of this trait. In addition, this cleansing of haughty pride concerns not only parents and teachers, but also concerns friends and contemporaries as well. This includes the arrogance you might display toward friends, whether because your mind is sharper than theirs is, or for any other reason, or for no reason at all. This kind of conceit is also like a stab wound inflicted by one's evil inclination. If your personality is contaminated with this kind of haughtiness, please: Rise up, cleanse, and purify yourself—or risk, God forbid, impairing your personality forever.

Instead of trying to rise above each other, you who are each so precious, you must realize that both you and your friends are like angelic beings of great purity, part of God's host and army, whom He sent to this world in order to vanquish it for Him. Hannah first used the expression "Lord of Hosts" while praying for God to grant her a child. The sages explained that in utilizing that particular name of God it was as if Hannah were saying: "Lord of the world, of all the hosts and armies that You created, is it so difficult to give me one little child?" Everything is clearly implied in this exegesis.

You, Jewish children, are each like one of the hosts and soldiers of God that Hannah requested. You have the same function that the angels do in the higher realms: to conquer the world for God and crown Him King. This will not be accomplished with sword or spear, but with the spirit of God that is within you. A special, holy nation will be established through you; through you, God's light will shine and the world will be sanctified through His holiness. When arrogance drives you apart from your friends, in reality you are distancing yourself from God, the Lord of Hosts. The sages have already told us that God has said of one who is arrogant: "He and I cannot live together." It is as if the arrogant person were literally pushing God's presence out of the world.

Pure-hearted students, love each other! Be scrupulous about observing the Mishnah's admonishment: "Let your friend's honor be as dear to you as your own." Do not let your love for each other seem forced; that is, as if you really loved only yourself, but since you've been commanded to love others you've compelled yourself to act accordingly, contributing from your ample store of self-love a little bit toward your friend. This kind of love is worthless even while it lasts, and it certainly doesn't last for long, but dissipates quickly and vanishes.

Your love for each other should grow out of your knowledge that you are all agents and messengers of God. None of you can rightfully feel independent of all others; none of you has the right to dismiss your friends as insignificant people. Everyone's task and position is set by Him who sent you. If you all serve God with all your strength, He will raise up all of you and make you spiritually great and physically prosperous, according to your effort and your humility. Many times we have witnessed young people with tremendous intellectual talents who have faltered because of arrogance and pride. This applies to adults too; even if they have succeeded in becoming great scholars, if they become arrogant, God will bring them low. And, of course, the opposite is also clearly true: many children who seemed of low stature as young people grew into majestic leaders of Israel in adulthood.

CHAPTER 7

THE ILL OF FALSE HUMILITY
AND ITS CURE

In writing this book, we have no intention of releasing you from the obligation and necessity of poring over the Talmud, *Midrash, Shulchan Aruch,* and all the other holy books that guide us upward on the path to God. On the contrary, the whole purpose of this book is to aid us in fixing ourselves and healing ourselves so as to be better able to deeply contemplate and absorb the sacred words of these works into our soul and body. Let us soak all our limbs in the spring emerging from the house of God and the holy chambers of paradise. We have not collected and copied in this pamphlet all the passages from the Talmud, the Code of Jewish Law, and other holy works that instruct us in proper behavior. These works are open to all. Whoever wishes to be close to God, to be one of His pure and righteous servants, should study them. We have reproduced only such quotations as directly relate to the matter at hand.

The first paragraph of the Code of Jewish Law states: "And one should not be ashamed by the taunts of those who deride his service of God." This kind of shame is a great obstacle because a person who is susceptible to it is unable to think independently, but instead is drawn and pushed by others. His fear of ridicule causes him to set aside his own opinions; he ends up doing only what he thinks his mockers would approve of. His performance of good deeds is thwarted by the possibility that a neighbor might laugh at him. He must conform to the expectations of an ever-widening group, in an effort to win their approval. A person like this has essentially handed over to corrupt people possession of his body and soul; he makes himself subject to their thoughts and decisions and domination. He himself is the only person who remains powerless.

This despicable affliction has its source in childhood. Children have not yet formed their own opinions about things; they must continually measure their behavior in terms of the words, acts, and behavior of the adults that surround them, judging constantly which of his actions will bring approval and which ridicule. This kind of thinking may continue even when the child becomes an adult. He may remain more concerned with what others find attractive than with true goodness.

Jewish child, listen to this principle, which applies throughout our discussion: Strengthen yourself with great courage and use all your might to uproot from within and distance yourself from every evil or foolish quality you possess while you are still a child, or it may well remain with you and cause you permanent damage. Have compassion on yourself and do not allow yourself to be seduced by your evil inclination, which will try to reassure you that your young age is the source of whatever character faults you possess, and that these will disappear or heal on their own as you get older. Do not give credence to this argument. Though time advances, people remain the same. There are adults, even old people, who are childish and even infantile in their approach to life and in their essence. Their immaturity is the result of neglect; they did not work on themselves at a young age, but instead relied on the advance of years to change them automatically.

Returning to our topic: How does this feeling of shame remain within a person from early childhood, and how can it be cured? At the beginning of his process of development, a child has no independent body of knowledge and opinions and is unable to distinguish between good and evil. He does not have an inner spirit to inform him and guide his actions. He must absorb his ideas from outside himself. His only means of discovering what to do in every situation is by assessing the behavior of those who are bigger and more developed than he is. If, as he grows older, he does not become independent in his thinking and establish his own internal means of judging and deciding, he will remain extremely sensitive to the opinions of others, and this will become his sole criterion for action. He will bend himself to accommodate all their foolish whims and will be shamefully aware of the possibility of their scorn. All of his efforts will be directed toward making a good impression on others.

Incredibly, there are people who have been stricken with two seemingly opposite plagues at once: feelings of inferiority and lack of independence in their thinking as well as the haughtiness and egotism we discussed in the last chapter. They arrogantly dismiss their rabbis and teachers and declare that they have arrived at an independent conclusion of utmost clarity on their own: They must set aside all considerations and opinions in favor of the ideologies of the decadent outside world, to which they are drawn like sheep to slaughter. Are not their distortions laughable? They display such arrogance and haughtiness, all in order to devalue, nullify, and destroy themselves!

That this arrogance has been accompanied by feelings of degradation and insignificance is natural because this arrogance itself is an alien characteristic. This rancid arrogance has a spark of idolatry at its source. Its purpose is to ruin and destroy the people of God, those who have survived the onslaughts of Nevuzradan, Nero, Caesar, and Titus. It is impossible that such a quality would emerge on its own from a Jewish soul. Arrogance is an affliction affecting the whole world right now. Jews who show this characteristic do so because they have no independent opinions and thoughts of their own. As they bend to the influence of the whole world, they are also exposed to this putrid fungus, and therefore they rebel against their parents and teachers.

To rid oneself of this corrupt disease, whose corrosive influence

has been active since childhood, it is not enough to acquire a body
of knowledge and opinions. It is crucial that this knowledge and
these opinions be your own. Even those people who are constantly
afraid of what others might say and consistently submit to the influence of others, have ideas and opinions. Yet, even if they have
already grown into adulthood, their ideas and opinions are not their
own and did not grow out of their own inner spirit. They were
absorbed from the external world. A child who wishes to imitate
an adult puts on the hat and coat of an adult, and everyone laughs
in amusement. The kind of people we have been discussing have
already figured out how to imitate the whole world without being
laughed at. But in both cases, there is a monkey-like aspect to their
conduct. It is just like a monkey who is trying to make his actions
conform to those of human beings. If the world decides that good
is bad, they too will begin to scorn Torah and Torah scholars. If
the world becomes insanely fascinated with childish ballgames, they
too will bow and scrape and bend to this new fashion, and submit
to the enthusiasm of the fans.

Our concern is to awaken in you your own autonomous source
of knowledge and judgment. You are, in your essence, a Jew. The
spirit of Israel will be revealed from within you. The spirit of your
ancestors, which is dormant within you, will begin to unfold and
grow. This spirit will urge you forward and compel you to serve
the God of Israel and observe His commandments, to listen to God's
voice as it speaks through your parents and teachers. You will find
those people who have distanced themselves from Torah worthy of
ridicule. Where Torah is concerned, you will be mighty, fierce as
a panther, utterly fearless and unashamed.

We do not need to warn you about the kind of people who
openly attempt to sway you, God forbid, from the path of God
toward certain spiritual destruction and darkness. You instinctively
know how dangerous they are. You will treat their words as if they
were a scorching fire, or arrows shot at you from a bow. You will
distance yourself from them and all their associates.

No, it is the hypocrites that we must warn you about. They
will approach you innocently and say: "We also fear the God of our
fathers and serve Him as you do. But at this particular time in history,
we must compromise a little bit. You have already studied Torah;

now it is time for you to learn a craft or business." They will even have the audacity to use the words of holy teachings to bolster their argument: "Even the Mishnah says that it is good to combine Torah with labor."

They will also attempt to sway you to compromise in regard to your worship of God: "Times have changed," they will say, "and it is no longer necessary to be as careful and precise in observing all the commandments and customs or as cautious in avoiding sin as it used to be." You shouldn't argue or dispute with them; in your heart respond to them thus: "If it's true as you have said that times have changed, they have changed for the worse. In former good days, the merchants and laborers all served God; now, most of the young men who leave the yeshivah to work for a living have been completely lost to spirituality. Do you want to murder me too, to burn my pure soul in the fire of this hell, and to cast my body, this innocent fledgling of a dove, into a pot of boiling excrement? I will not listen to you, I will absolutely not agree with you, I grasp the scroll of Torah, which has divinity within it, and embrace it with my two arms. As long as my soul remains within me, I will not part with it.

"As for their claim that I must begin to worry about how I will support myself as an adult, what are they talking about? Are they blind? Haven't they seen that, both in times of economic crisis— such as now—and in times when it was easier to make a living, everyone suffered or prospered equally? Many tradesmen and laborers go hungry, and many Torah scholars are wealthy. Our sages have already taught us that neither wealth nor poverty come from professions. God answers whomever He wants, and gives wealth to those He sees fit to give it to." As for now, you should say: "I will fill my body and soul with Torah and holiness. When I grow up, I will start to make an effort to make a living, and God, whose path I follow, will aid, sustain, and save me."

If, God forbid, you were faced with powerful obstacles that you could not overcome, and were not able to remain a full-time student of Torah, but were forced at a young age to leave the yeshivah for the marketplace, do not despair. Do not give up being a Jew with your whole heart, and do not abandon God. Trials and tribulations more difficult than those that forced you to leave the house of God, the yeshivah, await you. Be strong and withstand them, bind yourself to God and He will reciprocate and be with you in everything you do.

No day should pass without the study of Torah. Pray to God from the depths of your heart. Pour your soul out to Him in whatever way you wish to, whether in the manner we are going to suggest or in any other way, whether in words or in the silence of your heart: "I beseech You God, who knows the hearts of men, You know that I did not cease my study of Torah in a spirit of rebellion or treachery. I did not deliberately leave the world of truth for the world of vanity. You know the suffering and hardship I experienced that broke my strength and depressed my spirit until I was forced to leave the yeshivah in search of sustenance. Please do not think that I have abandoned or will ever abandon the Torah or Your holy service. I still pray to You, learn more than I would have thought I could, all my thoughts find their end point in You. Oh God, my heart is fearful and my soul shudders. I am a tender lamb, and a long and menacing way stretches out before me. The world I have entered is full of foes and adversaries; savage beasts and scoundrels are waiting to ambush and attack me in body and soul. But if I am like a lost sheep, are You not the shepherd of Israel? This is my whole hope—let Your glory guide us like sheep—this is the source of my strength. When a lamb is lost in the forest and is about to be torn up and devoured by lions or bears, its whole soul cries out in fear, and the shepherd hears, his mercy is aroused and he speeds to the rescue. I take it upon myself to cry out to You during my entire long and difficult journey: 'Save me!' You will hear me from heaven and will grasp unto the fringes of my mind and the strings of my heart in order to save me and guide me toward You."

Keep what we have just discussed in your awareness at all times. Do not distance yourself from your companions who were able to keep studying Torah day and night and who inhale the atmosphere of paradise and the breeze formed by the sweeping wings of the angelic beings that inhabit all the spiritual universes. Try to see your yeshivah friends from time to time and especially on Shabbat and on holidays. Schedule for yourself a period of Torah study every day. Recite from the Psalms every day. Pray with deep intention and attentiveness. Be certain to add time to the Sabbath and holidays. Make your Shabbat and holidays completely holy. Wait for the Shabbat all week with the awareness that on Shabbat the noise and din of hell recedes and we enter the Garden of Eden. Spend the Shabbat learning and speaking holy words with your companions; from time to time study chasidic and ethical texts.

And you who have merited to learn Torah constantly, do not distance yourself from the unfortunate soul that has been forced out into the hail that fell in Egypt, ice with fire inside, a hail that falls on everyone whom God does not wondrously save. Have mercy on him. You who are sheltered beneath the wings of the *Shechinah*, draw your friend toward this protection too, as long as he still feels close to God and longs for the time when he used to dwell with you in paradise. And if you detect in him signs of fermentation and change, speak to him gently, and from your heart—once, twice, three times. But if this does not help, distance yourself, so as not to be burnt by the fire that is engulfing his soul. For even after he reads everything we have written here, after we have cautioned him and warned him, he will still need miracles and great compassion from on high if he is to remain a faithful Jew. For have we cautioned him any more than the soul is cautioned and commanded before its descent into this world? And yet there are many who are led away and lost, may God guard us against them and all their multitudes.

CHAPTER 8

THE IMPORTANCE OF SPIRITUAL AND CHARACTER GROWTH

onscientious student, review what we have said so far, and reflect on each specific kind of *tikun*—fixing—we have recommended. Internalize each teaching and attempt to use the guidance it provides to mend your areas of deficiency. Don't be disheartened if you are not able to succeed in improving yourself all at once. To fall toward spiritual destruction can be accomplished suddenly; fixing requires much difficult and constant effort. On the contrary, if you are aware of a certain character flaw, and, after reflecting on what we have written, you begin an attempt to repair this flaw, and you imagine that you have corrected it all at once, you can be sure that you are deceiving yourself. It takes many attempts and much time to work on yourself, little by little, until you successfully vanquish an undesirable trait.

You must also be aware of the basic fact that we have not even begun to discuss the means through which one is able to spiritually ascend to one's proper level. What we have discussed so far is comparable to cleaning out a room—removing the dust, chasing out the mice. The room has still not been made ready to serve as a proper place to invite the king to come to live in. Its walls need whitening, it needs to be decorated with flowers and enhanced with beautiful furnishings and so forth, all according to the customs and temperament of the king.

A person afflicted by laziness or one who lacks an independent center of judgment exists in such a state of ruin that he will find it impossible to even arrive at the outer boundaries of serving God. That is why we began our discourse with instructions for washing away the poisonous and corrupting dust of these qualities. To be a Jew, a member of the special people who have been drawn close to God, the people He desired and with whom He made a pact, more is necessary. Even after everything dirty and repulsive has been expelled, there is a need for beautification and a continual process of drawing close.

Look at these astonishing words in the *Midrash* (*Kohelet* 1). The *Midrash* asks: "Was Israel created for the sake of the Torah, or was the Torah created for the sake of Israel?" The *Midrash* concludes that the Torah was created for the sake of Israel. The Torah, which is so holy, and which the angels longed for, was created, in its essence, for the sake of Israel! The infinite One came to Sinai accompanied by surrounding minions of holy beings, filling the skies with thunder and shaking the earth to its core—all for the sake of Israel. The purpose of God's appearance at Sinai, and of everything that went on there, was to draw you and your companions close to Him, so that you would become part of the special people that are His intimates. This closeness should be the goal that you constantly long for; your heart and soul should yearn to feel the presence of the Holy One of Israel who dwells within Israel. You must work toward this goal; you must awaken your soul, which seems shut up inside your body as if in prison, and lift it closer to its divine source that waits for it expectantly. Much work, activity, and practice is necessary to accomplish this task.

Conscientious student, I suspect that our words have frightened you. Up until now, you thought that the spiritual advancement demanded of you involved cleansing your character and clearing

away the poisonous dust of bad traits. This, you believed, would
be enough to allow you to ascend and become an authentic and
true member of the Jewish people. But now it has become apparent
that even after the cleansing and mending of undesirable characteristics, more is being demanded: spiritual ascent and closeness to
God. You are being asked to ascend until your whole inner being
is drawn close to God. This level of spiritual achievement is something you have doubtless seen as a goal that only great *tzaddikim* and
the unusually gifted are required to strive for and pursue, while the
average simple Jew is exempt from such efforts. You are greatly
mistaken. It is true that great *tzaddikim* have achieved a closeness to
God and have elevated their souls to a degree that is far beyond
the capacity of a simple person. But it is also true that it is virtually
impossible for any Jew to be a servant of God if his heart is arid
and his soul is in a state of concealment and sleep. It is necessary,
even for the simple person, to at least intermittently raise himself
up beyond himself and beyond the world. Moshe told the Jewish
people: "To you it has been shown to know that the Lord is God;
there is none else beside Him." Moshe was not speaking only to his
generation, for the Torah is eternal, and Moshe is our eternal leader
and guide. He is still calling out and proclaiming to every Jewish
heart and soul: "To you it has been shown to know that the Lord
is God; there is none else besides Him." The kind of knowledge
that causes us to think that God exists on high, outside of us, is
not enough: "We have been shown to know"—it is most important
that we see and feel Him, may His name be blessed. You, diligent
student, have already been shown a little of this kind of knowledge.
We may not see Him as the prophets and the great *tzaddikim* did,
who actually saw His presence right in front of their eyes. But
Moshe, our teacher, has already hinted at the kind of knowledge
that is readily available to us: "Know therefore this day and return
it to your heart, that the Lord is God in heaven above and on the
earth beneath: there is no other." Return it to your heart, think
about the experience of your own heart, and then you will know
that the Lord is God. For what is the trembling before God that
you feel in your heart, and what is the longing and desire for Torah,
for the commandments, for true prayer? And why, when you start
to imagine how good it would be to be a great *tzaddik*, as close to

God as the *tzaddikim* of previous generations, or how happy you would be if you could pray like the Maggid of Kozhnitz, for example, and cleave to God and unite with him in a state of supernal purity, why does your heart begin to shake, and your whole body shiver from the yearning that burns like a fire within you? What could inspire you to such feelings but the Lord, God of Hosts? For it is before God that the soul trembles, and it is for Him that the soul yearns to the point of dissolution. "Know therefore this day and return it to your heart, that the Lord is God." When you return to your heart, then you will know that the Lord is God.

Moshe, our teacher, did not only say "Know therefore this day . . . that the Lord is God in heaven above" but also "on the earth below, there is no other." This is of primary importance: to see and know that below here on earth there is no other but God and God's holiness. A person who has a foreign god dwelling in his heart will be unable to realize or declare this. The *Gemara* (*Shabbat* 105) states: "What kind of foreign god dwells inside a person?— the evil inclination." How can a person claim that he is a Jew and a servant of God if he also serves the foreign god inside himself, worships it, listens to it and fulfills its desires. How can he approach God and address Him, saying: "Blessed are you, O Lord, our God"— calling Him "our God" when facing Him, while in his heart, a foreign god has made itself a nest and forces him to submit to its rule.

Your main task is to expel the evil inclination from your midst. We certainly don't expect you to accomplish this all at once, to wake up one morning and find yourself purified in every fragment of your being, healed of every trace of malady. That is an impossibility. All that is asked of you is to begin the task, to begin and to completely give yourself over to it. We can compare our situation to that of a king, whose enemy has stolen in and is dwelling in his palace. If the minister in charge of the palace attempts with all his strength to expel the enemy, the king won't be angry with him, nor will he abandon him. The king will help him with the battle and will quickly move in to occupy each room and every foot of the castle from which the enemy is ejected. But if the minister stays idle and neglects to do battle with the enemy and wage war, and especially if the king feels that the minister has made a secret pact with the enemy and is taking orders from him, the king will become inflamed with anger. Incensed, he will reproach the minister and accuse him of being a deceitful traitor. "You have given my home to my enemy," he will say, "and have made peace with him, and you have the audacity to try and fool me by declaring that I am your king and you are my servant?"

You have certainly grasped the meaning of the parable on your own. Your body and soul are the palace of the Infinite One, the place where He dwells. The evil inclination has stolen in and set up house within you. The King of the world will become very angry at you, the minister of the palace, once He sees that you have not only allowed this enemy to take over the palace, but have made peace with it, have submitted to it and listen to its demands. He will become incensed, will accuse you of treachery and deceit at having continued all the while to repeat: "Blessed are you, O Lord, our God." You must begin, therefore, to cleanse and purify your character traits and your thoughts so that you cease to be like a cistern filled with muddy waters. You must work wholeheartedly to bring holiness to your thoughts and your character; God must be their king, so that all your actions, words, and thoughts are governed by Him.

A Jew's whole ability to drive out whatever evil is within him, to transform himself and become good, and to make himself inwardly holy, has its source in the power of choice with which God has endowed us. While animals are compelled by instinct in all their actions and thoughts, in everything they do, God has given man the power to choose life or its opposite, God forbid. Like a compassionate father He asks all of us to "choose life, that you may live." For a man to choose between two possible paths, however, he must stand over and above them, outside of them. The *Midrash* (Genesis 22) states: "Happy is the man who stands above his sins, and woe is the man whose sins stand over him." Would it be possible for a drunkard, while still intoxicated, to decide not to get drunk anymore? Who could possibly come to such a decision with his mind deranged and his spirit confused by wine? Similarly, how can anyone decide to choose the path of holiness while his spirit is being pulled downward by base instincts, or while his mind is still afflicted by the evil inclination, which causes him to confuse evil with good and good with evil?

It is imperative, therefore, that a person, at least occasionally, lift himself up, above his sins, his petty desires, his spiritual afflictions, and the whole world. At this moment of ascension and purity, he will see and feel that he is, in his essence, a Jew who is very close to God. He will suddenly realize the foolishness of his childish actions; he will see that his evil inclination, with all its temptations, is like a poisonous viper. He will feel ashamed and frightened and say to himself: "These evil qualities are so degraded and despicable. How can I cut myself, as well as my soul, which is the root of my ancestors, off from the source of life and holiness? I have cast myself into a nest of vipers, a place filled with a rancid stench, a place of death." He will shiver and shake; with all his strength he will attempt to rouse his soul and body, to free them from the quicksand and the serpents that are coiled around him; he will gather strength and resolve to choose a life of purity and divine holiness from now on.

Don't you yourself feel, on days that you learn Torah with perseverance and pray with proper intention according to your capacity, during moments that you draw yourself a little closer to holiness, ashamed of your foolish actions? Don't they seem tainted in your eyes? Isn't it easier to exercise self-control and to straighten yourself out? This is why we have instructed you to spiritually ascend. Ascension is not only for great *tzaddikim*. It is a necessity for every Jew, one that must be accomplished within the context of whatever his spiritual condition is. At least from time to time, he must ascend with all his being.

CHAPTER 9

ADVICE FOR GROWTH
AND SELF-IMPROVEMENT

Diligent student, you have certainly asked yourself the following questions: The Torah contains within it every spiritual level, it is even the dwelling place of God. Why has my learning not brought me to states of spiritual ascension? Yes, it is true that at times I feel a little spiritually uplifted, but does this tiny increment represent the entire distance that I may ascend? Have I arrived already at the spiritual state that this book seeks for me and promises, and that my soul has been waiting for? Why do some people learn Torah and then stop learning and plunge into the lowest depths? What happened to the promise that our holy sages made, that the light that is in Torah will suffice to transform one to goodness?

It is true that those who learn Torah connect themselves to "the One who teaches Torah to His people Israel," that is, to the God of Israel. But you need to know how to learn Torah. The *Zohar* states: "A person that thinks that the garment covering the Torah is all there is to Torah, has no portion in the world to come." This means that according to the *Zohar*, a person who utilizes only dry human intellect in learning Torah, as if he were engaged in any other intellectual pursuit, has no portion in the world to come. The manifest intellectual content of the Torah is only the outer garment of the Torah. And who is wrapped in this garment? God is. When one learns Torah, one must attempt to reach the hidden God who has concealed Himself in the Torah. You wish to purify your soul. Rabbi Akiva has already stated: "Just as a mikvah purifies the defiled, so does God purify Israel." But only someone who arrives at the mikvah and then enters it achieves purity. Penetrate, therefore, by way of the Torah's garments, to the Holy One blessed be He who exists within them, and be purified.

It is true that during the time you are actually learning it is very difficult to arouse your soul with lofty thoughts; you need to concentrate on the subject matter deeply, with your entire mind and your whole self, you need to work intensively, with the kind of effort that spends one's strength. You must therefore arouse your soul before you begin to learn, become aware of it, reveal it, and bind it to God. Then, as you learn Torah, while you labor at uncovering the simple meaning of the text, your soul, aroused and revealed, will speedily pierce through the garment to its king, the one to whom it belongs; it will unite with Him.

But the fact that your soul, through which you wish to ascend and draw near to God, is hidden from you, concealed within your body, asleep within your physical being, is not a good state of affairs. If you do not awaken your soul from its eternal sleep, extricate it from the woven mat of reeds that is its grave, how will you ascend and draw close to the Holy One of Israel? You must know, however, that you cannot awaken your holy soul the same way you rouse a sleeping body. A sleeping body need only be awakened once, while the soul can be roused only by constantly forcing it to labor and work. For it is possible to fulfill the commandments, using your hands and all the limbs of your body, including your mouth, during prayer, while the soul remains veiled and asleep. It is necessary to force the soul into activity and toil; this will cause it to awaken and be revealed. You must therefore remember at all times, even when you are not studying Torah, that you are a servant of God and that

you must bind yourself to Him. Strengthen your faith in God.
Several times a day repeat to yourself affirmations of faith: "I believe
in God truly and with all my heart. It is clear to me, my Father and
King, that You are the Lord of the world and of all the worlds that
You created, and of everything that is in them. You are the Lord
of the heavenly angels and of all the tiny creatures that crawl beneath
the earth. You surround me, and fill my body and my spirit. I am
Your servant, and I hereby give myself completely over to You."
Let this thought circulate through your consciousness until you have
examined its every aspect; it contains everything within it.

Gradually accustom your heart and soul to open and pour
outward toward God, in meditation and prayer. Both children and
adults whose spiritual knowledge is undeveloped think that the troubles and concerns that are the impetus for prayer are really what
prayer is all about. Their approach to prayer is comparable to the
approach a poor man might take when asking a rich man for help,
or that of a commoner imploring a king for aid or salvation. But
only an ignorant person thinks of praying in this fashion, thus
depriving it of its spiritual significance as if its whole meaning derived
from calamities and disturbances, and believes that if he had no
pressing necessities he would not need prayer. In reality, it is the
process of prayer itself, during which the heart is drawn close to
God and the soul flows out toward Him, that is the most important
aspect of prayer. Moreover, as you will see in the following words
from the *Midrash*, not only does prayer not derive its importance
from our crises and troubles, but at times God sends troubles and
concerns our way in order to provoke us to pray. The *Midrash* (Exodus
Rabbah 1) says: "Rabbi Yehoshua ben Levi stated: 'To what can it
(prayer) be compared? To a king who was traveling and heard the
voice of a princess who was being attacked by bandits crying out
for help. The king saved her. After a time, he decided that he
wanted to marry her. He tried to speak to her, but she refused to
speak to him. What did the king do? He sent the bandits out to
frighten her again, so that she would cry out to him for help and
he would have the opportunity to hear and respond to her.'"

You certainly understand on your own the significance of this
parable. Your soul is a princess that the Holy One blessed be He
wishes to marry—that is to say He wants the soul to draw near to

Him and unite with Him in holiness. To accomplish this it is necessary to speak to God and to pray to Him. For through inner prayer that emerges from the recesses of the heart, the soul is awakened from its slumber. It longs for and then unites with the King, the King of the universe. This is the primary purpose and goal of prayer. Certain problems are visited on a person specifically to cause him to pray and cry out to God from the depths of his heart and soul, just as the king in the parable sent the bandits to frighten the princess so that she would cry out to him. When you wish to awaken your soul and to prevent it from sleeping or withdrawing deeper under cover during prayer, you too should rouse yourself at first by concentrating on those things that pain you or that you need. To this end, you should focus during the formal *Amidah* on your immediate needs and desires, both spiritual and material. For example, during the prayers for spiritual knowledge ("You grace man with wisdom") and repentance ("Return us, Father, to our Torah"), focus on the longing inside you that God open your heart and soul to Torah and divine service. During the prayer for a bountiful year ("Bless us with a good year"), which is not only about agriculture and crops, but about material sustenance in general, pour your soul out and stir up your heart as you ask God to send your parents a means of livelihood. While you pray, your soul will awaken and be revealed, and will unite with its King, to whom it belongs. Soon this will occur not only when you are praying for your personal needs. Once you have accustomed your soul to rise and to awaken, you will find yourself even more suffused with true fiery passion when you are focused on godly matters. When you recite "You are holy and Your name is holy" your soul will become activated and will actually feel itself standing right before the source of holiness, directly addressing this source and praising Him. Inflamed, your soul will dissolve into the lovely, holy pleasantness of the Holy One of Israel. You will be similarly inspired during all of prayer.

You should not confine this kind of prayer to the three obligatory services of the morning, afternoon, and evening. All day, you should try to find free moments when you can meditate before God in prayer and song. The more you accustom yourself to this kind of soul-meditation, the softer your heart will become. Your spirit will lift, and your soul will draw closer to God.

You will be able, however, to rouse your soul to speak to God only if you strengthen the cognitive basis of your faith. You must think about how God's glory fills the whole universe, and how you yourself exist within Him and His holiness, even though you cannot see Him. More than a single thought is necessary. The more you reflect on these matters of faith, over and over again, constantly, the easier it will become to stimulate your soul to speak to God— Who faces you at all times.

It may still be difficult for you to imagine that you are standing before God, and that your soul, during prayer, has become stirred and inflamed because it is actually in the presence of Him whose glory fills the whole universe. You exist, after all, in a material world; your eyes see only the physical universe, and your hands touch only concrete matter. Look then toward the sky and contemplate, focus your mind and think: I exist on this side, while on the other side of the heavens, there is another world, completely different from this one. There are angels there, and seraphim; the souls of the patriarchs and of the prophets and *tzaddikim*. The throne of glory is suspended in their midst, and God, great, holy, and awesome, is present on the throne. In this world, God is hidden, while there His splendorous presence is very much apparent and revealed. Strengthen yourself, look, and think some more. "I stand on this side of the divine,. and I say 'Blessed are You, O Lord.' It is You, Lord, the one toward Whom I lift my eyes, whether I see You or not, it is You that I bless. I shut my eyes and look at You, and bless You and speak to You."

Listen and you will hear how far your gaze reaches, what you reach when you lift your eyes toward God. The *Tur Orach Chayim* quotes some of the following passage, which is found in the *Sefer Heichalot*: "The Lord has said, 'Oh, you heavens, and you angelic beings who descend past the holy Chariot, you will be blessed by God if you tell My children how I respond when they sanctify Me and recite "Holy, holy, holy." Teach them to lift their eyes toward where their prayers are received (that is, toward heaven—"and this is the gate of heaven"), tell them to lift themselves upward. My greatest pleasure in the world is to see them lift their eyes toward Me; My eyes gaze back into their eyes, I grip the throne of glory, which has the image of Jacob impressed upon it, I lovingly embrace and kiss every Jew, I remember their exile and speed up the process of their redemption.' "

What can we say in the face of such a description? Picture it to yourself. Our eyes look upward, as if we were looking directly into His eyes. He gazes back at us and is delighted by our gaze. It is as if parent and child were looking at each other's face; the father cannot restrain himself, his love overwhelms him and he reaches out and hugs and kisses his child. The heart dissolves in bliss and longing, the soul bursts out of its confines and in fiery enthusiasm calls out: "Toward my Father, my Holy One, I rise, I fly."

Look at the sky and meditate on these things. Strengthen and give courage to your eyes and your heart, and gaze with intensity and concentration. Be especially aware when addressing God as "You"; even if you are not gazing skyward at that exact moment be very aware of the meaning of "You." Focus your mind on the fact that it is God Who is before you, God Whom you are addressing as "You."

Please do not think that the only ways to arouse and awaken your soul are through the techniques we have described. This is not the case. Every Jew who has a minimum of internal self-discipline, every Jew who works on himself, will from time to time discover methods and means that aid him in arousing his soul, igniting and inspiring it to transcend the body, its usual hiding place, and draw close to God.

At times, thoughts and flashes of awakening that you had neither anticipated nor prepared for will visit you. For example, you may be in the middle of the prayer service during the Days of Awe. The congregation is beginning to sing songs of praise to God, such as "You are our God," and you begin to sing with them. All of a sudden your heart is gripped by fear. Now is the time, you realize, that all the beings of the supernal worlds, along with beings of the lower worlds, sing to the great God Who transcends all of them. What connection do I, degraded as I am, have to them? How do I have the audacity to blend my voice in with the voices of those who sing to God and cause Him to rejoice?

Suddenly, it is as if a spirit of life, of strength, were blown into you. You realize: This is the way it is when great joy is manifest in the world! The bands and orchestra with their instruments march, playing through the streets, accompanied by the wedding party, while all the important guests celebrate joyfully. The ragged barefoot children, their clothes tattered and their faces blackened with dirt, chase after the wedding procession, racing and clapping, singing and celebrating. This is also considered part of the honor accorded the bride and groom and the wedding. Your soul perceives, at that moment, the great choir of angels that is singing before God. The children of Israel join them in song from the lower worlds. Together they sing to the King of glory while He listens attentively, joyful and majestic. Like a barefoot, raggedy child, you have chased and joined this group, and along with the holy choir you sing a song to the God whom you have longed for. Your joy increases, your spirit expands to the breaking point in a state of great excitation, until at times your heart seems to melt and you begin to cry more freely even than you cried at Kol Nidre.

This spontaneous arousal will occur only if you labor over and over again to awaken your soul so as not to sleep away the seventy years of your life with a heart of stone. Know that even among our *tzaddikim* and holy men, who elevated themselves and achieved a closeness to God that is impossible for us to even grasp, there were those who used all kinds of different methods and techniques to rouse their pure and holy souls when they were first setting out along their paths. The book *House of Aaron*, for example, describes how the *tzaddikim* would imagine, just before they got up to pray, that they were lying in their graves, experiencing much suffering, until someone came by and said "Rise, stand up and pray." You yourself can picture how imagining that scenario in a vivid way would add tremendous vigor and intensity to prayer. And you, diligent student, if you make use of different techniques and work at them, you are also capable of reaching greatness that is beyond your capacity at present to imagine.

This is the fundamental choice that is offered you: to awaken and uplift yourself and draw a little closer to holiness. And at the moment of your ascent, look down from the perspective of your pure and elevated soul on the smallness that you usually keep yourself locked into. Look at your capacity for laziness and at the other undesirable qualities that affect you. Look at the lowly state of consciousness you normally exist in, with your petty thoughts and desires. You yourself will feel ashamed of them. Address yourself antagonistically: "Why do I lie around all day in a muddy pit, a virtual outhouse of childishness and foolishness? From now on I take it upon myself to become a Jew who is a servant of God. Master of the Universe, I want to be a Jew! I accept upon myself to be Your true servant." Repeat these kind of thoughts and speeches a number of times; with God's help they will aid you a great deal. One of the natural laws of the soul is that it will submit to words that are spoken powerfully from the heart. You can seduce and convince another with words that emerge from your heart and soul; certainly you can influence yourself decisively in the same way, providing you speak your words at a time when you have raised yourself to spiritual heights and are in a state of self-transcendence.

It is not enough, however, to merely resolve, in a general way, to serve God as a Jew. You must attempt, during moments of spiritual elevation, to mend and correct the undesirable qualities you recognize within yourself. It is true that while a Jew is engaged in intense prayer, it is better for him not to make all sorts of accounts, to dirty his hands with his faults. It is better that he pray and learn with fire and enthusiasm and draw near to God, as it says in the sacred books. But directly after praying, even during the reader's repetition of the *Amidah*, or during moments of fiery spiritual awakening that occur independently of prayer, you should try to mend your personal defects. For it is impossible to search for leaven except by candlelight. When you are aroused and inflamed by a spark of holiness, search and fix yourself before the light is extinguished. For example, if you have a bad temper, meditate as follows: "Is it good for me to become angry and be banished from before God? For the Talmud states, 'One who becomes angry does not even consider the *Shechinah* as important as himself' and also 'Whoever becomes angry—it is as if he worships idols.' Should I be so debased as to continue to allow myself to get angry? Will I rebel against the God of Israel, God of my life and soul, whose presence I feel within me at this moment? I resolve not to become angry from now on; with all my heart I resolve this. Master of the world, help me to stick to this determination not to get angry." You must establish this resolve and these thoughts within your heart and soul so firmly that when you begin to lose your temper and become angry, you will remember how shameful anger seemed to you, and the resolution you made not to become angry; it will be easy for you to gain control over yourself and calm down. Your main task, when anger begins to strike, will be to stubbornly attempt to remember and picture for yourself in the strongest possible way, and with the clearest possible conception, the time that you felt spiritually uplifted and the resolution you made then. You must use the same strategy when combatting the other character defects you perceive in yourself as well.

Do not imagine that in this fashion you will be able to heal all of your defects and spiritually ascend without working at it. Do not make this unseemly mistake. The only thing one can accomplish without work is to rot in the grave. To fix yourself and to become a servant to God is possible only through work. It cannot be occasional and incidental work either: it must be constant work. The Torah states "All the days of your life," and the rabbis interpret: "The days of your life—that means during the day. All the days of your life—that comes to include the nights." Thus you may never shift your awareness from this work. If you do work on yourself in this way, we can guarantee you that, with the help of God, your work will grow much easier, and you will not turn out like one of those men who, despite their good intentions and their desire to be a true Jew, find themselves at the end of their life looking at themselves and crying out: "In what way have I grown spiritually since my youth? How did I spend all my years?"

For with the strategies we've been discussing, along with other, similar strategies, you will, with the help of God, ascend from strength to strength.

You may also utilize physical techniques that will help you in correcting your undesirable qualities. A tendency toward anger, for example, can be helped if you take it upon yourself, when you feel the first flush of anger, to recite a section of Torah. You may recite for example, the teaching that begins: "In the study house of Elijah it was taught that whoever learns Halachah every day is assured a place in the world to come." Even better would be to recite something that demands more concentration, if you are able. First of all, the portion of Torah that you will think about in depth will actually defend you and rescue you from the urge to become angry. Also, the nature of the physical body makes this strategy effective. Anger is a kind of temporary insanity. It is difficult therefore to rely on the reasoning of a healthy mind to overcome anger because during the actual moment of anger, one's healthy mind has been superseded by insanity. But one has become insane only concerning the one matter that the anger is about. It is therefore only a thought that directly confronts the anger that is ineffective. One cannot tell oneself "don't be angry" since one is insane insofar as the subject of the anger goes. A different kind of thought, not directly opposed to anger, will be much easier to bring into consciousness. It is possible therefore to recite words of Torah that are not formulated in direct opposition to anger. As soon as you move your awareness away from your anger for a moment and concentrate your mind on the words of Torah, the intense feeling of anger will pass away. Your healthy mind will again be able to exert itself and restrain you from your anger.

In general, it is lamentable that in our day and age anger has become known as "nervousness"—or "weakness of the nerves." This classification leads men to resign themselves to it, without attempting to obliterate this evil quality, because in attributing it to a bodily weakness they no longer feel responsible for it as they would if they considered it a character trait. It is true that overstimulation of the nerves causes anger. Still, let us examine the fact that when a gentile becomes angry, he may actually kill the person he is angry at. A Jew who is on a base spiritual level may hit the person in a similar situation, while someone who has purified himself to a greater extent will neither hit nor kill, but will express his rage verbally and reproach the person with words. Despite the fact that all have had their nervous systems weakened to the same extent, not all of them are capable of the same kind of terrible acts when angered. A person is able to limit his actions even when he is asleep; his tossing and turning stops at the edge of his bed. Before he falls to the ground, he senses that he must roll the other way, back toward the center of his bed. Although he is asleep and unaware, the awareness that he possesses when awake continues to limit his movements, even in its apparent absence. The same is true in all matters. Those thoughts and opinions that are permanently established in a person have the capacity to restrain him completely even when he has lost his normal conscious awareness. In a Jew at a low level of consciousness, these limits prevent him from killing, even if he is angered and his nerves are provoked. In a person who is on a higher level of purity and consciousness, these restraints prevent him from hitting as well. And if you consider and resolve many times not to become angry, you can have weak nerves and even lose your awareness in the midst of anger, yet you will still be governed by the understanding that you have fixed into your consciousness. Even when your temper flares, you will not give in—even verbally—to rage and reproach.

Perhaps you harbor feelings of hatred toward one of your companions. You wish you could rid yourself of these feelings, but you are unable to do so. Of course, because you hate him, you see in him all kinds of faults and sins. If you were able to undo these feelings of hatred, you would truly be able to see whether his sins and faults exceeded your own. But, as we have said, you wish you could push the hatred out of your heart, but you are unable to do so.

This is what you should do: Write him a letter. Don't send it to him; hide it somewhere in your home. In the letter, insult and shame him as much as the serpent of anger in your heart desires. For some days, read the letter aloud, and imagine that you are standing right in front of him, taunting and abusing him with all the expressions of the letter. After some days, you will find your anger has dissipated, and, if you are a sensitive person, you may discover yourself running to reconcile with him.

Don't be astonished at this advice, and don't decide that one of two things must be true: either the description of what will happen is a lie, or there is magic or sorcery involved. How could writing an abusive letter and then reading it aloud make one forget one's anger and wish for a rapprochement?

This method is not false, nor is there magic or sorcery involved. Rather, it is a law of the soul that when a person taunts and abuses his erstwhile enemy, some of his anger dissipates. Since, however, when one insults one's enemy he returns the abuse in kind, the total result of the interaction is to increase the hatred. After having written a letter as sharp as the intensity of your anger, and after having read this letter out loud, degrading and debasing the object of your hatred, you will find your hatred has slightly diminished because of the abuse you've expressed. When you begin to read the letter for a second time the next day, after your anger has subsided, you will feel—while reading the expressions and insults you composed when your anger was still burning at its height—your heart beginning to rid itself of the intensity of the anger. You will be surprised at the number of curses and taunts you composed, and will be unable to read them with the kind of anger that you felt the day before. Since you have taken it upon yourself to read it, you force yourself to continue to do so, and on the third day you find that your anger has diminished even more and it is impossible for you to read it again. You already regret the things you expressed, saying: "Did I need to insult and degrade him to such an extent?" You already begin to think of strategies of reconciliation. If you are good-hearted, you will rapidly find a way to reconcile; whereas if you are stubborn, you will need to read the letter a few more times. But, with God's help, whoever uses this method will eventually make up with his estranged friend. However, don't use this technique often, and be careful not to lose the letter or to show it to even your closest friends, lest what you have written will reach your erstwhile enemy and the anger between you will spring up again.

It is possible to seek and find practical advice concerning all your spiritual work. For example, if you are trying to correct your tendency to be lazy and sleep too much, or if you are especially tired after a hard day's work and are afraid you will oversleep in the morning, try this: Instead of sleeping across the length of your bed, stretch out across the width and rest your legs on a chair. In the morning right when you awaken, kick the chair away and you will find yourself with your feet already firmly planted on the ground. Do this, however, only if you won't damage your health, and don't do it if it causes you to walk around tired all day because you didn't sleep comfortably the night before. And even if you don't experience these problems, don't attempt this technique more than twice a week.

CHAPTER 10

TO TRANSFORM BAD CHARACTER INTO LIGHT

People often perceive contradictions because they don't look into the inside of things, but see only the surface that covers the exterior. If they would penetrate to the inside, to the soul of things, they would see that in reality there is no contradiction, there is no question and no answer; everything is one, straight and direct; it just branches out into many separate paths. You most certainly have found all that we have discussed difficult and contradictory. First, you must be saying, they promised me that I would rise and grow and become one of the great people of Israel. This would occur, I was told, despite the fact that I felt no special inner distinction and I was not especially prepared for greatness. It would happen because within me there are hidden resources of lofty spirituality, holiness from higher worlds, concealed even from me. Through my bodily labor these resources would be revealed; through my soul's efforts, I would ascend. And yet afterward they acknowledge that I contain evil characteristics, and I am then directed as to how to mend them. It is not enough that I don't feel any sense of the holiness that is within me; must I also confront the evil and the sicknesses of my soul? And how is it possible that these evil qualities are imprinted on my soul, as if they were part of its essence and its nature, if within me a treasure house of holiness is stored?

A contradiction appears to exist, as we have stated, only when we confine ourselves to looking at the outer surface of our concern. If we limit ourselves to shallow perceptions we will never reach our goal. The way we have approached the mending of character traits until now has been to describe how one may restrain or overcome these traits so as to impede the destructive effect they can have on you and on others. This is not enough. If we are to achieve our goal, we must transform these evil qualities themselves into shining lights and blazing fires of a highly spiritual nature through which we can serve our Creator. We must be able to make our entire inner being consonant with the phrases "a holy people," "unique treasure," and "kingdom of priests" according to God's will and the original condition of His agreement with us.

For though it seems to us, whose eyes see only the outer surface of our character traits, as if these traits were evil, God has sent us the Baal Shem Tov (may the memory of the righteous be a blessing), a holy man of God, and his holy disciples who illuminated Israel. They taught us that the qualities inherent in a Jewish person's character are holy manifestations emanating from on high. It is only when we don't know how to act properly in this world, and with our physical bodies, that they change their appearance and seem evil. This is comparable to pure water placed in a dirty glass. When we look through the outside of the glass, the water looks dirty.

You may know that there exist holy qualities, *Sefirot*, on a higher plane. The light and holiness of God is clothed in them, and through them God acts and is revealed in the worlds that He has created. Even if you have not yet learned about the *Sefirot* because you have not yet reached the appropriate spiritual level for learning Kabbalah, you must still be familiar with them. They are hinted at in the daily prayer, where we recite "Yours, O God, is the greatness and the strength and the beauty and the victory and the glory." And you must have recited, during the counting of the Omer, the meditation that asks God to repair "that which I have damaged in the *Sefirah of Chesed within Chesed,"* or *"Chesed within Gevurah,"* and so on. The Holy One of Israel drew down light into our inner being from these very *Sefirot.* Just as God desires to clothe Himself in the supernal *Sefirot,* so does He wish to be enclothed in the *Sefirot* that He shined into us and to reveal Holiness through them.

The quality of loving-kindness is an emanation from the *Sefirah* of supernal love and kindness. The love of God for Israel, and of the angels for God as they serve Him (as it is written, "and they give permission to each other with love"), flows in and from this *Sefirah.* This quality should appear in us only in a holy way. We should use this quality only in holiness: to love God, His holy Torah, and the people of Israel. Our quality of awe should be, likewise, authentic and true. The qualities of love and awe that we possess should not just slumber within us. Love and awe towards God are part of the essence and nature of a Jew, even if he is unaware of them and even if they don't cause his heart to tremble and shake. But a person must, at the very least, set aside times to attempt to awaken his love toward God by actively longing and yearning for Him. He should pray: "Please God, bring me close to you. Why have you hidden Your Face from me? Why have you sent me far away from Your holiness?" His longing and yearning should be like those of a child longing for his distant father; his whole being is directed toward his father, he trembles until his heart hurts him. The same is true of awe. A Jew should not be satisfied with the awe inherent within him that has remained concealed and has not yet shaken up his soul. He must allow this awe to reveal itself at times. He should practice feeling as if he stood before a powerful king. His whole being should be filled with fear and trembling because of the splendorous glory and the great power that stands before him.

Examine the words of Maimonides that are quoted by the *Shulchan Aruch, Or HaChayim:* "When a person realizes in his heart that the great King, the Holy One blessed be He, whose glory fills the earth, is standing above him and sees all of his actions, as it is said in Scripture, 'Thus says the Lord: If a man conceals himself in hidden places, will I not see him?' he will be immediately struck by feelings of awe and submission coming from fear of God, and he will experience a constant sense of shame before Him." The important principle here is that your sense of fear should not be dormant. It should not be like the fear one feels in relation to a distant king, when your mind is aware that somewhere far away there is a king that you must fear because he has the power to help or harm you. Your awe, submission, and fear should be of God who stands right over you and sees your actions. You should vibrate with fear, your limbs knocking against each other; you should submit yourself and become annihilated before His glorious majesty that shines directly before you. This kind of awe will not be weak or faint; it will not get pushed aside or dissipate before some physical passion or desire. Even during times when this awe is not manifestly present within, the mere memory of the intense fear and trembling that you experienced an hour or two ago will chase away every particle of sin and even any permissible physical desire that is contrary to the will of God. And if you look within yourself and see that you have performed an action or spoken a word or had a thought of sin, or just wasted time doing nothing, which is the basis of all sin, you will become angry and upset at yourself and say: "Oy Gevalt! What have I done against God! I am worse than the lowest sinner in Israel! Forgive me! From today on, I take it upon myself to be a Jew with my entire being."

Our character traits are, in actuality, supernal *Sefirot* that have been drawn into us. That these chambers of holiness, these shining lights, have been damaged and corrupted is cause for great lamentation. With the very same attribute of love that God drew into us from His holy dwelling place in order that we should love and serve Him and be like divine angels, we feel attracted to foolish things. And with the attribute of might, which was meant to enable us to feel the fear and awe of God as the angels do, we experience undesirable fear, anger, and causeless hatred.

Precious child, as we have already repeated several times, you, yourself, are your own principal educator. You must rise up and take the reins of government into your own hands, become the captain of your own ship, or you may break apart and drown in the raging sea of this material world, filled as it is with the miserable aspirations of men. Your teachers and rabbis will not be able to help you then, God forbid. Therefore we must attempt to make you understand, in a way that will make sense to you at this stage in your development, that the qualities within you that you feel are evil are essentially shining lights and supernal *Sefirot* that have undergone a process of contraction and have been drawn down through the various worlds into you. You must understand this in order to ease the process of repairing them and returning them to their original state of holiness. For this is the first stage in any kind of healing: to recognize the source of the disease, its etiology and symptoms.

For this is the difference between the process through which internal attributes of character are stimulated and aroused and the way in which other strengths that a man might possess—such as intelligence or physical power—are stimulated. A person can stir up his physical power on his own, independent of any outside force or object that might provide stimulation. He can flex his muscles and tighten up his fist and say, "If so and so, my enemy, would show up right now, I would beat him thoroughly." At that moment he feels his strength gathering, ready to flow out of him and overcome any obstacle, even though his enemy is not present. In fact, people of extraordinary physical power feel a compulsion to wrestle with each other from time to time, not out of mutual hatred, and not just to show off their strength, but because they have tremendous power stopped up within that is pressing to be released and revealed. That is to say, it is not their opponent that forces them into combat, but rather their powerful energy that forces them to seek a partner with whom to struggle and reveal their strength. The same is true concerning the activation of the intelligence. At times a person may be stimulated to search and study something not because the object of his interest appeared on its own right in front of his eyes, but because the intellectual power, stored in his brain, became aroused—independent of outside forces—and compelled him to find something of interest to look into. This is the reason that men of great intelligence are never intellectually idle: the power of intelligence that is within them presses them to become interested in various subjects, to study deeply, to learn and to discover.

This is not the case with attributes of character. They do not become stimulated and aroused unless something acts upon them to arouse them. People become angry and fearful because something or someone angers them or makes them afraid—without this stimulus, they would not experience the emotion. Becoming angry or fearful for no apparent reason is a sign of mental illness, as is well known. The same is true of love—a person does not spontaneously feel love unless there is something or someone that arouses the feeling. In certain situations it may be easier to arouse feelings of love in a person rather than feelings of anger, or of anger rather than love. There are also people who by their very nature are more easily aroused to love rather than anger or vice versa. However, even in these situations or with these kind of people, there must be an external object to arouse them. Unlike the faculties of intelligence or physical power, love and anger do not spontaneously arise within and then stimulate the person to seek an outlet—someone toward whom to feel angry or someone to love.

This is the reason that, in man, these attributes first appear in a degraded form. When a person feels one of these attributes, he doesn't experience it as a manifestation of holiness, as holy love or holy awe. He also doesn't experience it in a neutral way, as unadorned love or fear which he can then decide to direct toward holiness or its opposite. Instead, he first experiences these attributes inside himself as debased qualities—love for foolish, unworthy things, and anger as evil hatred. He does not feel these qualities in the same way he experienced intelligence or physical power, which he felt within himself as pure and autonomous forces that he was then able to use any way he wished. Intelligence and physical power develop within a person spontaneously and independently; therefore he experiences them as neutral. Character attributes—emotions—that develop and appear only in response to something confronting them from outside, are thus perceived in an image molded and shaped by material concerns. This is because from childhood on, man is sunk into this material world, and it is material things that stimulate and arouse his attributes.

The earlier one begins to educate and accustom a child to stimulate and reveal his character traits through holy matters, the more their form changes for the better. From the very beginning he will experience these qualities in a positive way: as love for God, for Torah, and for Israel, as awe before God, and as anger at those who transgress His will, and certainly at himself when he perceives within himself any evidence of a low level of spirituality. Accustoming oneself to utilize the holy dimension of these attributes is an effective strategy not only in childhood. During the whole of a person's life, the more he employs these qualities in a negative way, the more these inner qualities, which originate from a very high spiritual station, are drawn into defiled garments. He experiences his inner attributes as growing worse and worse. How can a person such as this become holy before God? From where will the garments appear through which God's light can become manifest and dwell within him? And likewise, if a person continues to mend his character, and transform his inner qualities toward holiness, the result will not merely be that they won't cause any damage, like an ox that's prone to goring and has been tied up so he can't do any harm. Nor will the corrections that the person accomplishes through his efforts become apparent only on the physical, bodily plane. The exalted nature of the attributes will now be easy for him to reveal. The supernal *Sefirot* that were drawn into his midst will become manifest. The *Sefirot* originated in a place of great spiritual elevation; he will now be able to utilize these heights and this holiness in his service of God. Just as God clothes Himself in the divine attributes in the higher realms, so will God make Himself manifest through a person who has repaired and corrected his attributes. Through these qualities, God will come to dwell within; He will illuminate every manifestation of such a person's life energy and will embrace and commune with his soul.

CHAPTER 11

CONSISTENT WORK, CONSISTENT SEARCHING, AND EXALTED ATTITUDE

You must already have come to realize that you are not just a simple denizen of this world, nor are your labor and task a merely personal matter. You merge into high spiritual worlds; within you, *Sefirot* and spiritual light are to be found. Because of this, everything depends on you: to damage your character and your self is to cause damage in all the palaces on high, whereas when you mend your attributes, you heal and repair all these palaces as well. And through these attributes you yourself rise and draw closer to the One who is pure and whose attendants are pure, rise so close that the ministering angels will envy you. With these attributes you will draw into yourself the light of the One who dwells in supernal holiness, and these attributes themselves will become dwelling places for the light.

Diligent student, having reached this point in the book, you must already feel in yourself some sense of positive change. You already know that we have no interest in mere sermonizing; our intention is to make you realize that you yourself are the main end and purpose of the entire Torah. The whole goal is for you to become a true Jew. Holiness is divided into many levels, and one of them—the main one—is being a Jew. The purpose is for you to become a Jew in accordance with your potential. Since you have been studying and absorbing the thoughts we have presented—and not merely intellectually; you've begun to attempt to work and practice in the manner we've described—even if you haven't completed your task or the fixing you need to do, your heart has already softened, and you've begun to labor, with your whole being, to fix and reveal from within yourself God's supernal holiness. This is a cause of rejoicing for your Father in heaven; the small gleam of light emerging from you shines in the heavens as well as on earth. The people of Israel have been likened to stars. Stars shine from the heavens and illuminate the earth, and you, as a Jew, exist on earth and your light shines both on the earth and in the heavens.

It is most important, however, that you don't straddle the fence: one moment moved to draw close to God, while the next moment tumbling downward to the lowest depths, to foolishness, waste, laziness, debauchery. True, it is impossible for anyone to constantly remain on a high spiritual level. It is impossible to remain all day in the spiritual state achieved during prayer, just as it is impossible to retain all year the spiritual state attained during Rosh Hashanah and Yom Kippur. Still, you must strengthen your will and your inner holiness with what you attained on Rosh Hashanah and Yom Kippur in a way that will last the whole year. You must not neglect the spiritual resolutions you took upon yourself then, or the path you traveled, or the cloud of God that appeared overhead on Rosh Hashanah and Yom Kippur. Even when you don't feel these same feelings, you must not retreat backward. For if you do, your whole year, along with Rosh Hashanah and Yom Kippur and the fragment of light that shone into you then, will be dragged down into the pit of destruction. In the same way, it is impossible for you to remain constantly in the elevated state you experience when your soul draws close in a great outpouring into the very midst of your Father in Heaven. Still, you must bind yourself to, and strengthen yourself with, the holy matters and good deeds that you resolved to accomplish during that auspicious and exalted time, and be sure to carry them out.

It is most important that one's service of God be continuous. It is impossible to be internally connected to the unceasing service of God unless one is continuously in the process of seeking Him. King David asked of God: "Show me your way, O Lord; I will walk in Your truth, unify my heart in awe of Your name." King David had already annihilated his evil inclination. He had risen to great heights of holiness until he had merited to become one of the legs of the throne of God. Yet despite all this, he approached God as if he were still outside, and had not even begun to serve Him: Show me Your way, O Lord, ways through which I can travel to You. King David did not make this request once in a while, or at certain times; this was his constant request, as it states in Psalms: "For I cry out to You all day." And what about us? What would we answer if we had to compare our determination to his? Picture a prince, lost among mountains and uninhabited wilderness filled with wild beasts and bandits who might ambush him at any moment. He knows that there is a path leading to his father, the king, but he doesn't know where it is—he can't find it. Can you imagine how much and how continuously he searches and seeks the path, and how fervently he cries out to his father: "Father, show me the way?" The only way you will continuously seek the path toward God is if you see yourself like this prince, far from the King, your Father in heaven, lost in the wilderness of a material world full of foolish matters that hurt the body and wound the soul. If you see your situation in this way, you will call out continuously from the depths of your heart: "Lord, show me Your way." And your constancy in serving God will be in direct accord with your constancy in seeking Him. If you do not continuously seek Him, from the depths of your heart, you will find that it is impossible to be constant in your service of Him as well.

Also, as you already know, your task is to draw into yourself light from high above and to reveal within yourself the holiness of the divine attributes. This power is inherent in the will of a Jewish person, which is capable of awakening the divine will and causing it to shine down and illuminate it. Your will and your constant search are not in vain, for in utilizing them you are drawing down light and holiness from the supernal attributes. This should suffice as explanation.

Precious child, as we've already told you, the purpose of this book is not just to order you to walk in the path of God, for that is something you already know that you are supposed to do, and something your soul already longs for. Our purpose is to aid you and to accustom you to walk this path. As we've already written: You must be constant in your service of God, whether when you are rising spiritually, or when resting in one place, or even when you are falling. This constancy is completely dependent on the constancy of your quest for the true path that rises from the material world to God. But in telling you just this alone we have not fulfilled our obligation to you—the obligation of a supporter and helper. For how is one to stimulate oneself to reach this level; how does one acquire the trait of constantly caring about one's spiritual state and seeking after God?

The natural tendency of a person, even if he is aware of his Jewishness and of his responsibility to shake off the dirt that has encrusted him, to cleanse and purify himself and return to his Holy King, the Holy One of Israel—is to realize these things intellectually, while his heart remains unpained and unconcerned. Sometimes a few moments may pass when he feels these concerns in his heart, but even then, his concern is not very deep, and these moments occur very infrequently. Feelings of heartache and constant seeking are reserved only for the concerns of this world: "How will I achieve? How will I grow more powerful and gain more honor?" What good will there be in our charge to search for and be concerned about God if we do not help you and accustom you to search and be concerned? It's true, as we've repeated numerous times, that without your effort, your labor, and the application of all your strength to the spiritual task, our words won't succeed in moving you one inch out of the mire in which you're stuck up to your neck. Still, even once you have begun to make an effort, we must continue to instruct you as to how you can reach this state of constant seeking.

Listen well: Heartache and continuous seeking depend on your outlook. Take for example a once wealthy person, ruined by financial disaster. As long as he continues to see himself as a wealthy person and is troubled by the fact that other wealthy people are living in abundance in the lavish way he and his family used to live, his concern will remain strong and he will constantly keep coming up with ideas to become wealthy again, with the help of God. But if he changes his outlook, stops seeing things from the point of view of a wealthy man, and begins to see himself as a poor person like all the other poor people, his concern will cease and he will stop trying to find ways to become rich again. He will still harbor hopes of winning the lottery, or discovering a treasure and becoming suddenly rich—but he'll do no more than think about these things. He'll do no more than weave fantasies of wealth. His heart will not ache after what he lost, and his concern will be merely to earn enough for a crust of bread and a comfortable apartment in a warm basement.

So, too, what becomes of you depends entirely on your perception of what it means to be a Jew, and what spiritual level you believe you must attain. You know all this intellectually, we have discussed it before—but it is just like the poor man who was once rich but has now come to see himself as poor who also remembers what it was like to be rich and still wishes to become wealthy again. Since his memory remains only mental, however, and his desire to be wealthy is not etched upon his heart as it once was, since he has adapted a new outlook toward himself and no longer has the urgent concern and drive to find a way to become rich that he once did, he will doubtless lose his motivation to work hard or engage in commerce. The same is true of your knowledge; if it remains merely intellectual it will not suffice. God has said: "And I have trained Ephraim to walk, I have taken them by their arms" (Hosea 11:3). The merciful Father longs to bring every Jew toward Him, through the teachings of His prophets. But it is necessary to train and accustom the wandering soul and the child who has been banished to this material world to return to their Father and, so to speak, to jump into His arms. "And I trained Ephraim, I have taken them by their arms"—God is training us, and we must train ourselves in this matter as well. From now on let your faith in God cease to be hidden and concealed within you; let it be clear and strong. Remember, be careful and constant in practicing what we prescribed in Chapter 9: Several times a day you should reflect on how God, may His name be blessed, fills the whole earth with His glory, and how you are always standing before Him, wherever you are. Contemplate these thoughts especially when you have free time. Why should you inject emptiness into your mind, why destroy it with foolish pursuits? Instead, concentrate your thoughts on your faith in God. And according to the amount of time and energy that you devote to these matters, you will become more and more accustomed to faith, until faith in God will not seem like something that transcends human understanding, but knowledge filled with certainty, a clear and strong vision. Your knowledge of the truth of your faith will be clearer to you than the shining of the sun. For this is the way a Jew works even in regard to matters that transcend his intellect. The more he reflects on them the more potent and certain they become to him, eclipsing in their strength even those things that he can see with his eyes. This is simple to explain. A Jew's soul sees things that are higher than what his mind is able to perceive; it is just that his soul is hidden from him. The more he thinks about these spiritual matters, the more he accustoms his soul, with its special kind of vision, to emerge and gaze upon these things. It is able to perceive the true nature of things.

You should not only accustom yourself to contemplate faith in God and the fact that He fills all the worlds; you should also constantly reflect on your purpose, and the purpose of all of Israel, as we discussed earlier. You should consider the agreement that God forged with us—that we will be unto Him a unique treasure, a kingdom of priests, and a holy people. You should think about this often, until you don't perceive this purpose as exceptional, an additional demand that it would be possible to do without. It should seem rather that there is no other way to be a Jew. And according to the measure to which you accustom yourself to think these thoughts, so will your outlook change; your outlook on the world, on the people of Israel and on yourself. Supernal holiness and Israel will not continue to seem like two separate and distant entities, but will become the same thing.

As you become accustomed to these thoughts, as your outlook becomes more elevated, your heart will naturally begin to become concerned when you feel inside yourself even a tremor of corporeality and foolishness. You will begin to constantly ask of God:

"Show me Your way, O Lord, I will walk in Your truth. Save me, that I may serve You in truth, in awe and with love." And your constancy in serving God will be in direct proportion to your constancy in seeking and beseeching Him.

Become accustomed to thinking holy thoughts and maintaining a spiritually elevated outlook, in the fashion we have just described. Compare the former exalted condition of the Jewish people with our present lowly state. For according to the testimony of the prophetic writings, prophecy was not seen in earlier times as something extraordinary, unusual or wondrous. When God wished to announce to Manoach and his wife that they were to have a son, Shimshon, He did not tell them in a dream or inform them through a heavenly voice. Why go to so much trouble when He could simply send them an angel? And since one angelic visitation was not enough, God sent the angel a second time. This happened despite the fact that Manoach and his wife were not among the great spiritual lights of Israel, as our sages tell us. Yet just the fact that they were Jews, part of a holy people, meant they were able to see and speak to an angel as if they were having a conversation with a friend. King Saul, who was not a prophet, found himself once in the midst of a band of prophets—this happened even before he became king—and began to prophesy. This did not happen only to him. The men he sent to pursue King David were also visited by the spirit of God and began to prophesy when they came upon Samuel and his disciples, "the children of prophets." This did not happen just to save David, for would God transform into prophets a group who were out pursuing an innocent person if all He wanted was to delay them? He would have effected some other miracle, as He did in other situations when He saved David. But why bother with miracles that transcend the natural order—God doesn't perform miracles when they are not needed—when it is so simple to transform these men into prophets? For even if they had strayed from their spiritual point of origin and had become affected by the material world, they were still Jews, and on encountering prophets, the spirit of prophecy that was inside them burst forth. Saul too, who chased after David, prophesied the whole night through when he encountered the prophets. Our sages said that the number of Jewish prophets was double the number of the population that was taken out of Egypt—

that is, 1,200,000 people. There is no account of them in Scripture because only those prophecies that were going to be needed by future generations were recorded, and those that were not needed were not recorded (*Megillah* 14a). The *Midrash* in the Song of Songs says that there were 1,200,000 prophets in Elijah's generation alone, not to mention those that lived at other times. The greatness of someone who was known as a prophet, what distinguished him from other Israelites, was the constant nature of his prophetic activity, and the much higher level of prophecy that he achieved. For example, in our generation there are *tzaddikim*, saintly men who consistently serve God in a righteous and abundant fashion, each according to his spiritual level. Yet every Jew also serves God and acts righteously—if not continuously, at least at times. Even if their service and their deeds are not on the same level as the saintly person's, they are still considered righteous acts and divine service. This is how it used to be with prophecy. The forty-eight prophets who have become renowned developed into great prophets, each according to his spiritual level, and reached the stage of constant prophecy, as the Scriptures have stated: "I have given you over to be prophets for the nations." But occasional prophecy, when it was necessary, as with Manoach and his wife and as with the people who encountered the bands of prophets—this was something that any Jewish person might aspire to and merit. For in former times, the children of Israel were close to God, and the windows of the heavens were open, and whenever it was necessary, the divine Father spoke to His children.

We were in such a holy and exalted state then, but what about now? We have fallen, our spiritual senses have been dulled, we have become alienated from God. First prophecy ceased, then the divine spirit as well. Now, how great is our abandonment, and how thorough is the state of divine concealment! Even to ignite a spark of spiritual awakening, a tiny glow of spiritual fervor—just a fragment of the illumination, a spark of a spark of the great light of prophecy—a Jew has to put himself through much great exertion and struggle.

We don't want to turn you into a prophet, or even into a master of the divine spirit (at least not all at once). But a prince who has been thrown into a musty, decrepit basement must have reached a very advanced stage of depravity if he is not at least anxious over his fate and does not long to return to his previous life, to his birthright, to the time when he was so close to his father. His change in self-perception—where he once saw himself as a refined and noble prince, and now he sees himself as crude and degraded—is itself the turbid, muddy pit in which he is mired. And who knows but that this degraded self-perception will cause him to decide to remain forever in his decrepit state.

Leave me alone, let me cry bitterly, for my spirit forces me to ask: Who will concern themselves with the spiritual descent of the Jewish people if not you, Jewish youth? Who will yearn for the restoration of the Jewish people to their exalted state of holiness and to their spiritual purity? Who will completely devote themselves to the task of causing this return if not you? You are free of the demands of commerce and labor—Torah alone is your craft. You are still tender and soft—it is still possible for you to transform your flesh into holy flesh, your spirit into a consuming fire, your whole being into an embodiment of the splendor of Israel and of the spiritual beings who dwell in the palace of the King.

Jewish youth, why should you perceive yourself or any other Jew as an intelligent animal whose intelligence is applied merely in the pursuit and discovery of sustenance, and who is absorbed all day in such meaningless endeavors? When there is no sustenance to be found, you are anxious and concerned; when you are successful in attaining it, you are satisfied. You can waste your entire life in such a way! Why don't you demand greatness of yourself? Why do you consider yourself righteous merely when you refrain from injuring someone else or committing blatant sins? Tell yourself: "I am not demanding anything novel; I just want to return to the state that once existed. Our bodies and soul will return to their original state of purity and brilliance, and we will return to our Father, who was our Father then as well."

Behold, Jewish youth, the glorious shining of Israel as it once was, and the essence of the Jewish people, which was like the sky itself in its clear purity. Care about the terrible darkness in which we exist now. Let your concern fill you with longing to serve, to return, to arise, to draw close, at least a little bit, to our God. Arouse your soul from time to time, yearn for God, pour out your heart and wrap yourself in meditation, conversing with God like this:

"O Lord, you have always been our Father and we, Your children. It has always been true that from the very moment Jewish boys and girls burst from their mothers' wombs, they are beset by many bitter troubles. We have gone through difficult and intense suffering, and that has caused our separation from You. Still, each and every one of us is prepared to sacrifice our lives for You, Lord. And even though the smallest of us has been willing to stretch our neck out to be slaughtered for Your sake, we have been burned alive on countless altars; and our troubles, which suck out our lifeblood, have been endless. For Your sake, and so as not to be separated from You, we have accepted everything joyfully and with love. We have all lived this way, and I have too. This is how I am now and this is how I will always remain. But our Father, our King, in previous eras You guided us; we saw Your presence with our own eyes, You spoke to us like a loving father to his children. How good things were then! Now, because of our sins, You have ascended on high, and have closed the heavens up after yourself. There is nothing to be seen, nothing to be heard. No one speaks and no one responds. There are no prophets and no seers. O Lord, You have banished Your tiny flock, the remnants of Israel, to a desolate wilderness, filled with entities that can damage body and soul. My Father in heaven, I am afraid to be without You for even one minute; please draw us close and approach us as You once did."

CHAPTER 12

SOME THOUGHTS ON CHASIDISM AND HOW TO CONNECT TO TORAH THROUGH IT

You have already been shown, and have come to understand, that a Jewish person—even in his youth—is not material in his essence like an animal or wild beast, but is a spiritual creature, a heavenly being that God has placed upon the earth. Even his body is not like the body of the other physical creatures; it is pure and refined, a body compatible with such an exalted soul. But in this world, for various reasons—Adam's sin, the evil choices mankind has made—the body has itself become more material, and now covers and conceals the soul and all of a person's spiritual essence to such an extent that he is unable even to recognize himself, and is unaware of the heavenly treasure that is within him. His principal task is to awaken his soul until it is even more powerful than his body. Then he will be totally transformed. He will return to his essential nature and will serve God like the supernal angels, the divine seraphim, of his own free will. In previous chapters we have already delineated various techniques through which the soul can be awakened, through which your general outlook in life can be raised to a higher spiritual level, through which you can increase your concern for yourself so as to really begin seeking the path that ascends to the house of God, so as to advance upon it with your soul in a state of exaltation.

But please note, diligent student, that what we have outlined and discussed are only techniques of arousal. What is most important is to serve God on your own, in every aspect of your life. We can compare this to a person who has fainted and is revived by medicinal droplets. If he eats bread and milk and other nourishing foods, then with the help of God he will survive. If he foolishly reasons, "Since the droplets were efficacious in reviving me, they will certainly continue to strengthen me in my day-to-day existence—why should I have to chase and labor to earn my sustenance?" and then stops eating or drinking anything but the droplets, he will certainly become ill. Our words are only droplets meant to arouse the holy Jewish soul and body to accomplish its task. If you set yourself to work along the paths we have mapped out for you, and in the ways we have listed for you, with the help of God you will ascend and become a Jew who is close to God. You will feel the inner purification of your soul within you, and will be moved by flashes of holy fire that will spark from inside of you whenever you encounter words of Torah, or of prayer, and in everything pertaining to the performance of the commandments. If, however, you do not set yourself to work—to cleanse and sanctify all your character traits, and to labor intensively, with your whole body, like a servant before his master—and instead rely on techniques of arousal such as those we have discussed, you will be like the man who fainted and then wanted to nourish himself merely with the droplets. You will lose everything, and will cause damage, heaven forbid, in the higher worlds of holiness.

We are confident in you, however, and we have faith that you will not regress and backslide, will not be too lazy to work—and will not expect to effect everything all at once, but will work gradually and constantly, a little at a time, as we instructed you in Chapter 11. Our whole intention is that you accomplish this. And in doing so, you have already begun to be a "chasid."

You may ask: What is Chasidism and in what way is a chasid who serves God greater than someone who serves God but is not a chasid? Be aware that this is impossible to explain. Chasidism is not something merely intellectual, and thus explainable. The intellectual component of Chasidism is only one part of it, and is itself revealed only after one has engaged in the service of God. This is the same as in prophecy. It is impossible to rationally explain prophecy. A prophet is the only one who actually understands the nature of prophecy—and for him, the phenomenon seems so simple and obvious that he cannot understand why others do not see what he does, as Scripture states in Amos 3:8: "The Lord, God, has spoken, who will not prophesy?" Amos was unable to comprehend how anyone would not experience prophecy when God had spoken.

This is also the case in Chasidism, which is the revelation of the tiny spark of prophecy that exists within each Jew (as the Talmud states in *Pesachim* 66a: "Jews are children of prophets"). It is impossible to explain Chasidism with the intellect. Neither the chasidic way of serving God nor the chasid's perception of the world can be explained rationally. It is impossible to intellectually describe how a true chasid prays, how his soul becomes inflamed and bound to supernal holiness, or how he sees in the Torah and in the commandments the lovely splendor of God, the world's glory, how he sees a spark of His presence everywhere in the world. It is difficult even for the chasid himself to comprehend these matters. When he sees and perceives these things during his periods of spiritual ascent and burning enthusiasm they seem simple and certain, yet if he falls from his spiritual level, he himself cannot understand them. You have yet to advance to these stages; this is as yet beyond your grasp and even your desire. However, if you have begun to internalize all that we have discussed, you have at least reached the outermost edge of Chasidism, you have tasted the tip of the staff dipped into the honeycomb. If you continue to constantly work in the manner we have described, you will surely become a chasid, you will find refuge in the shade of God, and He will spread His radiant presence over you.

As we have already mentioned earlier, the totality of holiness may be found in the Torah, and through the Torah you can become connected to the holiness of the infinite One. It is necessary only to know how to study Torah. First, you must uncover your soul, which is hidden within you, slumbering and faint, and place it in the Torah. Previous chapters have already described briefly how to arouse and reveal your soul. And if someone should ask you: "What good will these chasidic practices do for you if they cause you to neglect times set aside for Torah study? What will you gain in disclosing your soul if you do not labor in Torah?" or if he argues, "You will certainly not gain entry into Chasidism either in this manner, for an ignorant person cannot be a chasid," then answer him by exposing his error. For everything we have spoken about so far will not lessen your hours of Torah study one whit, but will serve only to weed out the thorns, by utilizing the free fifteen minutes here and there that would have been wasted otherwise. You will be robbed of vain and empty daydreams, and in their place you will be filled with wisdom, holiness, light, and Chasidism. How can one deny the obvious? Look and see for yourself: Has the chasidic camp in past generations lacked people devoted to Torah study as compared to the other groups of Israel? And if in previous generations the chasidic world merely did not lag in producing Torah scholars as compared to the rest of Israel, we can see clearly that now, in this generation, the number of Torah scholars from the chasidic camp exceeds the number in all the others. That is to say, in this degraded generation, the amount of Torah students among the chasidim did not diminish, and the number of their students who abandon God and Torah did not increase to the extent that it did among the rest of the Jewish people. As I heard one God-fearing rabbi, who is not chasidic, say: "In Poland, Chasidism is what is still sustaining the Torah and the service of God." And certainly, to you, diligent students—you who will return the crown of Chasidism to its rightful place and become like the original chasidim, with a heart that is a sanctuary for the presence of God, with a living Jewish soul burning with a flame from above—to you and to those like you, Chasidism calls out: "Those who are for God, come unto Me." Not only will the number of Jewish youths dedicated to the study of Torah and the service of God increase, but also the quality and quantity of each individual's Torah study will grow and multiply. Everyone will learn many more pages, will study for many more hours, and will gird their loins to serve God and to study Torah in greater depth and with more concentration.

There is a simple solution to the riddle of why there has been such an increase in the number of people who have abandoned the study of Torah, which is the basis of our connection to God. Before we reveal the solution, let us add to the riddle. Why have so many weakened their grip when toiling in the field of Torah study out of laziness and neglect and then chosen to do physical labor that is much more difficult than Torah study? And even in the midst of this economic crisis, when everyone has already seen that neither labor nor commerce makes one wealthy, and many workers and merchants are starving and thirsty, God have mercy on them, why do they still find toiling in Torah and serving God much more difficult than profane work?: Why do they still abandon the labors of the holy Torah and run to work in bricks and clay which is so physical and so difficult? We may as well add this to our list of wonders: Why do Torah students and young scholars who have entered business remain idle, bereft of Torah study, for hours or even days at a time, sometimes without any reason at all? They are surely aware of the *Midrash* on Lamentations, which states that God may forgive even very grievous errors but will not forgive you for rejecting Torah. Yet they still remain idle and do not engage in Torah study, though they are careful not to transgress even the most minor sins.

The solution is as follows: The nature of a person is such that his mind, and the benefit he believes he will derive from something, strengthen him more than the mere power of his physical body can strengthen him. When you do work that will benefit you, or that you believe will benefit you, your mind gives you strength to work ten times harder than you would at even the easiest labor that is not benefiting you now and may not benefit you in the future. As it is commonly said: "If you put a farmer in a field where there is nothing to cut, he won't be able to swing his sickle for half an hour without quitting from exhaustion." If, however, he's harvesting his wheat field, the benefit he is deriving will give him strength to keep going all day. The same is true of a person with a desiccated soul; he is able to learn Torah only when he thinks his learning will bring him some gain—either financially, or by bringing him honor. Since, to our sorrow, the respect in which the Torah has always been held has diminished, Torah study does not offer much chance for gain here in this world. Furthermore, the honor accorded Torah scholars has also diminished; in fact, they are often derided by the wicked and insolent. In the young generation, therefore, even those who do want to learn find it exhausting, if their souls are spiritually parched, since there is no immediate material or emotional gain in sight. Even what they do learn they learn only perfunctorily; they are unable to make any great efforts or to delve into the depths of learning, and instead will decide to do hard manual labor. They are able to accomplish this hard labor and even draw strength from it because they believe it will bring them gain.

You students who choose the unique pathways of Chasidism will not experience these aforementioned difficulties. Your soul will awaken and reveal itself; sparks from the Garden of Eden will flash within you. You will sense the Holy One of Israel whose being is concealed within the Torah, and will enjoy the radiance of His divine presence. This will be your reward; from this you will draw strength and vigor to learn for many hours and in great depth. Don't imagine that we mistakenly believe that you will instantly be transformed into holy men who learn Torah for its own sake with no hope of receiving any reward, material benefit, or even any honor. Only great saints merit this level; we are fully aware of this. But the relationship to the Torah that you will have can be compared to a father's love for his son: his great affection causes him to perceive all sorts of excellent qualities in his son. He doesn't understand why everybody else does not also love his son because of these same great qualities. It is possible that in reality his son does not possess even a single one of these qualities, but his love colors his thoughts and stimulates him to have a high opinion of his son, and to see in him all kinds of good characteristics. The Torah contains all hoped-for benefits, even material ones, but this is not really the reason that you constantly meditate upon it and are bound to it. Even if on the conscious level you believe that your connection to the Torah derives from all the benefits it contains, the truth is that all the goodness you see in it springs from your inner connection and love for the Torah, which colors your mind and stimulates you to see a great abundance of goodness and even physical benefits in it. The great saints who imbued both their bodies and their souls with holiness, who dedicated themselves, their minds, and their souls to the service of God and to the Torah, studied and served purely out of a love for Torah and divine service. You, young people, still derive your consciousness from your physical mind. You are aware of yourselves; and your own benefit, even your own physical benefit, is your primary consideration. Therefore, the love of Torah and of serving God that is inside you is expressed in your mind and thoughts in terms of your self: you perceive the beneficial qualities and potential that are relevant to you. Within these seemingly selfish motivations pure motivations are concealed and through them, expressed. Our sages of blessed memory may have been hinting at this when they wrote: "A person should always be involved in Torah and mitzvot, even if his motivations are selfish, because through the selfish motivations [he] eventually will come to learning for the sake of the Torah itself." The phrase "will come" can also be read as referring to the phrase "learning for the sake of the Torah itself," and be translated: "through the selfish motivation *comes* the learning for the sake of Torah itself." The saying would then imply that the kind of learning for selfish motivation that one should engage in is the kind that brings along with it, in a state of concealment, learning for the sake of Torah itself.

The opposite kind of dynamic also exists at times. There are men who imagine that they are learning for the sake of the Torah itself, but in reality they are engaged in self-deception, and their learning is actually based on selfish inner motivations. A sign of such a person is that when the benefit he hoped for ceases to appear, and he realizes that his learning is not going to bring him as much gain as he had thought, or he begins to believe that some other kind of commerce will bring him more gain, he will quickly abandon learning, along with his specious "pure motivations." A student who is inwardly connected to Torah, on the other hand, even though he may consciously believe he is studying for selfish reasons, will not stop learning even if all his material aspirations come to nought. Whether or not he can discover other personal motivations for continuing to learn, he will remain connected to the Torah and will constantly continue to increase his connection more and more.

It is important for us to continue to explain why so many young people, and adults as well, have come to neglect the study of Torah, for this will help you understand the great advantage the practice of Chasidism will bring to your Torah study. We have already discussed the fact that a person is strengthened in his labors by his anticipation of the benefits that he will receive from his work. There is an additional criterion that helps determine how hard a task will be for an individual, besides, obviously, the amount of effort that it is necessary to expend to do the job. This other criterion is the degree to which the task fits one's spirit and inner capacity. The *Midrash* describes the "hard labor" that the Egyptians inflicted on the Jews—which Moshe witnessed, as it says "and he saw their suffering"—in the following way: "[They placed] an adult's burden on a child and a child's burden on an adult, a man's burden on a woman and a woman's burden on a man." While we understand that an adult's burden on a child or a man's burden on a woman might be simply too heavy, why would a woman's burden on a man or a child's burden on an adult cause suffering?

The reason is that the difficulty of work is also gauged by how appropriate the work is to the worker, as we have just explained. A tremendously wild and powerful man might find it easy to carry boulders to the top of the walls of a city—this won't tire him out at all—whereas if you put him to work cutting gems, he might be overcome by fatigue right away. An intellectual might find it difficult to carry even very light stones around, and might become more exhausted from the effort than he would from a really challenging job that required concentration and precision. Similarly, a man will not become weary from plowing and planting and other traditionally male tasks as quickly as he will from cooking and cleaning and other kinds of activity usually considered woman's work. The Egyptians, whose intention was to embitter the lives of the Jews and to siphon off their strength, reversed the men's and women's tasks, the adult's and children's burdens—assigning work that did not correspond to the spirit of the worker.

This is why a person who is essentially part of this world will be more inclined to pursue this-worldly work, even if it is difficult, and this-worldly wisdom and studies. They are appropriate for him and for his spirit, while the Torah, which is from heaven, from the

Garden of Eden, and actually preceded the existence of the world, does not fit him and is arduous and wearying. But it is only to a person who is immersed in the physical, who has no heart, whose soul is faint and buried beneath his material being, that the heavenly Torah and the divine service will seem unfitting. You, chasidic students, whose souls are alive and at least a little revealed, will find that the physical labor and the wisdom of this world fail to correspond to your inner predilections, and thus cause you fatigue. Only the heavenly Torah and divine service are really in harmony with your heavenly soul. You will draw strength from it, courage, and blissful pleasure.

The Torah is from heaven, and when you learn Torah, you ascend toward heaven. You ascend toward God and unite with Him, and He, may He be blessed, is drawn into your mind and heart and even dwells in your body. For what is the intellectual content that is in the Torah you study? The Torah was given by God, and its concepts are the understanding of God. And what are the reasons for specific commandments? God's desire that they be commandments is what makes them commandments. And since you have awakened your soul, have revealed it a little bit, and have begun, with your soul, to toil and concentrate in Torah, you cause your soul and your mind to cleave to God. When you understand something from the Torah, it is as if the intellect of God is within you at that moment, as the holy books say. And when you arouse your will toward Torah and the commandments, this will is no longer yours, it is now God's will that is within you. For the essential reality of Torah and the commandments is that God desires them. This desire has now been revealed within you; you feel within yourself God's desire for the fulfillment of Torah and commandments. Is there any greater union than this? He Who transcends all the worlds, Who is infinite and endless, He of whom the angels ask one another "Where is His place of glory?"—He unites with you and dwells within you. Now the words of the Mishnah that state "One hour of penitence and mitzvot in this world is more lovely than all of the life of the world to come" should no longer amaze you. For what could be higher? What could be more like paradise?

You will feel this pleasure and this spiritual bliss during the time you study Torah and afterward as well. On the physical plane, you will not be aware of it, but your inner soul will experience joy and bliss as it draws closer to its Father in heaven. You will feel greater pleasure upon comprehending a more difficult matter in Torah than after learning a simple matter. This is because the difficult matter demands that you collect more of your spiritual and even physical powers together to work at understanding the text. Therefore, you have caused a greater portion of your soul and its powers to cleave to the Father of all souls and the Master of all spiritual life. This increases your soul's bliss. When you are engaged in an easier matter that demands only a slight effort, you will have lifted out of yourself only part of your soul and caused only this part to cleave to God supernally. Your soul will consequently feel less bliss.

If a Torah student feels more pleasure after learning something easy than after learning something difficult, it is a sign that his happiness is not really bliss from the Garden of Eden, but is actually pleasure at having been able to work less and rest his mind and neglect his task. For in reality, is there anything in Torah that is easy? For example, when one first starts to learn Talmud, one learns the case in *Baba Metzia* of two men who are each holding on to an end of a tallit. This is taught to children because it is supposed to be easy. But is it really easy? The *Tosefot* and all the other earlier and later commentaries struggled and wrestled and meditated deeply on the issues that are raised in this section of the Talmud; yet there still remains ample room to distinguish oneself in understanding these issues. If you put effort into it, you will merit to reveal much that was previously unknown. In every segment and every issue in Torah, it is possible to toil and think deeply and to cause a great part of your powers and your spiritual vitality and your soul to emerge and be bound to Torah and to what is within it: the infinite God.

When you learn Torah, therefore, do not attempt to make anything seem easy. Don't say to yourself, "This particular segment is simple, and no trouble to understand." For if you take this attitude, it will be difficult for you to really penetrate to the depths of the matter, and sometimes you will even fail to understand its simple, surface meaning. The sages said, "Old things are more difficult (to understand) than new things." This is because you think that you will be able to understand something with ease because you have already learned it once. Therefore you neglect to gird yourself and gather your strength so as to approach the matter in full force. Your spiritual powers do not emerge to grasp the matter, to toil and penetrate to its depths, and the result is that you fail to understand it. Who could fail to understand that every subject and segment in the Torah is very, very deep, and that if you put your effort into it, and penetrate deeply, you will reach "the depths where the King dwells"—the King of the world. And is there a Jew whose soul does not shake in complete readiness to emerge toward the infinite God, to serve Him with all his strength, to think God's thoughts and to understand His wisdom?

There must certainly be times, after you have just studied and been moved by a brilliant, original analysis of a segment of Torah, that you are struck by a spirit of holy envy. You are envious of the Tannaim and Amoraim and all the other great sages and saints, and you say to yourself: "They were also only human, and yet they merited to bring down so much of God's Torah into this world. They enlightened the whole house of Israel; and even in the supernal world, in the Academy of Heaven, God quotes Halachah in their name. I am just a tiny ant. What value could I possibly have when compared to these lions of the divine chariot?" But why should you be satisfied with this spirit of envy alone? Why not try to follow in their footsteps? Be aware that, despite the greatness of their souls, and their righteousness, which is beyond our conception, they had to toil and work and distance themselves from the whole world in order to dedicate themselves to the labor of Torah. When they were actually learning, what tremendous efforts they made! The Talmud (*Shabbat* 88a) says that once, while concentrating on Torah, Raba inadvertently crushed his fingers so hard that they bled—and he didn't even feel it. It is said of the Ari of Blessed Memory that when he would study Torah—simply the text—he would work so hard that the sweat would pour out of him. You are an ant compared to them, yet you do not even want to toil! You should approach every Torah matter, therefore, as if it were very difficult. Even before you begin learning, it should seem forbidding and arduous. However, don't make it seem so hard that you despair of understanding it. In the same vein, when you come across something that really is very hard to understand even at a basic level, don't get discouraged and begin to think that it is beyond your mental capacity to comprehend. Such self-discouragement will cause you to become spiritually lazy and mentally soft. Instead think: "This is quite a difficult segment—but I too possess spirit and divine wisdom; I will strengthen myself and will succeed, with the help of God."

The same principles apply when studying the works of the later commentators, both those that explain the meaning of the Torah text and those whose subject is ethics or Chasidism. As you begin to study, imagine that an angel of God has just poked his head out from the heavens and is speaking to you in God's name. For what was the *tzaddik* before God sent him to this world, and where is he now? He was an angel God sent to this world to utter His pronouncement, to speak the words God sent him to speak. When he had finished speaking his piece, he returned and ascended heavenward. Should you not, with an effort of your entire inner being, attempt to listen to him by powerfully focusing your complete attention, by listening to each letter spoken to you with the intention of learning from each precise detail of this communication from heaven?

Wouldn't you wish to be a disciple of all the various authors who are angels from heaven? The Talmud in *Berachot* states that whoever sets for himself a fixed place for prayer will be helped by the God of Avraham, and when he dies, he is called a disciple of our father Avraham. The Talmud further states that Hillel, the elder, was considered a student of Ezra, although he lived hundreds of years after Ezra had died. This is because one who listens to the words of a *tzaddik* of a previous era and adopts his ways is considered his disciple. Is there anyone who would not long to be a disciple, if given the opportunity, of our great sages, both from earlier and later eras in our history? To be a student of the Baal Shem Tov and of the Great Maggid, of the Maggid of Kozhnitz and his disciples?

If you find yourself getting tired while you are studying, either because you have been studying for some time already or for some other reason, and because of this fatigue you are not learning with the full force of all your spiritual and intellectual powers, it is best to stop and rest for a quarter of an hour or slightly longer. For why should you deceive yourself by sitting with the Talmud open in front of you and convincing yourself that you are learning, when your learning at that moment is not really worthwhile? It is better to "waste" the fifteen minutes or half hour and gently admonish yourself to become stronger from now on. Then you may return to your studies with increased strength due to your period of rest; and, with your renewed vigor, you will toil and discover new depths in the Torah.

It is proper, as a preparation for studying, to effect a change in your physical condition—for example, by changing your location. If at all possible, you should leave your house and go to a different location to study. If there is nowhere else to study, or if there are idle people who may disturb your studies at these other places, you should at least set aside a place within your home—a room or at least a particular corner—as a special location for study. A place set aside for Torah becomes sanctified as a result and thus becomes especially suited for learning. In addition, the very act of moving and the physical change you make for the sake of Torah work to transform your thoughts and all your ideas, and to sever the threads that have kept you bound to mundane matters. And, just like your body, so your inner being and your thoughts will be roused from their slumber or from their involvement in worldly things, and will say to themselves: "Enough! From now on let's gather our strength for the labor of Torah."

CHAPTER 13

DO NOT DELAY

A light warning is sufficient concerning some matters, but others require multiple warnings and explanations. This is the case concerning the matter we are about to begin to discuss. A faint warning will not do, nor will isolated mentions of the matter that have been culled from what we have written so far. We need to present considerable explanation and much guidance where this matter is concerned.

The Talmud states that when a mitzvah comes to your hands, you should not delay performing it. But while to delay the performance of one mitzvah is bad, one can still repent; however, to delay one's whole self and all one's actions is an evil for which there is practically no penitence possible. To our sorrow, many of our youth are stricken with this procrastinating attitude. We admonished earlier, in Chapter 8, not to rely on the advance of years or the maturation of the body in hopes that these processes will spontaneously lead to the expulsion of all one's negative character traits as you grow. For only the years advance and mature automatically, and not the person. This is not only the case concerning the purification of one's negative traits, but holds true concerning the acquisition of spiritually elevated character traits and the chasidic path as well. Not only someone who relies on the passage of time and does not toil at all, but also someone who wants to work and to serve God, but keeps delaying and postponing his efforts, is engaged in self-corruption. Therefore, chasid-in-training, if you wish to guard yourself against a sickness that is almost impossible to cure, guard yourself with great care against delaying anything, and refrain from saying to yourself: "Tomorrow or at some point I will do it." And after learning any of what we have spoken about so far—the concepts, practices, commands—do not deceive yourself by saying, "This particular matter does not apply to me. I am just a child or a youth. When I get older, I will choose to practice these things; when I get older, I too will serve God in this fashion." Words such as those should make you shake and tremble; such thoughts should cause you to jump backward in fear because—you should know this—such words come directly from your evil inclination, which has risen up against you to kill you and to erase you, God forbid, from both this world and the next.

As we have already stated, it is not sufficient for you just to do good deeds—you, yourself, must become good. And it is not enough for you to perform chasidic deeds—you yourself must become a chasid. The earlier in your youth that you begin to work on yourself and on your character, in the fashion we have described, the better. It will be correspondingly easier to transform every sinew of your flesh and every fragment of your bones until, in their purity and clarity, they embody the principles of Chasidism. And to the extent that you postpone and delay this work, you allow yourself to become soured in the ferment caused by delay; it will become more difficult to arrive at the goal toward which we have been directing you through our instruction from the very beginning. If one of a child's limbs is twisted—if one of his arms is tied behind his back, for example—it will remain crooked even after having been released from its bindings, while an adult's limb will return to its proper place and shape upon release. This is because a child is still growing, is still adding flesh to his flesh and bone to his bones, and the flesh and bone that grew during the period that his arm was tied behind his back were created and born into the world in a state of crookedness. An adult, whose flesh and bones have stopped growing and developing, will not be affected as quickly by actions in a way that will change the structure and form of his flesh and skeleton to conform to the physical and spiritual shape of the action. If, in your youth, you begin to take upon yourself the practices of the chasidic path (in a way appropriate to your age), the synapses of your brain and the tissues of your heart—which carry the ideas and desires drawn from Chasidism as well as the spiritual qualities of love and fear and so forth—will, along with all the other parts of your body and your person, grow and multiply, shaped under the influence of the fiery heat of Chasidism in all its various patterns and emanations. And just as every species of animal, whether wild or domesticated, every insect and every kind of bird, has its own particular nature and set of instincts because the structure of its brain and nervous system, along with all the various limbs and organs of its body, are different than in any other species, so too will your brain and heart and all your limbs, which will have been exposed to Chasidism during their period of growth, find Chasidism attuned and compatible to their spirit and nature. Your limbs will find it very difficult to act in any other way, or to behave in a crude or vulgar fashion. All their physical activities in serving God will be performed with greater purity, sincerity, and directness.

Keep in mind, young disciple of Chasidism, that many great and good men are envious of your youth. They say to themselves, "If only I could be young again—I would devote myself totally to God." Many of them long again to be in an unsullied body, to feel their soul yearning for God. This has become difficult for them because of the passage of time. You are yet capable of anything; should you cast away this pearl by saying, "When I grow up I will serve God and when I get older I will fix everything"?

The Mishnah states, "To teach a child is like ink on fresh paper; to teach an old person is like ink on paper that has been used and erased." This axiom holds true in all matters, both when what is being learned is simply information, and when it is chasidic philosophy or the methods that need to be employed in order to fix one's soul. For there are many people who know what serving God is, and know what fixing one's soul is about, and long to accomplish it. In fact, they force themselves to act upon this longing. And yet most of their years are spent in this effort to force themselves; they continuously waver between two courses of action. They force themselves to serve God for a moment; for half an hour or an hour, and then regress backward for a time. They force themselves again, fall backward again—and in this state of constant vacillation, they live out their lives. They fail to make progress; they are unable to advance even one step higher and transcend their condition, they spend their best years and their choicest measures of spiritual strength wavering and falling.

Precious youth, this will not be your lot if you begin to work on yourself when you are young; Chasidism will be the substance of your very flesh and blood. Even when you fall, you will not regress; even if you sometimes stop, you will not become mired in mud. You will not need to spend your years just trying to keep yourself from falling, and in lifting yourself up from dust and clay. The main thrust of your labors will be to carry yourself higher and higher. Even the times that you do experience spiritual descent, your times of constricted consciousness will be comparable to the mishaps of a mountain climber whose path takes him to the high places of the earth. He may sometimes grow tired, he may injure his leg—this does not cause him to fall, or to descend. He simply rests and then continues upward; he bandages his leg and then keeps walking. You will continue ascending and will keep revealing greatness from inside yourself.

And in truth, child of Israel, you are capable of bringing out from within you spiritual tendencies and of effecting cosmic repairs that you never even dreamed of, that you, yourself, might not even understand. For example, a will that is both good and powerful may emerge within you, a will that is stronger than you are, so that your whole being is in the thrall of this will toward goodness, a will that forces you to fulfill its desires without excuses or rationalizations. Within you, suddenly, you will feel as if the spirit of God, a spirit strong enough to break apart mountains and smash boulders, has struck you, and is carrying you to accomplish a task. It will break apart any obstructions and smash all obstacles. The Lord is God; you are His servant, and you must serve Him.

There are many specific practices that are part of spiritual devotion and the restoration of the soul that can become natural to you if you begin when you are young. You will have repaired yourself so that you will no longer have to keep reminding yourself of these practices. For example, you can reach a state where, when walking along the street, you will not need to shut your eyes so as to avoid seeing evil things—you just won't see them. "Transform my eyes so as not to see what is worthless"—the eyes themselves should be blind to what is worthless. Don't imagine that we mistakenly think that you can, in a very short time, become so holy that even when your eyes gaze at something forbidden they won't see it, as King David is requesting. Know, my precious child, that it is not we who are mistaken. Rather, those people are in error who think that this world, which God created, is some kind of storehouse of evil desires, thoughts, and tendencies. They mistakenly believe that one who wishes to serve God must leave the whole world and distance himself from it—and because of this belief, they remain far from serving God and holiness all their life; they remain enmeshed in the foolish pursuits of this world. They are like a person who witnessed someone drown himself in a river, and came to the conclusion that water itself is evil and was created just in order to cause death. How foolish is such a person! Is it possible to live without water? Because one insane person did not use water properly, and instead of using it to give life to plants, animals, and human beings, he used it to commit suicide, does this make water itself evil? This is true of the whole world as well. It is a world created by God, and thus even in the lowest depths of the world, in all its twisted labyrinths, there exist paths, caverns, and underground passageways that lead to its Creator and Master, to the Lord of the world. The defect is only in man, who does not use the things of this world to a good end, and, instead, employs them for evil. The Scripture announces, "The foolishness of man perverts his way, and his heart frets against the Lord" (Proverbs 19:3). For are there not paths that will bring you to God, and is it just you who pervert them? Why continue, then, to ful-

minate and speak falsely against God—implying, God forbid, that
He created a material world where one is incapable of serving the
Creator.

And so it is concerning the specific matter we were discussing.
You are capable of developing such greatness that you will see
nothing evil and nothing worthless while you are still in this world.
You can reach this level even before you have become such a great
tzaddik, even before your eyes have become so sanctified that you
can look at evil and not see it, if in your youth you become accustomed to the chasidic practices we have outlined for you. For it is
a basic and well-known fact that man's mind has thoughts and responses that he is not even aware of. For example, if a person is
bitten by a mosquito he may lift his hand to swipe at it without
even realizing it—and not necessarily just when he is awake. This
may occur even when he is asleep, and even in his dream he may
have no awareness of what has transpired. These thoughts did not
pass through any layer of his conscious awareness. (Our intention
here is not to explain how this happens—just to emphasize that it
does.) This does not occur only in patterns of behavior that are part
of a person's set of inherited instincts. Forms of behavior or mental
calculations and responses that were not imprinted upon a person
in his infancy or early childhood, but were acquired only later, can
also become deeply impressed upon the mind to such an extent that
the mind thinks them without the person being aware of the thought.
For example, whereas an infant, if left to his own devices, might
fall from a bed in the middle of the night, he will, upon maturing,
turn from one side of a bed to the next, always stopping at the edge
and turning back the other way even though he is not consciously
aware, nor did he see whether he is in the middle of the bed or at
its edge. He feels that he is at the edge with his shoulders and with
all his flesh; this knowledge travels to the brain, which thinks and
decides that now it is time to roll back the other way. Meanwhile,
he remains unaware, even in his dreams, of a thought so strong that
it causes his entire body to move. Even though as an infant he was
not able to think in this way, he has grown into the knowledge that
one must be careful not to fall, and this thought was absorbed into
his flesh and mind, into his arteries and nerves, and became part of

his nature. All the parts of his body have come to know about falling, and work to prevent it from happening, just as in the example of the person who slaps at the mosquito in his sleep.

And when you grow up from childhood with pure thoughts, studying and practicing Chasidism; if you carve into your heart and mind, and depict within them and absorb into the nerves and arteries of your eyes and awareness that it is forbidden to stare at certain proscribed things, when you grow older your eyes will instantly turn away from all they are forbidden to look at. Just as you begin to get nearer to a forbidden object, before your eyes have even focused and seen clearly and before your mind and consciousness are aware that you were approaching a forbidden object, you will have turned away, looked to one side or to the earth. You will not even be aware that your eyes are turning, nor will you even glimpse the forbidden sight.

This, of course, will happen only if you do not wander through the streets and marketplaces for no reason, like a loafer or idler. When you walk through the streets it should be because you have something that needs doing, and the yoke of divine service should not lift from your neck. Don't think about the fact that it's forbidden to look at certain things because these kind of thoughts are not very helpful, and, in general, your mind should be in a state of purity and not involved in all kinds of speculations about whether one should look or not look. Progress beyond such thoughts, and simply remember that you are a Jew, not an unbridled person, God forbid. And certainly you should accustom yourself to think about some holy matter, or at least a business matter, when you are walking through the streets.

If you are unsure of the veracity of the process we have just described, ask the sages and they will tell you; ask the wise men— wise in Torah—and they will say it to you. But why ask? Try what we have told you and see for yourself how mighty and strong are our words.

Dedicated student: Guard your childhood and be careful with your years of youth. How pleasant and how lovely is a youth blessed by God! Like a river of honey, like a stream emerging from Eden, all the years of a person's life are drenched in its nectar. Into old age and beyond one is nourished from its rich oils and can grow and blossom, watered by its continual refreshment. The body will grow old, your strength will diminish, but this fire from youth will still be preserved. You will warm yourself in its heat, and will burn with its flame. Who is foolish enough to forfeit this, who is so insane as to pollute or stop up the source of his life?

This is not to say that someone who did not begin the discipline of chasidic practices in his youth, who did not accustom his soul when he was still young to raise himself out of the bed of reeds in which he was enmeshed, to shake from himself the mounds of dust that he was buried under, will later be unable under any circumstance to come to God—one must not even mention such a possibility. The gates of heaven are always open for every Jew who girds his loins and wishes to bind all his powers to the task and the burden. And does the Mishnah (*Avot* 4:20), which states that teaching an older person is like writing on a paper that has been written on before and then been erased, lock the gates, God forbid, and prevent a person who wishes to return to the Torah in his old age from doing so? The difference is only in the sum of work that is necessary: an older person who wishes to learn Torah and take upon himself the work of the chasidic path must redouble his efforts and work ten or a hundred times as hard as someone who begins his learning in his youth. Since because of our multitudinous sins, not everybody fully applies himself even to the simpler sacred tasks, much less to such heavy and difficult work, we can safely say that if you do not begin early to sanctify yourselves now, in your youth, you will not, God forbid, be able to achieve your goals. And not only your own souls, but also the souls of all of Israel, of the prophets and the *tzaddikim* from this world to the next world, will mourn you, will weep over your destruction. And even the Master of all lives and the Father of all souls will, as it were, be saddened by your neglectfulness and vexed by your laziness. For the darkness of your souls is darkness and dread in all the worlds, and their light is light in all of them. We can say something else as well: even a person who completely dedicates himself to chasidic practices in his old age—and even if he achieves his goal, through much difficult effort—will still always be lacking the periods of his life that he passed through before beginning his practice. This applies to everyone save the original chasidim, who lived during the Baal Shem Tov's life-

time—like the Rebbe Reb Ber and the others, may the memory of
the righteous be a blessing—for they were already holy beyond our
grasp, and, in general, their service of God transcended time and
nature. They reached what they reached even though they did not
become acquainted with Chasidism until their later years.

To explain further: the Mishnah (*Avot* 5:21) says, "Forty years
old to achieve wisdom, fifty to achieve counsel." The meaning of
this statement is that a person's life is divided into periods—at forty,
one's mind is prepared for and capable of understanding; with the
addition of another ten years one reaches another period, that of
counsel. Not only at forty and fifty, but every five or ten years a
person's life can be divided into distinct periods. That which a person
is particularly capable of during his youth he will not be equally
capable of in the periods that follow, including his old age. That
which a person is particularly suited to and capable of when he is
advanced in years and has reached old age, he is not capable of
during the earlier periods of his life. See how wondrously this has
been described by the prophet (Joel 3:2) as he announced the word
of God. "And it will come to pass after this that I will pour out my
spirit on all flesh. Your sons and your daughters will prophesy."
Even then he articulated a distinction: "Your elders will dream dreams
and your young people will see visions"—the elders will perceive
the divine in dreams and the young people in visions. We don't
mean to discuss here the difference between a dream and a vision,
but there *is* a distinction, and the prophet has assigned each to a
different period of life—youth and old age. It is, of course, apparent
that this passage does not apply to God's prophets, who transcended
their physical bodies, time, and the physical universe, and remained
stable in the level of prophecy they had merited all their lives—
they were not bounded by the various periods they passed through.
This passage refers, rather, to the whole Jewish people, for as the
Scripture says, "I will pour out my spirit even on the slaves and
maidservants" (Joel 3:1). The people as a whole will remain bounded
by the period of life they are in even during the Messianic epoch
of greatness. This means that even in serving God, a person's life
is divided into periods, each specially suited for something else. For
example, there is a youthful period in which a person is more capable
of becoming spiritually enflamed, while in later periods a person is

more capable of experiencing the bliss of heavenly sweetness. There are periods during which a person feels nothing except when he is in a state of fiery spiritual excitement, and there are periods when, even when he is not in an excited state, he feels a lovely sweetness in every simple thing, from every letter of the Torah or of prayer that he recites. There are periods in which his spiritual excitation and all his divine service must originate in his brain, through the use of his mind to achieve deep understanding; there are other periods when he is capable of beginning from his heart as well.

Thus, if a person begins to serve God along the pathways of Chasidism while still in his youth, thereby allowing all his natural abilities to emerge so as to use them in serving God, they will all be established permanently within him. In his old age, his service of God will be a kind of crown of splendor in which all the various shapes and colors from all the different periods of his life will be visible. However, if one delays in accustoming oneself to spiritual practice, even if one eventually achieves it, the lost periods will be missing.

And now, students, children, and young people, you are doing the work of the holy, great, powerful, and awesome God. You have merited to become one of the hosts of He who is high above all heights, the infinite One who has no end. The supernal angels are unable to see Him; they ask, "Where is the place of His glory?" Yet He rests upon you and lives within you. Even His name refers to your designation—"hosts"—for he is called the Lord of Hosts. Say to Him: "Our Father, our King, we are Yours; we dedicate all our power and all of our souls to You and to Your Torah and to serving You."

And now, diligent, dedicated students, go out and conquer the world for your Father, the glorious King.

CHAPTER 14

INSTRUCTIONS AND ADMONISHMENTS

MANY OF THESE ARE A SUMMARY OF EARLIER CHAPTERS. IT IS GOOD FOR STUDENTS TO MEMORIZE THEM.

While you are still lying in bed in the morning, be aware that the Lord, the God of heaven and of earth, is already expectantly anticipating your arrival at the yeshivah, waiting to teach you His Torah joyfully and lovingly. Don't be lazy; get up quickly, gather strength and run toward the embrace of your Father in heaven.

But if you lie down at night without a feeling of responsibility and without joy, this is how you will awaken as well. At night, think expectantly about the morning: "How long will it be until I rise and find myself immersed in God's Torah, surrounded by the light of His holiness?" Set water by your bedside. Recite the *Shma* attentively, and meditate on these thoughts until you fall asleep. Then you will find yourself speedy and nimble in the morning as you rise; you will joyfully leap toward God's Torah.

Why whisper the blessing over the Torah and the early morning *Shma* as if they were insignificant, when the tenor of one's whole day depends on its beginning? Remember the yoke of responsibility that rests upon you. All the worlds, even the fate of God's holiness in this world, depend on you. Let this thought touch you and concern you, and from the midst of this concern either think or recite the following prayer: "Master of the world, I wish to dedicate myself entirely to serving You. Bring me salvation. Let me merit to be Your servant and to fulfill Your wishes." As you continue to focus on this thought, begin to recite the blessing before studying Torah, and ask of God, "Please make the words of Your Torah feel pleasant in my mouth" so that you too may taste the sweetness of the Torah.

Remember that you are a member of the host of the Holy One (blessed be He). It is incumbent upon you to proclaim His greatness to the world as soon as you open your eyes, and to make the Lord of the world the King in the world. When you recite the hymn "Lord of the World," pay attention to every word and let each syllable fill you with excitement.

Before you recite the *Shma*, pause for a few moments and think: "I am now taking upon myself the yoke of the kingdom of heaven. I now abnegate myself before God's greatness and His holiness." While focusing on these thoughts, recite the *Shma*, intending as you do so to bring God's reign to the heavens and the earth, and to the four directions of the globe as the sages have recommended (Talmud *Berachot* 13:6). Also, have in mind your preparedness to cast yourself into a raging fire for the sake of God's holiness.

Be conscious of all your actions and your conduct the entire day, for would you want, God forbid, to desecrate the name of God and have people say: "Look at that student who is supposed to be one of the hosts of the Holy One, blessed be He, someone who learns Torah. How petty and degraded is he in all his actions!"

Do not associate with an evil person. Avoid even the shortest conversation with him as you would avoid the path of an arrow. One cynical word from him, one wink of his eye can spoil all the vast stores of Torah and holiness that you have gathered into yourself through the efforts of ten years.

Arrive at the yeshivah on time. If you do come late, let this misdeed trouble you, and take it upon yourself to come earlier from now on. Take your seat in the yeshivah filled with awe and joy, for God is now with you, ready to teach you His Torah.

When you come home from the yeshivah, yearn to return there again. Think to yourself: "How good it is at the yeshivah; how pleasant, to be a disciple of the Holy One, blessed be He!"

Be extremely careful not to lie and not to use profanities. A person who lies becomes false himself, and his Torah is no longer either true or pure. A person who guards his mouth and tongue remains true and pure in his Torah and in himself.

When you become aware that you have done something wrong or that you didn't study properly one day, admonish yourself out loud in the following way: What have I done? Why have I brought my life so low? I have put myself into hell with my own hands! Repeat this rebuke angrily, several times, and resolve to conduct yourself virtuously from now on.

If you find yourself having trouble overcoming one particular bad trait—laziness, for example, or lack of concentration—think to yourself: "Will I allow this trait to cause me to lose everything, God forbid? Have I sunk to such a low level that I can't overcome even this one thing? I'm going to gather all the strength I have, and pound at the rock—the evil inclination—that has me trapped beneath it, until I smash it into a million pieces."

If the urge to do something grabs you, and it is not something expressly forbidden but you wish to restrain yourself from doing it for the simple reason that a Torah scholar should not be at the mercy of all his various urges and desires, try the following strategy if all other approaches fail: Decide that you will do whatever it is you have the urge to do, but not just yet—in another hour or two. Say to yourself, "Am I so depraved that I can't wait for another hour?" You will certainly succeed in postponing your action for a few hours. One of two things will then surely happen: either, after an hour or two, the idea will have lost its appeal; or you will give in to your desire one or two times but, by the third time, you will gain the strength not only to postpone, but to completely shatter these desires.

Be extremely vigilant in loving your friends and peers. A child whose parents are wealthy should under no circumstances be haughty about his wealth, nor should a child from an impoverished home feel low or debased because of his poverty. All of you are children of the Lord, His pure angels on earth.

To the extent that all of you bind yourselves one to the other in friendship and love, linking your souls together as one, to that extent will God also bind Himself to all of you. And the opposite is also true: every flaw in your unity, any distance between you, leads to distance between you and God, and causes God to cast you away from Him.

The students should sometimes discuss among themselves the greatness of God, and speak about matters of devotion and of the obligations of man to God, even if no one has anything particularly new to say, and everyone has already heard what is being said.

⟨decorative flourish⟩

The greatest evil is when a person considers himself righteous, as the prophet Jeremiah has said (Jeremiah 2:35): "Behold, I will judge you for your saying 'I have not sinned.'" This self-righteousness is caused by a lack of perception, by a person's failure to really look at himself. Even worse is when a person does not demand greatness of himself, when a person is satisfied to say: "I have already examined myself and have not discovered any serious sins weighing on me—and that's enough." Don't you at least want to be a Jew at the most basic level? Don't you want to fulfill the condition stipulated by the Holy One, blessed be He, when we received the Torah? Only if we fulfill its terms can we really be called Israel. Greatness and holiness are essentials for Israel; they are demanded of you. Don't be righteous in your own eyes; look at your own shortcomings, and let them humble you. Then gather strength and ascend. (See Chapter 4.)

⟨decorative flourish⟩

Hanging yourself is not the only way to commit suicide. A person who is lazy or halfhearted is also committing suicide. Time—precious hours, pieces of his life—he squanders and dissipates, and thus destroys. With a lazy person, it is at least possible that he will come to reconsider his ways, when he sees how many hours he has wasted and how the pieces of his life lie rotting in the mire. A person who does things halfheartedly is in a worse position because he is engaged in self-deception. He considers himself to be serving God and learning Torah, but since he is doing everything halfheartedly, he is also wasting his time and destroying pieces of his life. Only when he reaches old age will he wake up and tear his hair and scream: "Woe is me! Where have my years gone? Many, many weeks, days, and hours without end—where are they? How did I spend them? I am bereft of both Torah and divine service, of holiness and knowledge of God! It was all in my hands—and I lost everything. I caused harm to all of Israel, even to supernal Israel on high." Therefore, rise up while there is still time, cast away your laziness and your halfheartedness, serve the Lord joyfully and with strength, and use your valuable years to acquire what can be gotten with them. If you do, you will be happy in this world, and will benefit greatly in the world to come. (See Chapter 4.)

Yet no amount of resolve will help a person unless he learns to budget his time and utilize it for accomplishment. For an undisciplined person's days and nights are confusion, all of his time is confusion and is wasted. Every night he will say, "How did the day pass? I didn't even feel it passing; it stole away from me and escaped." In this fashion, the next day and the following one will also slip away, wasted and used up on inconsequential matters.

If you have compassion on yourself, you will learn to budget your hours; every hour will have its own task. You should decide before you begin how much time you want to spend at even mundane matters. When you begin a conversation with a friend, you should know beforehand how long you want to spend conversing. Your hours should not be left open, but should be defined by the tasks you set for them. Write out a daily schedule on a piece of paper and don't deviate from it; then, you will reach old age with all your days intact. (See Chapter 5.)

Both haughty and weak-willed students, both students who are stubborn and rebellious and those who are falsely humble, will come to the same end. The haughty and rebellious students hate their teachers, despise the Torah and even God. The weak-willed and the falsely humble abnegate themselves before everything, before any of the world's follies. They will come to the same end; we cannot hope to see any benefit emerge from any of them—not even one small ray of light. They deceive themselves in darkness; they will degenerate together in gloom and darkness.

Listen, my child, as we reveal the foundation of their sickness. Understand, strengthen yourself, guard yourself, and live.

What they are missing is the Jewish sense of worth, the "I"; this is their illness. This "I," which is a spark from the I of "I am the Lord your God" spoken when the Jews received the Torah, has somehow disappeared. Because of this their whole self has been broken and trampled on. They are like a ship without a captain, which is tossed in the waves by every gale, and in the end sinks to the bottom of the sea. So too every evil wind in the world affects their course, as if they were drifting and directionless, and every plague and disease in the world infects them. If a foolish spirit of sin, haughtiness, arrogance, or hatred of the holy should pass through the world, they are broken by its force.

Awaken the Jewish "I" that is within you, and be saved from this kind of fate. Be a chasid, and devote yourself to God. (See Chapters 6 and 7.)

◦◦◦

Is serving God just a way to fill your leisure hours, God forbid? Or perhaps a means of driving away the concerns you have about yourself and what you lack? You may say to yourself, "I am laboring to fix myself" although you haven't fixed yourself at all. Or you may say "I am ascending spiritually" when, in reality, your ascents are like the struggles of someone drowning in quicksand. He rejoices at having lifted one leg out—forgetting for the moment about his other leg, which is sinking deeper—and then he lifts the other leg, and the first leg sinks down. He is unable to lift himself, his center, out of the mud; thus he rises and falls, rises and falls, and still remains in the same spot. Eventually the mud reaches his neck.

But you, if you are wary of false ascents, and if what you really long for is to run to the true God—lift up the center of your being, raise up your soul. How can you possibly ascend if your soul is stuck in the mud? And how will you choose good if your soul is buried in evil? Hurry and rouse it, while it still has life. Quick, lift it up, before it suffocates beneath the mounds of foolish concerns that you have heaped on top of it.

Wake up your soul with prayer. Wake it with Torah, with devotion to God, and with any means of arousal that comes to you. Carve the following principle on your heart: If even the simplest Jew were to listen to the voices of his soul—the sighs of suffering, the songs of joy, the tremulous sounds of its climb as it ascends, and the noise of its descents—he would be able to write a huge, thick book from the events of just one day. But who will listen to the soul's hum? Who will pay attention to its fluttering? Listen to it, and you will spontaneously awaken; your thoughts, counsel, desires, will ascend toward God and will rouse you.

But the foundation, the beginning and the end of everything, is faith. Faith is not something that you should know only in your thoughts. You should enter the palace of faith with your whole being.

Therefore, engrave the following rule on your heart, for it is one of the laws of the soul. Repetition does not only aid the memory. It also broadens one's understanding, and makes it stand out and become visible to the eye and to the heart. When you return over and over again to even an insignificant thought, and repeat it in your mind and on your lips, it will become clear and certain and will stand out in front of your eyes until the whole room, and even your entire surroundings will be filled with this thought and you will find yourself completely immersed in it.

Think and speak frequently, therefore—to yourself and to your friends—about the substance of your faith: that the whole earth is filled with the glory of the Lord. If you do, you will feel and see, in your mind and in your heart, that your whole being has been placed in the palace of the holy, in the chambers of faith. And the stronger your faith is, the more it fills you inside and out, the easier it will be to awaken your soul.

Make praying with intention and with an aroused soul a regular practice. Begin first with those prayers that speak about your own needs—such as the prayer for knowledge, for repentance, for material blessing and the like. Later, habituate yourself to pray with concentration and intention throughout the whole prayer service.

If you wish to test your spiritual awakening, to see if you have experienced a true soul-revelation, and have really drawn closer to the supernal Pure One, or if all you have been experiencing is merely deceptive emotions—examine your character. If you have corrected, at least a little, some of your flawed traits of character, then you can be sure that you have stripped off some of the outer layer of evil that covered them, and have revealed, at least to a small extent, their source and their holiness. From traits that seemed evil you have aroused yourself to love and fear of God. If, however, your character traits are still as they were, if you have not managed to transform them and lift them even a little bit, you must come to grips with the fact that your spiritual awakening hasn't accomplished anything. You may even have done yourself harm by engaging in self-deception.

Directly after your moments of spiritual arousal, right after you have prayed with proper intent, when your spirit is still hot, and when visions of holiness are still dancing before your eyes, shift your sight to your own lowly character. Let the view of this snake pit, seen from the heights of the holy mountain to which you've ascended, shock and embitter you. Trample on your evil traits and correct them. Neutralize the evil of their outer garments and expose their essential holiness. (See Chapters 8 and 9.)

Just as it is impossible to serve God without a strong will, it is also impossible to serve Him without being decisive. It is more difficult, however, to achieve decisiveness than it is to develop a strong will because the will is aided in its development by other components of the personality, such as the mind and the power of strong thoughts. Decisiveness, however, in and of itself, comes to the fore as a separate quality only when all other factors have been eliminated. The time when one decides for the sake of deciding is when one does not have a strong desire or even a clear thought about what must be done.

In other words, a person's actions follow his will. Everything depends on the strengthening of the will, including, even, the elimination of all obstacles. If a person's will is strong, it can smash or eliminate obstacles; if it is weak, the obstacles will eliminate him. Fortunately, there are ways in which a person can assist himself in achieving a strong will. Through contemplation and meditation on what one should want and should do, one can awaken one's desire, and strengthen it and expand it once it has been awakened. But while the will is only used at certain moments—once it has been aroused—decision-making must occur constantly, even when one's desire is no longer awake and even when one's mind is cloudy. For this is how people operate: their thoughts arouse their will, and then their will reciprocates by instructing the mind as to the way to think. When both are silent, a person will cease to perform or to carry out even a deed that he may have been ready to give his life for previously, when his will and his mind were strong. However, if he is able to arouse his decisiveness, if he can say to himself: "This is what I decided to do before, and this, therefore, is what I must do," then he will be able to do, to act, and to fulfill. If he does not have this quality of being able to stick to his decisions, neither his will nor his thoughts will help him, since neither of them is constant and unchanging.

Decisiveness is a separate trait and quality that a man must slowly coax out from within himself. To be able to perform an action just because one has decided to, even after his desire has passed away, and even when he does not understand the reason for this particular devotional duty the way he understood it when his desire was aroused—this power comes from decisiveness. And this quality is difficult to achieve because in such situations one is not assisted by either the mind or the will. But it is a trait that is absolutely necessary for someone who wants to serve God. It is impossible to do without it. Little by little, it is possible to develop this quality and make it grow.

Just as it is impossible to accomplish anything without will, or to practice a discipline on a continuous basis without decisiveness, it is equally impossible to ascend spiritually without having faith in oneself and in the power of one's devotions.

That is to say, we have already established the fact that doing good deeds is not sufficient in and of itself; a person must himself become good. He must take his character traits and transform them to goodness; just as Israel as a whole is engaged in a process of ascent and of growth, so must he be. But it is very difficult for a person who is in a lowly state, who feels that his personality is composed of degraded traits and that even his essence is ignoble, to believe that his character will be transformed and made virtuous, and that he himself will experience spiritual ascents. Because of this, he will be halfhearted and will not make a real effort. He will perform good deeds, but that is all. He will not try to strengthen himself in order to transform his being itself to good. And yet, have we not said over and over again that you do not know yourself, that all you see is the outer covering—what is inside is concealed from you as well? Why doubt your own ability, thus destroying your own great future, when you do not really see and cannot really know? Desire, decide, and believe in the power of Israel that is within you and within your devotions. Then you will see whether or not you will become holy as others have, and whether or not you too will shine like a bright star.

Just as it is true of the earth from which he was taken, one cannot realize the potential of a human being, or uncover the treasures hidden within him, without sweat and effort. Anyone who imagines that he can do holy work without effort, without compelling himself even when he doesn't want to, is ordered away from the encampment surrounding the presence of God, and is subject to heavenly reproach: "You will remain degraded and of little account spiritually until the day you die."

How does a farmer force himself to work? With the knowledge that if he does not, he will die of starvation. Similarly, as long as you entertain even the slightest notion that the emergence of your soul, and your efforts to cleave to holiness, through Torah, prayer, and your other devotions, are not completely essential, that you could live without them, you will not make the necessary effort, will not compel yourself as you should, and will not succeed in uncovering even the smallest ray of your *Neshamah*.

Only if you remember that God's agreement with us came with the stipulation that we become His special treasure, only if you know that it is impossible to be called Israel if your soul is foul, only then will you work to uncover the cache of riches hidden within you.

Even the crazy thoughts and confused mind that sometimes disturb one's prayer and devotion are, most of the time, the result of insufficient effort. For the nature of thoughts is that they come bound together, one following the other, and one bunch entwined with the next. They flow through the human mind independently, and—unless something happens to interrupt the stream—in an unending chain. When you attempt to pray, even if a good thought stirs within you, since the thought has come without effort and without reinforcement, the thoughts that have been flowing within you wash it away like a torrent of water.

Take a moment, therefore, before you begin every prayer or devotional act, and think: "I am now gathering my strength, and with all my might I now attempt to intensify my love and fear for God and to center my thought around Him. Stormy waters will not be able to wash them away because my thoughts reach heaven; I will strengthen myself in God and will defeat all distractions."

Without strong effort it is impossible to achieve anything, and with strong effort it is possible to achieve everything.

But accustom yourself to rule over thoughts, so that you will not need to make such an effort while praying and serving God.

There are many kinds of thoughts that people like to think and contemplate continuously—not for any purpose, but simply for pleasure. For example, you may enjoy thinking about a celebration or party you have attended, or one you are looking forward to. In the middle of such a pleasurable thought, strengthen yourself and force it out of your mind loudly, and think about something else— not for any other purpose except to accustom yourself to have control over your thoughts so that you will be able to pray and serve God properly.

Remember that you should not only be involved in chasing away bad thoughts because focusing on bad thoughts will not get you very far. Rather, concentrate on strengthening and intensifying your good thoughts as well—your immersion in love of God, the awakening of your fear of God—all of your contemplations about holiness. If you concentrate on good thoughts, your disruptive thoughts will disappear on their own. Darkness cannot be dissipated except by light.

If it is hard for you to focus your mind, and you find yourself having difficulty overcoming all the many disturbances affecting your concentration, imagine that you are trying to push your way through a great crowd to the place where God is. And actually do it—move your body, your arms and legs as if you were pushing through the crowd. Screw up your face, and think: "Through all of them to God, with strength to God." The one thing you have to be careful to avoid is focusing your mind on your physical movements. Your body should do what it is doing, and strongly, and your mind should focus on its thoughts, namely "To God, with strength." You will actually feel your thoughts and your intentions drawing closer to God.

If you have tried, however, to take a stand against your mundane thoughts and have been unable; if you have stubbornly attempted to enter deeply into holiness with your thoughts and have been unable, imagine the following scenario: Your soul on high is running, trying to escape from thousands of angels of destruction and frightful wild beasts, toward the gates of the Garden of Eden. Your soul runs, and they chase it; they bite at your soul, break its bones, throw it down, block its way. In the immensity of its horror, in the midst of its terrified convulsions, your soul screams out, loudly and bitterly: "Save me, Lord! Bring me close!" Heaven and earth tremble, the gates of Paradise shake, even the hordes of wild pursuers are stricken by fear when they hear this scream. They stand rooted to their spots, and your soul escapes to the Garden of Eden.

Just as your soul on high, so too the soul that is within you, should fear the hordes of destructive thoughts that pursue it. Your soul should cry out to the Lord with a great scream that remains hidden within, in the heart. The thoughts will stand still, and you will draw close to holy prayer.

PART II

THREE ESSAYS
FOR SENIOR STUDENTS
AND YOUNG MARRIED SCHOLARS

INTRODUCTION

These essays discourse on Chasidism and on some kabbalistic principles necessary for chasidic practice.

The student must study carefully and remember each concept. All three essays contain progressive themes. If an earlier concept is forgotten, it is difficult to understand what follows.

It is a good idea to review after completing each essay. Or, one may review each separate subject within each essay. If any idea remains uncomprehended, either in the text or in one of the notes, even after reviewing it two or three times, continue studying the essay. Perhaps after becoming more familiar with the concepts you will understand what you were unable to understand before.

It is a good idea not to read too much at a time. Read little by little, according to your ability.

The descriptions of spiritual rapture—for example, on Pesach, dancing on Simchat Torah, or on Shabbat—shall not be read as descriptions of other people. Rather, visualize yourself as saying these words, and visualize your soul as being enwrapped in them. They are not mere words but expressions of the experiences of the soul.

ESSAY 1

HOW TO STUDY CHASIDIC TEXTS

❧ I ❧

My dear student, after having come this far, it is necessary to take another step together upward, toward a higher level of holiness. We have already discussed the crucial need to elevate one's whole approach and outlook toward life; I've also hinted at the need to constantly raise oneself to new levels of holiness. It is important to realize that these two necessities are interdependent. It is impossible to maintain a spiritually elevated outlook without constantly uplifting oneself and rising higher and higher in holiness. If one remains in one place mentally for any substantial length of time, one's thoughts become stale and stagnant and lose the power to affect and move one to real feeling. What good does it do you to know that every Jew is an exalted being, a descendent of prophets, if your soul and body do not tremble at this knowledge and at this thought, if your soul does not draw strength and encouragement from this realization that will enable it to guide you up the path that rises toward the House of God?

If you have been practicing, as well as reading, all that has been discussed in this book so far, a certainty that derives from trust in God assures me that "wings" will emerge from within you to carry you higher and higher along this path. Desires and thoughts of a pure nature will arise in your heart and mind, whose common theme will be a wish to study, meditate, and reflect on the words of our holy masters, may their merit protect us, in order to know what God has spoken. A modicum of guidance and help are essential if this study is to be conducted properly. Without guidance in how to learn, how to immerse oneself intensely in these texts, one of two things is liable, God forbid, to happen. Either you will not be able to enter and understand the inner significance of these texts at all, and your spiritual wings will be severed and fall away, or you will wander along crooked paths, your conceptions tangled and needlessly complex.

A Jew who purifies his body will, inevitably, awaken within himself ever more exalted thoughts and yearnings. These will lead to a desire to see beyond the obscuring screen of the physical body. Earlier, we referred to the talmudic statement about the Jewish people in *Pesachim* 66b: "Israel, if they are not prophets, are at least the children of prophets." This statement cannot mean merely that Jews are descendents of prophets. Would the fact that many generations ago a person's ancestor was a prophet guarantee that this person would retain a degree of prophecy that would enable him to intuit a law that the great sage Hillel did not know? Hillel was so certain of the prophetic nature of the Jewish people that he did not even begin to discuss or dispute the issue in question; he said, confidently, leave it up to Israel—they will independently fulfill the law in the proper fashion. We see in scriptural passages that minor prophets, whose names did not become well known, were called "children of prophets," as in the following passage: "And a man from the children of prophets" (I Kings 20:35). This expression is used in other passages as well. The *Targum* (Aramaic translation) translates the expression "children of prophets" as "students of the prophets." However, this does not mean that they were merely students; they received prophecy at times, as this text itself implies when it continues: "And a certain man of the children of the prophets said to his neighbor in the word of the Lord, 'Strike me, I pray thee.' " The meaning of the words "children of the prophets"—the reason Scripture did not simply write "students of the prophets"—is perhaps similar to the meaning of the expression "child of Torah," which is used to describe a person who has a small amount of ability to learn Torah, whereas a real scholar is called a *lamdan* (a learned person). The modifier "child of" teaches us something about the essence of the person, as in the expression "He is assuredly a child of the world-to-come." The meaning of that phrase is certainly not that his father is in the world-to-come and he is his son, but it does tell us something about the essence of the person himself, namely, that he himself is a child of the world-to-come. The same is true in regard to the expression "child of Torah," which is used to describe people who are able to learn Scripture and perhaps a bit of Talmud. The expression is not only one of delimitation; it also tells us something positive about the person's essence—that he doesn't act like a crude and ignorant person. The expression *amei haaretz* (ignorant people) also implies more than just a lack of knowledge of Torah—it refers to a pattern of crudity in behavior, as the Talmud explains (*Berachot* 47b): "Who is an *am haaretz*?" The Talmud goes on to define the *am haaretz* not only as ignorant, but also according to his actions: he does not put on phylacteries, does not raise his son to learn Torah, and so on. Even though the most important part of the definition is that he is lacking in Torah knowledge, since this quality has a deleterious effect on all his acts and on his very self, the name says something about his essence as well. Similarly, the "children of Torah"—even those who have not studied and do not know such a great quantity of Torah—since the Torah that they do know has begun to affect them and their behavior in a way that distinguishes them from other groups within the nation so that they do act according to the Torah—they have been given a name that refers to their whole person and distinguishes them from others. A scholar (*lamdan*), on the other hand, is not so different in his behavior or his bearing from other "children of Torah"—the additional Torah knowledge he possesses is not so apparent because the other "children of Torah" behave in a manner similar to his. His name, therefore, refers to his distinctive characteristic—his superior level of scholarship—which separates him from other "children of Torah." The disciples of the prophets, before they had reached a high level of prophecy, were called "children of prophets." This title expressed a quality that they themselves possessed, for they (already) contained within themselves a little prophetic power. In their whole being and behavior they were already distinct from the rest of the (Jewish) people, because of the essential quality of prophecy and because of their behavior. A person who was a great prophet received the title *prophet* through the greatness of his prophecy, just as the great scholar received the name *lamdan* through the greatness of his scholarship. When Hillel wished to say that the people of Israel would, when the time came for action and the proper hour for bringing the sacrifice arrived, express by their behavior their inner knowledge of the right law, he said, "They are children of prophets." Hillel himself, with all the knowledge he possessed, did not know the law; the people themselves would not have known it if he had asked them the day before the festival. The name "children of the prophets," which Hillel called them, expresses the fact that a spirit of prophecy is present in their essence and in their actions; when the time to act comes, the spirit of prophecy would inform their actions.

This is also what distinguishes the prophets of Israel from the prophets of other nations, such as Bilam *(lehavdil)*. Concerning Bilam, Scripture uses the expression "And it occurred" to describe his prophetic encounter. For a prophet to arise among the nations is a chance occurrence. For a great prophet to arise in Israel is not a chance occurrence but a constant and essential event, for prophecy is the life-energy and essence of the whole people. For a scholar to arise from among the *amei haaretz*, for example, is an accidental occurrence, an exception to the natural course of things. However, for a scholar to arise out of the class of the children of Torah, even though the other children of Torah are not scholars, is entirely natural—arising as it does out of the essential nature of the group—and not at all an accidental occurrence. Perhaps this is also the reason that God appears to gentile prophets only at night, as the *Midrash* specifies (Numbers *Rabbah* 20). For the gentile prophets, their prophecy and their own self are two separate entities; therefore, during the day

they go about doing their deeds, and at night, when their thoughts
and activities have dwindled, the prophetic vision is able to reveal
itself. Prophets of Israel, though, whose prophecy is their very life
and self, experience great prophetic revelations during the day as
well, even during times when they are fully awake and active in
their thoughts and in their behavior. The *Targum*, which translates
the phrase "children of prophets" as "disciples of prophets," does so
because of the following reason: the great prophets fully understand
what God had spoken and toward what He was hinting when He
spoke to them. The "children of prophets," however, whose degree
of revelation was not so great or outstanding, and who had not yet
become accustomed to the word of God, needed their teacher, the
prophet, to teach them how to reveal and draw out their prophecy
from within themselves, in order to know what God had spoken.
Whom do we consider a greater prophet than Samuel? Yet at first
he was not able to distinguish between the voice of God coming
from on high and the voice of Eli, the Kohen.

We are not trying to imply in the preceding paragraphs that
the children of the prophets who lived during the prophetic period
are to be equated with the multitudes of Israel that were called
"children of prophets" by Hillel. Nor are we claiming that our generation today is the equal of the generation that lived in the time
of Hillel. For the generations descend spiritually, each lower than
the one before, and because of our sins we (now) have no great
prophets, and even the holy spirit has ceased; there are no prophets
and no seers. Even this quality that we call "children of prophets,"
which is the essence of the life-energy and holiness of Israel, has
diminished to an astounding degree. Yet we can still say this: The
essence of the people of Israel, the energy from which Israel draws
life, is prophecy. This is true even now, though this essence may
have dwindled and diminished and remains present only in a small
quantity. Just as a certain quality of life-force separates animals from
plants, and the capacities of reason and speech are what differentiate
human beings from animals, it is the prophetic essence that distinguishes Israel from the rest of humanity. This quality, which is
alluded to in the expression "children of prophets," is the source of
all the good thoughts of a Jew, all of his beneficent desires, longings,
and ideas as well as the fiery enthusiasm that he feels as a result of

these thoughts or ideas. Even when a Jew has a simple and momentary realization of the need to repent, a flicker of awareness, it is this prophetic quality which is the source.

It was not only the predictions of the great and holy prophets that were prophetic. Their many words of guidance and of ethical teaching were the word of God as well; they heard His glorious voice and transmitted His word and guided Israel with His teachings. Their prophecy was great; they heard God's voice and perceived prophetic visions in a way that is beyond our conception. Because this power has diminished, Jews today, who are the children and the remnants of prophets, remain unaware when they feel the stirrings of goodness within themselves, that these stirrings are a spark of prophecy. And yet, as everybody knows, the Baal Shem Tov said that the heavenly voice from Mount Sinai mentioned in the Mishnah (*Avot* 6:2) awakens in every Jewish heart momentary thoughts of penitence. This thought is a spark of the heavenly voice, even though it seems to each individual as if it arose independently within him.

But what was true for the holy prophets of previous eras is still true today. Not all of the prophets were equivalent in their level of prophecy. The prophetic spirit would rest upon a prophet according to the degree to which that prophet sanctified and prepared himself for prophecy (see Maimonides' work, *The Eight Chapters*). The same is true in regard to the essence expressed by the phrase "children of prophets," which is to be found in all of Israel. All are not equal in this quality. In a person who has thickened his body into a state of materiality, who has stupefied his soul and buried it beneath earthen and clay mounds of worthless bodily folly, only a minute quantity of the spirit of prophecy will be found. At times, even that will not be heard or sensed at all, God forbid. On the other hand, if a person purifies his body and grasps the visible threads of his soul in order to draw it out, more and more the spirit expressed in the phrase "children of prophets" will be present within him to a greater and greater degree. This is why we said to you that if you have been practicing, as well as just reading, all that has been discussed so far in this book, we are certain, with a certainty founded in our trust in God, that from within you wings will emerge that will bring you higher and higher, to pure thoughts and pure desires.

This will awaken within you yearnings and ideas that will ca
on your own, to seek out the word of God in the writings
holy masters, may their merit shield us (from all evil). That
we must give you some instruction in how to reflect upor
understand, at least a little bit, their holy words. We have alre
mentioned that the term "children of the prophets" is translated
the *Targum* into Aramaic as "disciples of the prophets" because the
were in need of instruction that would help them to know and
understand the spirit of God that beat inside them since it was
manifested, but in small quantity. We, in our generation, so diminished in spiritual understanding—can we even compare ourselves
to them? We are a generation grasping onto the tiniest glimmer of
prophetic spark that is aroused within us.

The Mishnah (*Avot* 3:17) states: "One whose wisdom exceeds
his deeds, to what can he be compared? To a tree whose branches
are many and whose roots are few. Along comes the wind and
uproots the tree." Let us try and understand this in simple terms.
What measure can be used to determine which is greater, one's
wisdom or one's deeds? For according to the plain meaning of the
text, it is difficult to understand why it should be permissible for us
to study the holy *Zohar* and the other holy books that discuss very
elevated matters, including the worlds of Emanation, Creation, and
Formation. Are we going to ascend into these worlds? Why is this
study not also included in the category of "one whose wisdom
exceeds his deeds"?

The holy books teach us, however, that a Jew has five levels
to his soul, called *Nefesh, Ruach, Neshamah, Chayah,* and *Yechidah.* The
Nefesh, Ruach, and *Neshamah* dwell within a person's body; the *Nefesh*
in the liver, the *Ruach* in the heart, and the *Neshamah* in the brain.
Chayah and *Yechidah,* though, are far greater and holier than the body,
and they are unable to use the body as a vessel in which to enclothe
themselves and take on form. They encompass the body and surround it from above. This is not to say that these levels of the soul
are a surplus and are not absolutely necessary, God forbid. Quite
the contrary: they are essential for every person and for his entire
Nefesh, Ruach, and *Neshamah.* An illustration taken from the physical
domain should help you understand this, even if the correspondence
is not perfectly accurate. A funnel that is used for pouring water or

wine into a flask actually only enters the flask with its narrow end. The wide portion, the main part of the funnel where most of the liquid collects, remains above the flask. So it is with the light and holiness that is present in every Jew. Its source is in the holy heights of the supernal worlds; it diminishes and contracts until it takes the form we have called "the spirit of the children of prophets." It then is diminished further until what remains is the small spark of prophecy that our generation possesses. The light then enters the person in the physical world, only in the measure that can be received and absorbed by the body, according to its level of refinement and purity. This light then manifests within the brain as *Neshamah*, within the heart as *Ruach*, and within the liver as *Nefesh*. Each vessel receives the light and holiness according to its capacity. The liver and the other coarse organs receive only a small portion that serves only to give life and energy to the body. The heart, which is a more refined vessel, receives a larger portion of light, which manifests within it as spirit and as the emotional attributes of the personality. The brain is able to receive more; the light manifests within it as *Neshamah* and as holy knowledge. Above the head, the light is like the wide part of the funnel; it is a reservoir for the main part of the soul's light and holiness—*Yechidah* and *Chayah*. Like the wide part of the funnel, they cannot enter the body because they are too large, whereas *Neshamah*, *Ruach*, and *Nefesh*, which have been contracted and diminished and compressed to a greater extent, can enter.

Actually, the light and holiness of Israel does not begin with just *Yechidah* and *Chayah*, but is drawn from the highest worlds and from our Father, our King; and progresses and contracts, until it reaches the *Yechidah* and *Chayah* of a Jew. However, since we are discussing each individual Jew, we do not mention the lights and holiness that exist above *Yechidah* and *Chayah* because these lights cannot be said to belong to any particular individual. Although there is wine in the barrel, or in the stream pouring from the barrel into the funnel, this wine is not connected to the flask, but to the barrel, until it reaches the funnel. So, too, we can only begin to speak about the soul of an individual Jew (we will speak about the general soul of Israel in later essays) when we reach the level of *Yechidah*. At that stage, the light is already connected to a particular soul— we can say Reuven's *Yechidah* or Levi's *Chayah*. Above *Yechidah*, the light exceeds any particular person and cannot be called by any particular name.

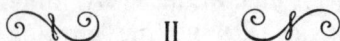

II

In order to enable you to more fully understand yourself, to understand the place from which you originated and your connection with the supernal worlds, we must broaden our scope a little and speak in a general way about the process of contraction and the creation of the worlds. However, you should always keep in mind the following admonition when you are studying this book or any of the writings of our holy masters, the seraphs of God, the lights of the world, may their merit protect us, who speak about similar lofty topics: do not attempt to understand anything beyond what is being explained to you, and avoid asking questions about other spiritual phenomena. For in these matters, you are like a child who is just beginning to learn his ABC's. If the child's teacher, at this stage, happens to be holding a volume of Torah or Talmud, and he opens the book in order to show the child how the letters look, and the child immediately wants to know everything the book says, the intelligent teacher would answer as follows: "If you succeed in learning what you need to learn now, later you will be able to learn everything in these books. But first you must learn to recognize the letters as I show them to you. If you try to rush the process, you won't even know the alphabet. You'll just fill your mind with foolish questions."

The same is true for you. Eventually you'll understand more. In the meanwhile be satisfied with what you are given.

We have a tradition from the patriarch Abraham, from the prophets, from the Tannaim and particularly Rabbi Shimon Bar Yochai, from the Ari Zal and from other kabbalists, that when God created the world he did so through various contractions (*tzimtzum*).

God's creation of the world is not like the work of an artisan. The artisan changes form, not essence. Out of wood or metal he forms an object. He didn't create the wood or the metal; he merely made, out of a simple piece of wood, a table, or out of simple metal, a key. God, blessed is He, on the other hand, created the world out of absolute nothingness. The essence of all things was made out of His divine light. The whole earth is filled with His glory.

The Baal Shem Tov and his holy disciples taught us that this does not merely mean that within every thing is a Godly vitality that gives it life—as, for example, the "growing force" of a plant or the "life-force" of an animal. Rather, even their physical bodies that we see and touch are a spark of God's light. For in His wondrous, hidden way He contracted His light again and again until the physical bodies we see and touch were created. His kingdom has dominion over all, for all the world is but an emanation of His light.

Our tradition teaches us that this contraction (*tzimtzum*) that revealed a finite world out of His infinite light, has various well-defined stages. It corresponds to the contraction of the parts of the soul named *Yechidah, Chayah, Neshamah, Ruach,* and *Nefesh.* This vitality descends within the person so that even his toes derive their vitality according to their appropriate level from the divine life-force that is particularly the life-force of the holiness of Israel.

Thus the particular holiness of the body of a Jew is different from that of the body of a non-Jew; the body of a Levite is different from that of the body of an Israelite; the body of a Kohen is different from that of a Levite or an Israelite from the moment of birth. For since their *souls* differ from each other, their bodies are different too, for the entire body draws its life from the source of the soul.

And if you are wondering at this point what the distinction is between the divine holiness that has contracted and condensed into Israel, and the divine holiness that is in the world, since His kingdom is everywhere, wait until you reach Section III of the second essay in this book and you will find it explained there.

You already know the names of the various stages of your soul's contraction; our holy masters have also handed down to us names for the various levels of the cosmic contraction. They are ten in number and are called *Sefirot.* The names of the various levels are *Keter* (crown), *Chochmah* (wisdom), *Binah* (understanding), *Chesed* (loving-kindness), *Gevurah* (power), *Tiferet* (beauty), *Netzach* (victory, eternity), *Hod* (glory), *Yesod* (foundation), *Malchut* (kingdom). However, we are not going to discuss the *Sefirot* at this point; when you have the opportunity to delve into knowledge of the *Sefirot,* you will find everything explained in the holy books. For it is not our purpose here to teach you Kabbalah; instead we would like to speak to you in a general way about study and contemplation, whether of chasidic or of kabbalistic texts (when you get to them). Our main concern is that you not approach the study of these subjects as if they were simply another kind of wisdom, areas for intellectual investigation to be accomplished by your mind and your intelligence alone. We want to help you realize the limitations of your understanding as well when it comes to these spiritual matters, so that when you do comprehend a concept from this body of knowledge, you won't mistakenly believe that you now understand the actual workings of God.

Since this is our purpose, we will not discuss the *Sefirot* at length, and instead will speak about the four worlds, which are also designations for various levels of the contraction of divine light. They parallel the levels of contraction that exist in man, in the parts of his soul. The world of *Atzilut* is the highest; from there God continued to contract His light and created the world of *Beriah*. He then contracted His light again and formed the world of *Yetzirah*. He contracted His light once more and made the world of *Asiyah*, which is the world of coarse materiality. And just as the body is nourished by the soul, so the body of the world is nourished by the divine light through the contractions of the four worlds, one from another. Our holy masters revealed the connection to and the dependence of the soul's contractions with regard to those of the worlds. They described the correspondence between the various levels of the soul as it emanates from the lofty divine realm down into the body, and the stages of contraction represented by the various worlds. *Yechidah* and *Chayah*, in the state of contraction and in the quality of light that illuminates them, correspond to the world of *Atzilut*. The light that is in *Neshamah* is from *Beriah*, the light in *Ruach* is from *Yetzirah*, and the light in *Nefesh* is from *Asiyah*. A person who merits to receive and absorb the light of *Yechidah* and *Chayah* has a degree of holiness that corresponds to the world of *Atzilut*. A person who has absorbed the light of his *Neshamah* is illuminated by light from the world of *Beriah*, which is a world that has contracted further than *Atzilut*, and whose light has diminished correspondingly.

Do not imagine, however, that the light of everyone's soul is equivalent, for do all flasks have funnels of the same size? When we want to pour something into a larger vessel, we will not use the same funnel that was sufficient when we were pouring into a smaller vessel. The funnel used for the larger vessel, in fact, may be as wide at its narrow end, the end that enters the vessel, as the widest upper part of the other funnel used for pouring into the smaller flask. Similarly, a coarser person who has thickened and become rooted in the materiality of this world is unable to receive the supernal light to the extent that a more refined and purified person is able to. That soul-light called *Chayah* or *Yechidah* in the person rooted in materiality, the part that is suspended above his body and cannot enter it, may be *Neshamah* or *Ruach* or *Nefesh* for a more purified person. There is much more to learn about these matters, but we have said enough already for our purposes here.

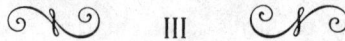

✺ III ✺

We can summarize the outcome of our discussion as follows: a Jewish person, his essence and holiness, is drawn from the lofty heights. This essence and holiness emanate into him as *Yechidah*, *Chayah*, *Neshamah*, *Ruach*, and *Nefesh*, which correspond to the worlds of *Atzilut*, *Beriah*, *Yetzirah*, and *Asiyah*. Although *Yechidah* and *Chayah*, which correspond to *Atzilut*, do not enter him, they are still his, and correspond to his level of purity and holiness, just as the measurements of a funnel correspond to the size of the flask it is being used to pour into. That is to say: each person has a portion in the worlds of *Yetzirah*, *Beriah*, and *Atzilut*. Even though they may have no understanding of these worlds, and though this portion is suspended above their bodies, still, rays and sparks are drawn into each person through the *Nefesh*, *Ruach*, and *Neshamah* that he has absorbed. Without these rays and sparks, the parts of his soul that are manifest within him would have no inherent holiness. A Jew who studies concepts and descriptions of the higher worlds (*Atzilut*, *Beriah*, *Yetzirah*) is in reality studying only those portions of these worlds that are his, even if he does not recognize them as such. Even when he does understand something of the worlds *Atzilut* and *Beriah*, this does not mean that he is able to rise up and enter them. They remain suspended above him.

When you comprehend something you have come across in one of the holy books that speaks of the higher spiritual realms, be very careful not to think that you now know something about the matter as it exists in reality in the worlds of *Yetzirah, Beriah,* or *Atzilut.* What you actually know is a part of your portion in those worlds, and some of the light from your *Ruach, Neshamah, Chayah,* or *Yechidah.* A person whose spiritual advancement has progressed far beyond yours might find what you understood to be of very little significance, for he understands these things on the level of his soul, which is his portion in the higher worlds and is much greater than yours. For example, if you come across an interpretation of the passage, "And on the image of the throne was an image like the form of a man," and you understand it, do not begin to think that you now understand what the prophet saw. Only a spark of a spark, the twinkling of a single ray, have you seen. The words of the prophet contracted themselves and traveled until they reached your *Yechidah, Chayah,* and *Neshamah.* What you understand is only your own *Neshamah,* which carries within it an illumination from the words of the prophet. It is with this awareness that you should study and contemplate the words of our holy masters.

In order to enhance your understanding, let me tell you a parable. You know that a person's body consists of various powers, senses, and capabilities. The power to see abides in the eyes, hearing in the ears, the power to move from place to place in the feet, and so forth. All these powers and capabilities receive their vigor from the life-force within; for we see that at death the body is left with all its limbs and organs, yet they are all bereft of their powers and senses. Are there multiple souls within man—a soul that gives life to the sense of sight, one for hearing, another for walking? No, one soul gives life to the body in a simple unified fashion; many different capacities and senses are revealed as this one soul becomes manifest in the various vessels of the body. When part of the soul becomes manifest through the eyes, the power of sight is revealed. When part of the soul becomes manifest through the ears, whose structure and design are different than the eyes, the sense of hearing emerges. If this same part of the soul had instead become manifest using the eyes as its vessel, sight and not hearing would have resulted. This principle applies to the other senses and powers of the body, according to the holy books of our tradition.

This example should help you understand our previous discussion of man's ability to perceive spiritual matters. The unique preparation required to understand these matters does not merely stem from the fact that they are completely sacred. Rather, the kind of understanding necessary to comprehend spiritual matters differs in its very nature from the kind of understanding necessary to know mathematics, for example, or astronomy. In astronomy, say, you contemplate things that are outside yourself and that remain outside yourself. Even after you know all about the stars, the stars remain outside you, in the heavens. They don't enter your brain. This is why it is possible to think about matters that do not exist at all, as one does in mathematics—for the science of mathematics is almost completely founded on abstract speculation. But holy understanding is the comprehension of that which is within; it is the actual drawing of the light of all the parts of one's soul into oneself. Through this process, each part is revealed within, in accordance with the physical vessel through which it has become manifest. When the soul is drawn down and becomes manifest within the liver, as well as throughout the rest of the body, it appears as simple life-energy. This life-energy, however, is not the same quality of life-energy that one would find within a domesticated animal or wild beast. There are various gradations of holiness, even at this simplest level. Humans are different from animals, Israelites from gentiles, Levites from Israelites, Kohanim from Levites. When the soul becomes manifest through the heart, the *Ruach*, or spirit, appears. This *Ruach* is the locus of such holy qualities as love and fear, as well as others.

When we speak here of love and fear, we certainly are not referring to foolish loves and fears. As we have already mentioned (see Chapter 10), the qualities that become manifest within a Jew are lofty and divine, even if this spiritual dimension remains concealed and invisible for reasons we have described earlier. When the soul becomes manifest through the brain, which is a more refined vessel, the *Neshamah* is revealed, which is the aspect of the soul that comprehends the Torah and the service of God. And when the light of *Chayah* and *Yechidah* surrounds and saturates him from above with a greater intensity, his desire and longing for matters of greater holiness, matters that transcend his grasp, will increase. He will not only long for that which is hidden, he will not only just wish he could be a great *tzaddik*, as if this could happen without tremendous effort and work; his whole being, body and spirit, will long to achieve a state of greater sanctity through the actual service of God. His brain will desire to grasp more, both of the simple meaning of the Torah and of knowledge of Chasidism and the path that leads to the ascent of the soul.

And this is the meaning of the Mishnah quoted earlier: "He whose knowledge exceeds his deeds, to what can he be compared?" and "He whose deeds exceed his knowledge, to what can he be compared?" We may study and contemplate very lofty spiritual matters, as long as we are aware that the kind of understanding we are achieving is not like the kind of understanding we achieve when we are studying other things. When we contemplate the supernal worlds, we are not contemplating things that exist completely outside ourselves. To study with the false assumption that we were understanding these worlds as they exist outside of us would be an example of "he whose wisdom exceeds his deeds." This would not be beneficial. Instead we should be aware of the correspondence between the higher worlds and the parts of our soul that remain suspended above us, yet still belong to us. If one keeps this in mind, the supernal light will manifest within him, starting from above the head and continuing down through the feet. Increased light and holiness will flow to every limb of the body and every part of the soul. His body will grow more sanctified, his heart will be activated with increased love and awe, and his mind will increase in the quantity and quality of its thoughts and contemplations. Even if he studies very elevated spiritual matters, matters concerning the worlds of *Beriah* and *Atzilut*, his wisdom will not exceed his deeds, for it will be his *Atzilut*, his funnel, that he is learning about. The outpouring of the flow from this funnel will exist within his body, in his *Neshamah, Ruach,* and *Nefesh.*

The mind and the body are thus interdependent. If you work on your body, refining it and purifying it using chasidic methods, the ideas that arise in your mind will be of a higher, more spiritual nature. However, if you do not know how to study and think properly, one of two things is bound to occur: one possibility is that your inability to increase the light informing your mental processes will eventually cause a corresponding downfall in your physical progress. This will come about because you have not allowed the additional light of *Neshamah* flowing into you to spread through your brain. This will have the effect of arresting the main influx of light, of cutting off the head, so to speak, of the added soul-light entering the body, thus leaving the body with only the portion of soul-light that it had previously absorbed. The other possibility is that the spiritual refinement of your body will automatically push upward, pressing on the thoughts and desires sparking within your brain. Since there is no straight path open to them, they will become twisted. If you do manage to understand something, you will grandiosely think that you have already reached the world of *Atzilut*. In general, you will be unable to recognize the paths that are straight and holy.

However, if you do continue to advance mentally, you will experience delightful sensations and feelings of spiritual excitation in your body as well. If it were just a question of comprehending certain matters with the mind, one would not feel such pleasantness and such passion. But we are not merely dealing with thought and intellect. Practicing the proper methods of refinement and contemplation is like adding a head to the *Nefesh* and *Ruach*, which already exist within the body, thus causing their light to spread to an even greater extent within the body. Does not every Jew experience this when learning Torah? A gentile studying the laws of Passover—the rules governing the baking of the matzoh, the order of the meal on Passover night—would find such study to be a dry intellectual exercise. The necessity of all the detailed laws would escape him. You, however, are moved so deeply! You find so much grace and delight in the laws; their spirit infuses you with a pleasant feeling of peace. As you study the laws, your tongue can already taste the matzot, your eyes can see the seder table laid out before you, along with the Haggadah and all the symbols of freedom from Egypt. This is not just imagination. The mind has drawn an influx of supernal light into itself. The *Ruach* and *Nefesh* are thus activated by the additional light pouring in, until the body, including the tongue, are affected and feel sensations. The same thing happens in the month of Elul, when one begins to review the supplicational prayers and the services of Rosh Hashanah and Yom Kippur. This study is not merely an arid intellectual experience. Rather, through the learning one feels the quality of judgment of the Days of Awe, until the laws have the same effect, at times, as one would expect from one of the ethical treatises admonishing repentance.

This is what you will find, and this is what you will practice, when you contemplate and study higher spiritual matters. You will realize that what you are studying, what you understand, are the portions of the worlds *Atzilut, Beriah,* and *Yetzirah* whose emanation is directed toward you and remains suspended above you. You have not understood the world of *Atzilut,* for example, as it exists objectively, in and for itself. And when, with God's help, you ascend further and wish to understand a passage or topic in the holy *Zohar* or in one of the other holy books, and cannot find any explanation written in a book, create an image of it in your own mind, and attempt to understand it within yourself, through the power of your will, your soul, your various qualities and attributes—all the four worlds that are yours. For in any case, whatever you grasp, whatever you understand, is from the light of the worlds and the qualities that have emanated for you.

Thus, you should look within yourself. If, through study and learning, your body has ascended and awakened spiritually and become holy, then your learning has not been merely external learning, "wisdom that exceeds one's deeds," God forbid. Rather, through your learning, light has been drawn down for you, and extends from above your head to the soles of your feet. You may not be able to recognize this after every time you learn Torah, or every time you do an act of service to God. Examine yourself every half-year, or, at the very minimum, each year, for this light. You will be satisfied and pleased; your life will be blessed with goodness.

ESSAY 2

TORAH, PRAYER, AND SINGING TO GOD

⚬❧ I ❧⚬

King David commanded his son Solomon, saying: "Know the God of your fathers and serve Him with a full heart and with a soul filled with desire."

Even the small amount of knowledge of God that a man may merit to achieve is not arrived at through research and investigation or through the human intellect; not at all. Only through serving Him does one merit knowledge. Even when we learn Torah, whether we are studying the commandments, or seeking knowledge of the higher realms, or studying Chasidism—where our whole intent is to know the One who conceals Himself in the Torah ("like a son searching in the King's secret treasure house," from the *Zohar*)—we gain knowledge only because studying Torah is a form of divine service. For God has commanded us to serve Him with the limbs

of our body, as well as with our minds and our capacity for understanding, by studying Torah and learning about the commandments.

We have already stated in the previous essay that the knowledge that the mind acquires of Torah and of divine service is not
of an intellectual nature, nor is it equivalent to other kinds of knowledge. Rather, this knowledge comes about through an unfolding
emanation from above; it is drawn into the mind from its source in
the soul. In the previous essay, however, our focus was on the
supernal realms, on the way in which the light contracted in its
progression downward from on high in various stages: *Yechidah,
Chayah, Neshamah* and so on. Now we wish to focus on man's internal
activities, on what occurs inside him, on how he draws light down,
connects himself to the light, and reveals it. For although we stated
earlier that the *Nefesh* of a Jew, which is holy, is drawn down into
his liver and throughout his whole body, and although we stated
that the body of a Jew has an added dimension of holiness because
of this *Nefesh*, still and all, we can't help but observe that when a
Jew becomes ensconced in materiality, the life-force sustaining his
holiness vanishes and he is left spiritually bereft of the distinguishing
qualities of a Jew, and is similar to other men.

And even if a person does not sink completely into materiality,
and still retains the quality of Israel, there are many possible degrees;
not everyone is equal in these matters. The great *tzaddikim* had bodies
that were completely holy; their senses, as well as their life-force,
were holy. With their flesh-and-blood eyes they were able to see
lights and souls and angels, and with their ears they heard God's
voice from on high. Men who are not of this stature possess the
spiritual qualities of Israel only in a small quantity. The qualities
they share with other human beings are more prevalent within them.
Even though their entire bodies are sustained by the life-force drawn
from the source of Israel, and though even their "animal" soul is not
equivalent to the "animal" soul of other human beings, still and all,
the aspect of soul they share with all men is more visible. For, after
all, we are men and we exist in the material world.

We may compare this to a rose with a sweet, lovely scent.
The scent of the rose is an organic part of its being, is inseparable
from the rose itself. It would be impossible to separate the scent of
the rose from the rose's life as a plant, as if the energy sustaining

the rose as a plant and the delicious scent were totally unconnected. In reality, they are one entity—a living thing with a delicious scent. The rose is a plant among plants—it's just that it happens as it grows to bring forth a lovely scent.

The special quality of Israel is similar to that of the rose. The life-force that animates a Jew's physical body is holy, yet a Jew is still a human being. Just as a Jew's body is identical in nature to all other human bodies, and has the same needs, so too, a Jew's mind, though it is drawn from his *Neshamah*, is not independent of the body's functions and activities. If the brain function of a Jew is, God forbid, weakened, his *Neshamah* will realize and understand this fact, for after all, the *Neshamah* dwells in, and is dependent on, the brain. The *Neshamah* will not be injured by the brain's weakness; however, the connection between the *Neshamah* and the brain will be damaged. This is an example of the relationship between the Jew's particular spiritual qualities and his physical being, which is identical to that of other people's.

If we wish to elevate Jews and make them holier, therefore, it is not sufficient to discuss the progressive unfolding of the supernal quality of Israel alone. We must speak about the human functions that Jew possesses and about his modes of perception. This will enable us to know how to harness these qualities as well and to transform their activity into holy activity. In this way they can be guided and made to receive the lights of *Nefesh, Ruach, Neshamah, Chayah,* and *Yechidah,* from the worlds of *Atzilut, Beriah,* and *Yetzirah,* which are unfolding in their midst.

Of the more spiritually elevated matters, which are not perceived or known about through the senses, there are some that are perceived by the intellect. But if you check closely, you will see that the human brain does not perceive anything spiritual very clearly, or from a position of much closeness. All the mind does is to guess or imagine them. This holds true not only in regard to those spiritual entities that exist beyond this world, but also in regard to those that do appear in this world. Man does not see them, does not know them, but only imagines and guesses at their existence, and at how to use them, and knows nothing more substantial.

For does man really know what electricity is, even though he uses it at will? It is a force created by God; man guessed it was

there, found it, and nothing more. This is all the more true about
the forces of life that exist in the world. Everyone knows that there
is a vegetative life-force that God created by contracting His light;
this life-force is manifest in the thousands of species of plants that
exist and in the millions of individual flowers and plants of each
species. This animal life-force is similarly manifested in the various
species of animals, wild and domesticated, and in all the different
kinds of birds and so on. But even though man knows clearly that
these life-forces exist, does he actually see or intellectually understand the nature of these various life-energies? All he knows is that
different species of animals have existed since God created the world
and that each individual member of a species ensures the biological
continuity of the species in the world. Insects, before they die, plant
their eggs in a safe place in the ground or in a crack in a tree branch
before winter, so that when summer returns, even though not even
a speck of their own bodies will remain, they will have participated
in the creation of new insects. The insect does not reflect on what
it is doing, but the life-force created by God, and made manifest
in species and in individual creatures, acts through them, and causes
them to act even though they are unaware of what they are doing.
Does man actually know or see what this life-force is? He hypoth-
esizes that it exists, after observing all the activity we described.

And if man's mind is not really capable of perceiving the powers
and life-forces of this world, how can he possibly come to know
about higher spiritual matters that transcend this world? How foolish
are those people who wish to investigate and know about spiritual
matters using their intellect alone! They will succeed only in ac-
quiring false and heretical opinions, and falling into a spiritual void.
There is, however, another kind of knowledge available to human
beings, knowledge of a slightly more elevated nature. This knowledge comes through feeling, through upliftment, and through at
least a slight revelation of one's soul.

We, whose spiritual stature, along with the spiritual stature of
our entire generation, is slight, have no authority to speak or think
about prophecy, which far transcends our reach. But as we have
already discussed, the phrase in the Talmud, "Israel are the children
of prophets," means that our essence, the life-source of our holiness,
is a spark of prophecy. About this spark we may speak. The Talmud

states that a wise man is preferable to a prophet (*Baba Batra* 12a). In the *Tikunnei Zohar* (*Tikun* 30), it says that the source from which the wise man draws his wisdom is higher than the level that prophets draw from. This refers to the supernal source from which the *tzaddikim* of former times drew their wisdom. Their wisdom came down to them from the *Sefirot* of *Chochmah* (wisdom), *Binah* (understanding), and *Daat* (knowledge), from the world of *Atzilut* and *Beriah* on high. Our wisdom, however, comes from the world of *Asiyah*, from the lowest of the supernal *Sefirot*, the *Sefirah* of Kingdom. This is similar to the example we used in the first essay, of the smaller funnel whose wide end was only as large as the narrow end of the larger funnel used for pouring into the water bottle. It is impossible for us to know, with our intellect or minds, what we sometimes perceive with the spirit that is within our hearts, or when our soul is uplifted.

The *tzaddikim* of former days were surrounded and filled with so much light and holiness that the selfish human dimension of their personality was greatly diminished or even annihilated. Their knowledge was not the self-centered kind of knowledge possessed by an ordinary man, but consisted of inspiration from above, wisdom that had the quality of prophecy. We can see this from a passage in the Talmud, which brings evidence that even after the destruction of the Temple, prophecy was not taken from the wise. The proof the Talmud offers is that wise men often anticipate conclusions and make statements that are later found to be identical to the statements that are discovered to have been made by sages generations earlier, or discovered to be *Halachah L'Moshe MeSinai* (laws revealed to Moshe at Mount Sinai). When the Talmud states, "Prophecy was not taken from the wise" and "a wise man is greater than a sage," it is not referring merely to unadorned human intelligence. The sages apprehended lofty and elevated matters, using their intelligence as a vessel to receive inspiration from their *Neshamah*, *Chayah*, and *Yechidah*. Their intellectual discourses are also holy, inspired wisdom. When we study their holy words, especially when the subject matter transcends the physical universe, we are not studying the product of their intellect, of mere human wisdom. What we are studying, what we want to know, is the spiritual content, the prophetic wisdom, the holy inspiration and divine service that inhere in their words.

But the fact that their works contain prophetic wisdom, an-nunciated from on high, is not sufficient. Everything depends on us as well, on the kind of power we activate within ourselves, the effort and work and study we put forth in learning spiritual teachings. The Talmud's statement (*Shekalim* 13b), "Those who preceded us plowed and sowed, and we? We have no mouth with which to eat" was said about us, about our way of knowing things. For since the light that is within us has diminished, and our self-centeredness has increased, it is difficult, generally, for us to intellectually compre-hend spiritual matters. When we focus our attention on something, we bring our ego into play. We say to ourselves "I am studying," that is to say the bodily I, the physical I. The holy content is once again transformed into mere human intellect. What we understand, more than the inspiration, is the human content, the garb in which the holy words are clothed. A person can learn Kabbalah all his life and still know only the sequence of the worlds or of the *Sefirot*— that *Chesed* (loving-kindness) precedes *Gevurah* (power, stringency); that *Tiferet* (beauty, harmony) mediates between the two, and so on. The human intellect can comprehend the order and sequence of the *Sefirot*. However, in trying to understand what a particular world or *Sefirah* actually is, a person will naturally use examples taken from this world, which his senses and mind can comprehend. He will then apply this same model to the higher spiritual worlds, and will remain ignorant of the actual reality of these worlds. We might compare this to a blind man who has never seen the sun. He imagines the sun to be round as a ball and hot as an open oven—just more so, better and more beautiful. Can this be called knowledge when, unfortunately, he has no eyes with which to see?

And even though the path of the Baal Shem Tov and his disciples is to draw down very lofty matters into the *Nefesh, Ruach, Neshamah, Chayah,* and *Yechidah* of each individual so that he can comprehend them utilizing the various levels of his soul—if he uses only his intellect in reflecting on these matters, he will understand only the externals, the allegory, but not what it is pointing to. This is not the case when the *Nefesh* and *Ruach* within a person are uplifted and reveal themselves a little. For to the extent that the *Ruach* and *Nefesh* are aroused and revealed, the ego is consequently diminished. One can feel in a non-egotistical way. The arousal of the soul and

the spirit and their subsequent revelation allow a person to comprehend, to a limited degree, the inner significance of the holy
words of our spiritual masters and other spiritual matters. One knows
these things in a different way than one knows, for example, the
intricacies of an intellectual debate, or things one sees with one's
eyes, or logical proofs. These last are capable of providing knowledge only about the exterior of things, and about the human intellect. Through feeling, and through a kind of knowing that
transcends human intellect, one is able to comprehend some of what
is beyond human intellect, beneath the garments. One is able to
glimpse the radiance of a particular world or a particular *Sefirah*, a
little at a time.

This principle applies in every aspect of divine service. It is
easier for a person to awaken himself spiritually if he begins by
arousing his *Nefesh* and *Ruach* rather than by trying to arouse his
Neshamah using his intellect. Our use of the word "intellect" is precise—we don't refer here to "thought" or "imagination." Thought
and imagination spring at times from the *Nefesh* and *Ruach*, from our
desires and even from our sense perceptions. It is not as difficult to
rouse oneself through thought or imagination as it is through the
intellect, through wisdom only. The great *tzaddikim* are able to arouse
themselves spiritually even as they utilize their intellect in study,
for their *Nefesh* and *Neshamah* are always manifest; they are always
ready to draw closer to God and to cleave to Him. Everything they
encounter arouses them spiritually. For an ordinary person, however,
it is difficult to become spiritually aroused even if what he is studying
is Kabbalah or Chasidism, even if he is engaged in intellectual
contemplation of God's greatness, of the development of the numerous spiritual worlds in descending order down to this world, of
how God is found within these worlds even as He remains separate
from them. While one is studying, using his faculty of wisdom to
increase his knowledge, although he may be inspired, it is still
difficult to awaken even the feelings of love and fear for God that
one would have while standing before a king. Only after one has
finished studying, has broadened his field of insight and is attempting
to integrate his knowledge within the *Sefirah* of *Daat* (knowledge),
the *Sefirah* that connects *Binah* (understanding, insight) with the

emotional attributes—only then will he be able to awaken in himself the feelings of love and awe. And even then, it is not at all simple for the average man to become aroused spiritually, into a state of love and awe transcending the human condition, a state of spiritual excitation in which the *Nefesh* is uplifted and revealed, through the path of the intellect, which utilizes mainly the *Sefirot* of *Chochmah* (wisdom), *Binah* (understanding), and *Daat* (knowledge). Such a person must continue to arouse and awaken himself, even after his period of study and reflection, in ways that affect the *Ruach* and the *Nefesh* directly, through prayer (which is called the service of the heart), for example.

That the task of spiritual awakening can be more easily accomplished by utilizing the *Ruach* and *Nefesh* rather than the intellect, can be partially understood by recalling our discussion in Chapter 10. There we concluded that the emotional attributes differ from such qualities as wisdom and strength, in that wisdom, intelligence, and strength are aroused spontaneously within a person, while emotions are aroused only by someone else, some external person or thing. That is to say, a person's intelligence is more thoroughly under the dominion of his ego than of his emotions. We can see that at times a person may feel love or fear or empathy against his own will—he may not have wanted to feel these emotions; these feelings were roused in him by others. This is not a phenomenon of the intellect; one never feels internally compelled to study Torah or to seek wisdom even against one's own will. Since intelligence is more completely governed by the humanly self-centered aspect of a person, it is harder for inspiration to use it as a vessel. Even though the *Neshamah* does flow into the mind from above, the mark of the human ego, which governs the mind and covers over the *Neshamah*, is more distinct. Since the *Ruach* and *Nefesh* are less dominated by the ego, it is easier for them to be aroused and inspired. The story we quoted from the Talmud, in which Hillel calls the Jews "children of prophets," brings out this point. Hillel didn't ask the Jews what to do, for they themselves would not have known. It was far easier for their prophetic quality to become manifest through their deeds and through their spirit than through their knowledge or wisdom.

II

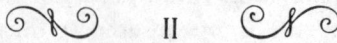

Since we wish to discuss the arousal of the *Ruach* and *Nefesh*, and not the intellect, we will not be able to explain ourselves using intellectual analyses or logical arguments. We will have to instead bring some examples from the world. Is it possible, for instance, to explain the following fact using logic or analysis? Take a person whose spirit is diffuse, whose thoughts are scattered and insignificant and have no general theme connecting them to a single great nexus. Imagine that such a person wishes to unite all his thoughts, direct them toward one central point; he will certainly find such a task very difficult indeed. Yet, say he arrives that evening at a Simchat Torah celebration and begins to dance with all his might. Suddenly he is transformed, healed. If he had refrained from dancing, his psyche would have stayed in its weakened condition. As he danced, he was not necessarily in a state of expanded consciousness. He may have had only simple thoughts, such as these: "This is God's Torah. For her sake, we have spilled our blood constantly. I will dance and rejoice with my God, with the Torah, which is my soul and my life." During the course of the dancing, he feels himself cleansed of all profane worries and concerns; they fall away from him like sand and dust from a coat one has shaken in the wind. His soul is refined and elevated, his inner thoughts and feelings become purified, bright, and clear as the sky. The fact that a physical activity—dancing—has had such a profound effect on his soul and mind cannot be explained logically. Yet this is true: physical activities stimulate the soul, strengthen it, and to an extent reveal it.

Take another example. At times, a person may wish to pray with an awakened heart and an aroused soul and yet he finds himself unable; his heart and soul are blocked. He starts to pronounce the words of the prayer out loud, as the holy books suggest, not for the sake of the volume, but as if he were straining to roll away a boulder that has been stopping up the source of his heart and soul. He says the words of the prayer as they were intended when they were written—that is, he doesn't just try to understand what each word means—he tries to mean the words. For example, when he says "Praise God, call on His name," he imagines himself standing opposite the whole world and shouting out to them: "Give praise to God—are you all asleep? Call out His name!" If he were to simply think this intention in his heart, as he whispered the words, it would not have the same effect. Calling out loud awakens his *Nefesh*, to an extent, and excites it to pray passionately. Why is the voice more capable of arousing the soul than the intellect? The *Nefesh* and *Ruach* are both spiritually higher and lower than the intellect. They are lower because the *Neshamah*, which is the source of the life of the intellect, is higher than *Nefesh* and *Ruach*. They are higher because they have an ability to reveal the soul that surpasses that of wisdom and mind.

So it is that in our generation, our condition is such that we are incapable of investigating or knowing any spiritual matter utilizing the intellect. Even more: our attempts just to awaken ourselves, to reveal a little of the inner quality of our soul as it exists beyond the obscuring barrier of our body, are more successful when we use techniques that grip the *Ruach* and *Nefesh*, rather than using study and reflection (which appeal only to the intellect). We don't mean to suggest that the soul can be awakened and become manifest only through the efforts of the body and its activities in fulfilling the commandments; these must be combined with the right intentions and with thought. Even in the two examples we provided— dancing and praying—nothing would have been accomplished without the accompaniment of thought. Dancing alone would have done nothing. Only when the dancer concentrated fiercely on God and the Torah—and these thoughts were the focus of his dancing and rejoicing—were his *Nefesh* and *Ruach* aroused. Similarly, shouting out the prayers would not have worked to stimulate his *Nefesh* and *Ruach*; this method was effective only after he had grown concerned about how closed his heart had become, and after he had imagined himself standing before God at the very moment of prayer. Actions are ineffective without thought, as are thoughts without their appropriate actions. But only clear, powerful thoughts can assist actions as they are being performed. Intellectual reflection will not be effective, and thus the Talmud says: "One should get up to pray only from the midst of a clear decision of Halachah." It is worth studying the letter included in the *Siddur HaRav* (Rabbi Shneur Zalman of

Liadi's prayerbook) that says that one should not attempt to keep in mind all the individual details of the meaning and proper intention of all the various prayers as one is praying, even if one is intellectually capable of doing so. One should instead keep in mind only the essence of the right intention. Concentration on all the details of the intentions should be during study period only; this does not apply, however, to the recitation of the *Shma* wherein one must concentrate in detail. The main thing is to think with great strength about God, and how He fills the entire world with His glory.

As we have already said, this kind of thinking has its source in our *Ruach* and *Nefesh*, and unites with our actions in causing the *Ruach* and *Nefesh*, as well as the *Neshamah*, to become more clearly manifest. We need not hesitate to say this, for the *Pardes* (Gate 10:1) has already written that a person can become spiritually aroused all the way up to the *Neshamah* through his physical senses. The text there talks about seeing colors; white or black, for example, stimulates the *Ruach*, and through the *Ruach* the *Neshamah* is stimulated as well. This is because the special "Israelite" aspect of the soul has contracted itself so as to abide within the human dimensions of the person too. When the physical "human" aspect of a person is stimulated, his *Nefesh*, *Ruach*, and *Neshamah* are aroused as well. This general principle applies to all matters of the *Ruach* and *Nefesh*: our generation, and, in particular, individuals who are beginning to serve God, and wish to uncover their *Nefesh* and *Ruach*, should concentrate on and grasp hold of the human part of their being in order to accomplish this awakening. This is just like the fact that someone who wants to understand the lovely scent of the rose must first learn all about its biology and structure as a plant. Only afterward can the delightful scent be truly reached and known.

We are not suggesting that a person can be spiritually awakened and filled with holiness without devoting his intelligence and his mind to holiness and Torah. We are merely saying that it is difficult for the ordinary person to become spiritually aroused through the activities of the intellect. Still, it is crucial for such a person to be immersed in Torah and holiness. And to the extent that he devotes himself—not just part of himself but his whole being, his body and his *Nefesh* and his actions, his emotions and his *Ruach* and his thoughts, his mind and his intellect and his reflections—to that extent will spiritual phenomena, such as *Sefirot* and the supernal worlds, become increasingly manifest in him.

At first he will feel only the kind of attraction and awe one might feel before a king. Then his feelings will begin to come in the form of fiery passion. For since the light of God's holiness is shining upon him with greater intensity—and even if he does not perceive it consciously, his soul feels it—he is standing closer to God. His spirit burns passionately with love and awe; he experiences shame as he feels the eyes of God looking at him, penetrating his entire body and soul with their glance. At times, he longs for God so much, he actually feels his heart ache with yearning. On occasion, the spirit called "children of prophets" rests upon him to such an extent that a spark from the supernal source of splendor and harmony appears in front of him; his soul glimpses the brilliance of heavenly beauty and a ray from the lustrous majesty of He who lights up the whole world. He will not be fully conscious of what he is experiencing; he will just feel within himself a sense of absorption and bliss, a pleasantness and joy emanating towards him from above and drawing him upwards, until he feels compelled to sing songs and praises to God.

This phenomenon cannot be explained in a rational way, as it is not a rational phenomenon. However, we can try to grasp it with an illustration. Imagine a child, so filled with love for his father that he can't hold himself back; he runs over to him, kisses him, and still filled with love hovers about him and says: "My dear father, my sweet father, my wise father!" He is not in the middle of telling his friends how great his father is—what causes him to pronounce such endearments? Why does he suddenly compare his father to a sweet honeycomb? The passionate love induced by the presence of his father overwhelmed him; he had to express himself, and his expressions took the form of familiar thoughts and words.

This is the distinction between the kinds of praise that one is forbidden to add to those Moshe Rabainu annunciated and the Men of the Great Assembly fixed in our prayer; and the songs of praise that have been added since, such as "The Song of Unity" (*Shir Hayichud*), "I Shall Sing with Pleasantness" (*Anim Zmirot*), "Every Living Soul" (*Nishmat*), and others. It is forbidden to attempt to add to the description of God's greatness, as we learn from the words of Rabbi

Channina in the Talmud. Rabbi Channina recognized that the person he had rebuked for adding to the praises of God was engaged merely in trying to describe God's greatness—which is forbidden. But we may add to those hymns and songs that we sing out of the great passion and longing of our souls. We preface the song of praise *Anim Zmirot* with the verse: "I shall compose pleasant psalms and weave hymns, because my soul yearns for You. As I speak of Your glory, my heart longs for Your love." Only afterward, because of our yearning, do we continue, "Therefore I shall speak of Your glories and shall honor Your name with loving songs." We do not attempt to describe or complete the praises of God. All we desire is to reveal the spark that was ignited within us. Nor do we merely want to tell the praises of God as we would a story. We don't want just to convey the content and meaning of the words and phrases. The words and phrases of God's praise are enveloped in an additional level of soul. To merely describe a specific act of God might take only two or three words; to extract the divine spirit above and beyond the words—to do this we need to add anew.

One who simply describes God's greatness and His praise is like a person who reports that somewhere far away, there is a great light. But to actually sing God's praise is like bringing a candle back from the faraway light to this world. It is thus connected to the prophetic dimension that is within us; through song and spiritedness, some of this aspect—the aspect of prophecy—is revealed. The *Targum* renders the verb "to prophesy" as "to praise" in its translation of the following passage: "And a chain of prophets approached, and the spirit of God poured out over him, and he prophesied among them." The spirit of prophecy called "child of the prophets" was aroused within him; he looked and perceived a spark of God's lustrous majesty; his soul trembled in great agitation until he was unable to bear it, until he felt compelled to speak and express himself in words and praises and inspired descriptions. Not that this kind of praise is all that prophecy is about, all it contains. Here we are only describing the lesser prophetic spirit that is present in every Jew.

Sometimes a Jew will be moved to sing without any reason or cause, simply because his soul became impassioned at that moment, just as it does sometimes as one performs acts of devotion to God.

This kind of spontaneous arousal is especially likely to occur on Shabbat and on the holidays, when one experiences a heightened degree of sanctity, and when one is filled with joy—joy being one of the necessary preconditions of song. Then there are songs composed or sung after a miracle. After a miracle, one is obligated to thank and praise God; but aside from the obligation, one's soul itself presses one to praise God. This kind of praise is not only thanksgiving for the miracle, equivalent to the homage one would pay to a human king who has been generous toward one. It is also the result of the closer bonding to God, in faith, love, and joy, that the miracle has created. The additional suffusion of *Ruach* and *Neshamah* that radiates with a hint of the shine of the beauty and glory of the higher worlds must be expressed through words of praise. The *Midrash Rabbah* (*Beshalach* 23) says that through their faith, the children of Israel merited inspiration from the holy spirit that enabled them to sing the Song at the Sea. They were not simply telling about an event they had witnessed. The inspiration of the holy spirit was a necessary prerequisite to their singing.

Moreover, the salvation God sends to Israel is also an emanation of His light and holiness. It unfolds through various stages and penetrates into all of a person's physical vessels, into all his needs, until even his bodily desires, such as his need for physical sustenance, are fulfilled. This is in accordance with the principle that we stated previously, that the special holiness of Israel descends all the way down into all the human aspects of a Jew. The *Kedushat Levi* (*The Holiness of Levi*) by Rabbi Levi Yitzchak of Berditchev, states that salvation originates from above as a formless ether. It takes on form in this world according to the needs of the recipient. Therefore, since in receiving salvation each individual is actually receiving divine light from on high, his heart rings with song to God.

The prophets and *tzaddikim* of previous eras saw the precious light of God and His splendorous glory explicitly, because they were suffused with much light. A great deal was revealed to them. They were therefore able to sing new songs, and in this way to express through the holy spirit that enveloped their words, what they had seen. They praised His glory, His majesty, the precious beauty of His greatness. One of the phrases from the Song at the

Sea, "This is my God, and I will glorify Him," expresses this notion. A person who has perceived a level of spirituality, of holiness, with such clarity of vision and such explicitness of knowledge that he can say "this" (as if he were pointing right at the object of his praise), will then be able to glorify and praise God with a new song.

In our lowly generation, our vision is so limited that we are confined to merely feeling passion, longing, bliss. Our experience is not clear and precise enough to express ourselves with exactness and explicitness, especially in the diaspora, where we are bereft of even the holiness of the Land of Israel, which in itself inspires an added level of vision and song. We are unable, therefore, to add to the songs composed in previous generations, which were inspired by prophecy and the holy spirit. All we can do is sing to God in the words of the sacred songs of earlier eras. Through the words of their songs, which are filled with all the visions of God that a Jew might see, we arouse our souls to perceive with the special prophetic capacity; our prophetic spark is uncovered, becomes manifest. Even though we are not composing new songs or adding to the words and phrases, we are adding something new—new soul-light, new vision that our soul perceived in its state of excitation.

We can compare this to a short-sighted man who sees something in the distance but is not certain exactly what it is. He sees a white shape, surrounded by green and black and other colors. A man who has excellent vision comes toward him and says: "See that white? It's the palace of the king. The green is the garden surrounding it." Quickly, the short-sighted man jumps in and adds: "Yes, yes, I see it now! What a beautiful palace and garden! The black— why those are the ministers of the king! It seems to me that I even see the king's splendor shining out from among them." The man is moved and excited by the beauty of the kingdom, awed by its glory.

But this will happen only if the short-sighted man is able to see a little bit at least, even if he can't quite distinguish or express what it is he is seeing. If he can see nothing, or if he closes his eyes and does not look, the descriptions conveyed to him by the clear-sighted man will not have any effect on him.

Only a person who sings in this fashion is really singing to God. Otherwise, he is just repeating the words a prophet said thousands of years ago, words that everybody already knows.

꧁ III ꧂

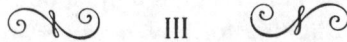

The festival of Pesach as well, which contains within it the essence of song, cannot be understood without arousing one's *Nefesh* and *Ruach* through song and joy, thus utilizing the prophetic spark every Jew possesses. On the first night of Pesach, it is praiseworthy to tell the story of Exodus in as much detail, and with as much elaboration, as possible. On this night, according to the *Zohar*, God and His retinue of angels come to hear Israel sing and give praise to God. The last days of Pesach also center around song—the Song at the Sea, which the children of Israel sang after God had saved them from their enemies. It is clear that if you do not arouse your soul in the manner we described earlier, it will be impossible to really comprehend the significance of Pesach and all the customs and practices of the first night of the holiday. Why, for example, are we commanded to elaborate so much in telling the story of the Exodus when a few words might have been sufficient? What is the meaning of the feast that is eaten in the middle of the recitation of the Haggadah? Why do we sing the *Hallel* during the evening prayer service in synagogue, when we are going to sing it during the seder anyway?

However, a Jew who experiences moments during the course of the year when his soul is aroused and ascends, and who perceives phenomena whose source is in the higher worlds, will long for the approach of the first night of Passover as if he were yearning for paradise. He will already have experienced, on the occasions of his soul's ascent, feelings that cannot be readily assimilated by his intellect, either during the spiritual journey or afterward. His mind, he will have already seen, was unable to grasp the nature of what he saw, that which brought him so much bliss. Thus his soul will have grown accustomed to ascending, and pulling him up as well, beyond the particular situation of his life, and above the barrier between this world and the higher worlds.

The days of the Pesach festival are not of this world—they are days of light and joy and the music of paradise. As Pesach approaches, a Jew who has prepared himself spiritually during the course of the year begins the physical preparations for the holiday. His soul begins to heat up from the light appearing in the distance. The ceremony of searching for leaven arrives, the first step on the threshold of the holiday. Our sages have said that Pesach expresses the quality of divine love; a person whose heart is still closed will need to sit and think and reason to understand the connection between Pesach and love. But a Jew such as the one we have described will not need to search for allusions or reasons. He will feel all the commandments of Pesach, all their complicated details and all the special care necessary to ensure their proper fulfillment, as if he were a child hearing the loving words of his father who, from the midst of an embrace, coaxes him to do a task. The child runs with all his strength, accomplishes what his father told him to do, and then turns to look at his father. He remains excited, full of love and respect for his father; he adds extra embellishments to the task that his father assigned to him out of love; he does everything joyfully. Out of love for his Father in heaven, and because he feels the compassionate eyes of God that watch all he does, our Jew adds stringencies and anticipates all the possible implications of the laws of Passover. He searches for *chametz* everywhere, both in places where he might have brought *chametz* in and where he almost certainly did not. He wishes he could enter every little crack and hole to search; he leaps on top of the stove, and pushes himself under the bed, for his heart is full of longing that will not be calmed.

It is difficult for him, at this point, to talk of anything but Pesach; all his thoughts and words concern the preparations necessary for the holiday—dishes that must be koshered (scalded), food and wine that need to be purchased. He is completely immersed in Pesach. He continues to learn the laws of Pesach, studies their allegorical significance and what the seder is hinting at, and so on. He is quick to lie down at night and then rise again in the morning in order to burn the *chametz*, and, most of all, to bake the matzoh that will be used to fulfill the mitzvah. He bakes his own, even if he already has matzoh in the house. When the Holy Temple was standing, and we lived in the palace of the King, we would travel for Pesach to the Sanctuary. There we would offer a sacrifice to Him. We would experience with our own eyes the splendor emanating from the holiness of our Father, our King. The whole community of Israel, the rose of Sharon, would join together and reach the lofty heights of song, and praise the glorious King. All this has been taken from us, but God is still with us and we still have our love and fear of Him. He has saved us from the sword and from fire. We have hidden Him deep within our hearts. Just as we once did, we will sing *Hallel* to Him. It is not a time for mourning or sadness, but for yearning for the sight of His holy splendor and the peace that His presence brings. The soul breaks down all obstructions such as the distance of the Temple, in space or in time. The soul knows no boundaries, is not material. Together with the Jews who went out of Egypt, and with the people who offered up sacrifices at the Temple, we will perform our holy tasks. Our bodies bake the matzot, our souls yearn, desire, and sing out the *Hallel*.

It is true that only a person whose soul is aroused, whose soul rises and ascends at least a little during the course of the year, will be able to feel what Pesach is. But during the year there are times when a man's heart falls within him, and he says to himself: "Am I really a Jew? And even though I keep the Torah, who can assure me that what I do is accepted in heaven, or that I am even counted among the least worthy, the smallest members of the people with whom God made his covenant, declaring 'You will be My special treasure, a kingdom of priests and a holy nation'? Yes, at times I feel an awakening, I experience holy light, but what does this guarantee? Didn't Bilam receive greater prophecies when God deemed it necessary? Who knows what necessities cause the awakenings from above that I experience? Perhaps they come at times when I am about to sink entirely into the mire; in order that I not be lost completely, an angel descends, pulls me up by the locks of my hair, and my soul then feels a little of the supernal light. Then, though I don't immediately begin sinning like Bilam, I do fall. The added light my soul experiences disappears. And can I really know that these descents are all part of my spiritual work—that my service to God consists of a pattern of small and large ascents and descents? Perhaps the opposite is true. Perhaps my ascents are just a kind of rescue, God's rescue assuring that I don't sink completely into the depths."

These doubts occur during the rest of the year. But on Pesach, a person knows that he is a Jew. One *Hallel* is not enough, one song will not quiet the agitation of the soul. As if in the days of yore, the Garden of Eden has descended to this world and he is in the midst of it. He has become another man completely. He has reached, at least, the lowest rung of what a true Jew should be. His heart and mind are different than they are the rest of the year. By the time the evening of Pesach has come around, he has become a smoldering mountain; the fire bursts forth, he cannot hold himself back until the seder. Right away, during the evening services ushering in the festival, he must say *Hallel*. His body must be very strong to stand in its place as his heart and soul dance with abandon, yearn, and shout in song to God. And as he finishes the *Hallel* with the phrase "for it is good to give thanks to You, to sing to Your pleasant name," his heart almost melts within him. "This is really the truest good in all the worlds, those above and those below, to give thanks to You and to sing to Your pleasant name." He then sits down to the seder, makes Kiddush, recites the Haggadah and sets the table for the feast, which is like the feast of the world-to-come. The limbs of his body and his senses now begin to lose their physical nature; they are absorbed in God who has become so close. Even the table, the candles, the walls, gather with us into one unit; together we bow and sob and, in ecstasy, praise God's splendor and beauty. It is really like the world-to-come, when "The fields and everything in them will rejoice, and all the trees of the forest." All are pure, holy souls, all serve God together and praise the splendor of His holiness that has been revealed in front of all our eyes. How great is a Jew who can draw the spirit of this night into the whole year, and live continuously immersed in purity and holiness, in this clarity that is akin to the clarity of the higher spiritual planes!

Yet even what was seen or experienced during Pesach, the time of year most propitious for glimpsing the supernal glory, is difficult to describe or explain after the holiday is over. The most a person can do is to distinguish between the arousal and passion and feelings he experienced on Rosh Hashanah and Yom Kippur, and those he felt on the night of Pesach. On Rosh Hashanah and Yom Kippur, even the light and joy he saw and felt were part of an overriding experience of awe, dread, and fear, while on Pesach even the awe was part of an overwhelming love. On Rosh Hashanah and Yom Kippur all the feelings, all the passionate excitement that moved the soul, took the form of awe, while on Pesach everything took the form of the glory and preciousness of the supernal kingdom. It is difficult for him to express more than this; the requisite *Ruach HaKodesh* necessary to sing a new song is hard to come by because his vision is quite limited. Instead, he infuses the songs already composed by our holy masters with new energy, praise, and exaltation, through the inspiration and vision he received utilizing the power of prophecy within him.

At times during the year he also comes forth with new insights in Torah that express the greatness of God, or thinks of new ways to serve Him, new strategies of drawing close to Him. These new insights also come from this spark of new song that is within him. Since he is unable to express in song what his soul glimpsed, this spark therefore stimulates his mind and heart to think of new ways to approach God. This spark is concealed in his subconscious, however. For this spark of new song is the manifestation of the light and vision of each Jew's inherent prophetic capacity when it is brought down to this world, and appears here in this particular place. And it is very difficult for our generation to reveal this light, especially in the diaspora.

IV

What emerges from our discussion is the following: just as God cannot be apprehended through the physical senses, so too no spark of His light and holiness can be comprehended with the human intellect. This holds true even if this light has contracted and been drawn right inside us, into our very midst. The mind is capable of surmising the presence of something holy and spiritual, but cannot see it or know its essence. Only with the inherent prophetic capacity we possess, that is stimulated when our soul is aroused, are we able to glimpse sparks of the supernal light. We must prepare ourselves in order for this *Ruach HaKodesh*, this prophetic capacity, to enter and dwell within us. We must devote ourselves completely to our task of purification and sanctification. The body is purified and sanctified through the avoidance of all transgressions or even the atmosphere surrounding transgression, and by the performance of the divine commandments. The heart is purified and sanctified through the service of God wherein we utilize our various emotional attributes, through the voice of Torah study, and through prayer. The brain is purified and sanctified when it thinks holy thoughts, or when it is occupied with the intensive in-depth, study of Torah. This is the meaning of the biblical admonishment: "Know the God of your fathers and work for Him." Only by working for Him can you know Him, through the knowledge that is drawn into you as you work for Him.

For this is the difference between *avodah* (work) and *shimush* (service). Almost everywhere the word *avodah* is used to describe man's service to God. *Avodah* implies a kind of activity that demands a person's strength, and can even exhaust him, while *shimush* can mean to accomplish things for somebody else without any real work or effort. It is impossible to know God through *shimush* alone. In our first essay we explained, using the example of the funnel, that whenever a Jew perceives spiritual phenomena, he is really perceiving only his *Nefesh, Ruach, Neshamah, Chayah, and Yechidah.* This concept would seem to imply that the light of all the levels of a Jew's soul is for him alone, that it touches and concerns only him. However, since with the help of God we have reached this new stage in our discussion, we would like to enter into this concept a little deeper, and to explain that a Jew is not merely a private individual— he or she is the soul and foundation of the world, of this world and all the worlds, the lower worlds and the upper worlds. For the vessels and contractions of a Jew's soul are not for him alone. Rather, in general, they cause God to be revealed, and without them, it would be impossible to apprehend God at all because of the absence of any revelation.

Let us preface our remarks with a quotation from the holy *Pardes* (Gate 10:2), which asks a question about a section in the *Zohar* that assigns various divine attributes to limbs on a symbolic *sefiratic* body. *Chesed* (divine love) corresponds to the right arm, *Gevurah* (power) to the left arm, and so forth. The *Pardes* asks why the sides are not reversed, since the *Zohar* is describing the heavenly realm—that is, my right arm should correspond to God's left arm, just as when I face somebody, my left arm faces his right arm and my right arm faces his left. In fact, when we bow down we turn ourselves leftward, so that we are bowing toward God's "right."

Among its other answers to this question, the *Pardes* says the following: "In actuality, in the high spiritual realms there is no left and no right; everything is one undivided essence, united in a true and absolute unity. Moreover, man as a whole and all his limbs have been created in the image of the supernal form, and he is a shadow of the divine that materialized into a (more solid) image in coming from on high to this world, and the shadow of his right corresponds to the right at the root. Therefore man's right corresponds to the supernal right and his left to the supernal left." Our purpose is not to explain this answer—why when we bow we seem to be using a different model of the heavenly realm than we use in our understanding of the *Sefirot*. We want only to explain a portion of the answer in which it is stated that above there is no left or right, but only unity. This principle is a constant through all the answers and a foundation of our whole faith. And yet in the second answer we quoted, which begins "moreover," it seems that there is a right and left in the heavenly realm, and it appears as if the *Pardes's* holy words contradicted one another, God forbid. We can understand this seeming contradiction according to the method of the Baal Shem Tov and his holy disciples.

In the third part of Essay 2 we used the relationship between man's *Nefesh* and his five senses (seeing, hearing, etc.), to illustrate the process through which all the various parts of man's soul are revealed. Let us now expand a little on this example: Even though all of the various senses and powers that a person has are infused with life by the *Nefesh*, we don't see the *Nefesh* as consisting of many separate, individual *Nefashot* (plural for *Nefesh*)—one for seeing, one for hearing, and so on. Instead, we see the *Nefesh* as one simple, indivisible unity, whose nature corresponds to the sum of all the individual physical vessels which receive its light. All the various powers of the body are included within it, in a hidden way and in a completely simple form. When a particular vessel, designed for a specific task, draws power from the *Nefesh*, the power or sense that is revealed corresponds to the nature of the vessel through which it has become manifest. The eyes, through their specific design, reveal part of the soul as sight; the ears, through their design, reveal hearing; and so on.

The senses and forces, as everyone knows, are drawn from the soul and become manifest through activity. For example, if someone were to keep his eyes closed for a long time he would eventually lose his sight, because the flow of power from the *Nefesh* to the vessels would be completely interrupted. This holds true of the powers and senses that are particularly human as well as of those we have in common with other forms of life. Even the various powers of the *Neshamah* are made manifest through the activity of various bodily vessels. For example, wisdom is revealed through the activity of the brain. In order for the wisdom contained in complete simplicity within the soul to be revealed in a specific fashion—as, for example, in knowledge and comprehension of the Talmud, or of the secret of the calculation of the calendar, or of knowledge of numerology—one has to actively labor in these fields. If one is not active, even if one has great potential for wisdom, he won't know anything, no matter how much he wishes he did. If a child were to grow up wild in the forest, far from people or civilization, he would not have any understanding of even basic human wisdom. His soul might possess great intelligence, hidden within it in utter simplicity. But the brain must be activated and engaged in order to bring this wisdom out and allow it to take the shape of specific forms and words. The wisdom of a child who grew up in the forest remains hidden because he has had no opportunity to take his innate intelligence and reveal it in proper forms and specific fields of knowledge.

This is the only difference between physical senses such as sight, which is revealed from the soul, and the more spiritual ones such as wisdom. The eyes are always seeing things; they are in a constant state of activity. Therefore, it is not apparent that it is only through their activity that a part of the soul is being drawn out and revealed. Only if one closed one's eyes for a long period of time and then discovered that one's sense of sight had disappeared would this become apparent. With the intellect, however, since it is not constantly in the presence of matters of great wisdom upon which to meditate, it is more readily apparent that work and effort are involved in drawing wisdom from its simple, pristine form within the soul, and into specific kinds of knowledge.

This is true of all the various powers of the soul. Yet, as everyone knows, all the different limbs and organs in humans and animals and even in plants are not really individual vessels—they are all part of one larger vessel. All the parts of a plant, for example— the roots, the stem, the branches—are all directed toward one purpose: that through their interaction, one plant, with one plant soul, be revealed. The same is true of animals: all the many limbs and organs of the body are parts of one vessel, through which the animal's soul is revealed. The greater the revelation of soul in a form of life, the more will each individual part of the body be absorbed in the task of the collective revelation. The individual parts of an inanimate object, through which only a small amount of life-force is manifest, are not absorbed to such a great extent into an encompassing unity. A stone that is broken in two does not lose its entire identity—both parts are still stones—they are just smaller than the original stone.

With plants, however, it is immediately apparent when leaves or branches have been torn off—it is apparent that something is missing. This is because there is a greater revelation of life in plants than in inanimate objects, and consequently, the various parts of a plant are each absorbed to a greater degree in one unified whole. With a plant, however, you can at least take the single branch that has been torn off from the whole and replant it: an entire tree can grow from the one branch. With animals, this, of course, cannot be done. If a limb has been torn off, it will always remain conspicuously absent and missed. This is because animals manifest and reveal even more of the life-force than plants do. The purpose of every animal is this one unified revelation.

The purpose of a human being is to be a human being—to have the consciousness and the will of a human being. The difference between humans and animals is, however, that human beings have a choice of whether or not to manifest their ultimate purpose. If a person does not, he will seem more like an animal—that is what will be revealed by the conjunction of all his organs and vessels and limbs. If a person labors to understand the wisdom of the Torah and to serve God, he will reveal his Jewish soul and will have made his purpose and end manifest. In addition, all of his bodily vessels that manifest the life-force that gives him his simple vitality, what we call his animal soul, will also readily become absorbed, bend, direct, and shape themselves toward this one task of revealing the Jewish soul.

The level of absorption and submission of individual limbs in a greater unity depends on the extent and quality of the open manifestation of the end purpose—the revelation of the Jewish soul. If this revelation has occurred only to a very limited extent, the limbs and organs of the body will not submit themselves to this larger task; instead, they will be vessels for the animal soul. If, however, a person, through his own choice and effort, reveals his purpose to a greater extent, the limbs of his body will also submit to this task, and all of them together will manifest his Jewish soul. Then his hearing, seeing, and eating will all reach a level of refinement unlike that of an animal or a human being who is still operating on the level of the animals. His whole body will become refined, until "the wisdom of a man shines on his face" (Ecclesiastes 8:1). His flesh and bones and skin will have been transformed for the better.

What emerges from all of this is that the soul is simple and undifferentiated, and becomes manifest through the various bodily vessels. A Jew manifests his ultimate purpose—the revelation of his Jewish soul—when all of his limbs and organs are working in concert, even the limbs and organs of his body that seem to be vessels for his basic life-energy. Just as, in general, the life-force is revealed through all the various parts and limbs of an organism, so is it with the Jewish soul, which becomes manifest when a Jew fulfills the Torah and all of its commandments. By utilizing all the parts of his body in fulfilling the Torah, they are all united as the means toward one end—the manifestation of the Jewish soul.

If this is the process through which the soul of a person becomes manifest, what should be the process through which the light of God is revealed? A person's soul is, after all is said and done, not completely simple and unified, for after all, each soul is individual and particular, and is the result of a process of contraction through the various worlds and Sefirot. Even Chayah and Yechidah, which remain above the body, are still identified by the name of the person they are connected to, so that it is proper to say, for instance, "Reuven's Yechidah" or "Shimon's Chayah," because the process of contraction whose ultimate end is Reuven or Shimon has already begun. This is the process we illustrated with our model of a funnel and a pitcher. The light of the soul is revealed through the vessels of the body, through the Torah learning and fulfillment of the commandments a person accomplishes with his brain and body.

But God's light is completely and utterly simple, simple beyond our conception. We cannot even call God "simple" or "unified" because His simplicity and unity are so transcendent that it is beyond the ability of any creature to evoke or describe or even praise these divine qualities; this is what our holy books say. This is the meaning of God's pronouncement: "I am known through My acts" (*Midrash Exodus Rabbah* 3). We do not apprehend God himself, nor is God ever really revealed. What we do apprehend, what is revealed, is light from the line that extends from His light into all the worlds, and sparks from the illumination of His glorious presence that have been drawn into the vessels of the worlds of *Atzilut, Beriah, Yetzirah,* and *Asiyah.* In *Asiyah,* the sparks enter all sorts of vessels and bodies. This light (that has emerged in the form of line and sparks) is what we call by the various holy names of God. "According to my acts, so am I called": if *Chesed* (love) is manifested through all the various worlds, we use the divine name *El.* If *Gevurah* (might and stringency) is what is coming through, we use the name *Elohim,* and so on. This is expressed in *Petach Eliyahu:* "And each *Sefirah* is known by a name— but You, You have no name, for You fill all the names."

But you must also know this: the correspondence between the process through which the human soul is manifested and the process through which the supernal light is revealed is not exact. There are many differences. A man's *Nefesh, Ruach,* and *Neshamah* spread into his body and are contained within its bounds. God does not spread out into the worlds, nor is He bounded by them. For He is much higher and more exalted than all the worlds; what shines in the worlds is only a glow cast from His light. Also, whereas the vessels and limbs of a human body precede the *Neshamah* in this world, and are needed by the *Neshamah,* all the spiritual and physical vessels of all the worlds, including this world, were all created by God according to His will.

Since we've begun using man as a model from which to understand a little bit about the divine—and the Torah hints at the possibility of learning about the spiritual worlds by looking at man in the passage "and I will see God from my flesh" (Job 19:26)—let us continue to pursue this path a bit further. God's actions in this world reveal only His power, just as a man's physical activities and senses reveal the power of his *Nefesh*—the power that gives him life. His Jewish *Neshamah*—that is, his consciousness of holiness, both his overall knowledge and all his individual thoughts or meditations, as well as his desire and longing for Torah and for the service of God—are manifested through the performance of the command-ments and through learning Torah. The study of Torah and the fulfillment of the commandments are vessels for the revelation of the *Neshamah* that operate on the level of thought, word, and deed. The very first words of the Torah hint at the primacy of Israel in the plan of creation. The *Midrash* states that the word *b'reishit* (in the beginning) alludes to Israel and the Torah, which are both called *reishit* (the first) so that the word *b'reishit* is an acronym of "for the sake of Israel, who are called the first" and "for the sake of the Torah, which is called the first."

For through the world, only God's power is revealed, while through the people of Israel, the light of His holiness is revealed. For as a Jew meditates on the Torah, and fulfills the commandments, and as holy thoughts and light from the higher realms appear within him, supernal holiness is revealed. Every holy thought or desire that enters his brain or his heart is just such a revelation. Using the terminology of our model, we can say that the world manifests the level of *Nefesh* of the light of God that is revealed in this world, while a Jew manifests the levels of *Ruach* and *Neshamah*. The light that a Jew manifests comes from God's very essence (if we may say such a thing) and from His holiness. This light is the purpose of the entire revelation, for, as we have already said, the *Neshamah* of a person or thing is always its end and purpose. And this is what the Torah means in hinting that the world was created for Israel (and as the *Midrash* also states, Israel was on God's mind at the beginning of creation): the ultimate end and purpose of the creation and revelation is the manifestation of the *Neshamah* level of the light of God that is shining into the world.

You may ask: "Don't the sacred Scriptures also say that God's wisdom and understanding, as well as just His power, are manifested through the physical universe, as in these passages: 'He created them all with wisdom' (Psalms 104:24) and 'He counts all the stars . . . how great is our Master; His power of understanding is unfathomable' (Psalms 147:4, 5)?" These passages do seem to imply a revelation of wisdom and understanding as well as power. But let us recall an earlier part of our discussion, where we distinguished between a person who brings word of a fire somewhere else, far away, and someone who actually brings a torch of light from the fire. Through the world, a spark of God's power is revealed for all to see. But as far as God's wisdom is concerned—this the world only tells about, as if from far away. For the world appears as if it were completely material, though it testifies to the existence of its Creator—elsewhere, in lofty realms—and to His wisdom. A Jew, however, when he thinks holy thoughts or is filled with holy desires, has the wisdom and the holiness of God right within him.

In our discussion of plant and animal life we saw the extent to which the whole being and all the various limbs and parts of an organism are aimed precisely at realizing their one central purpose. This is so despite the fact that they are not as infused with life-energy as human beings are. We also described how a Jew who realizes his ultimate purpose, manifesting his Jewish *Neshamah* through the study of Torah and the practice of mitzvot, will find that all his limbs, organs, and senses, even the base physical ones, will direct themselves toward this task and become absorbed in it. This occurs even though the existence of a person's body and the development of his senses and physical powers precedes the manifestation of his *Neshamah* in this world. Imagine, then, to what extent the world and everything in it must be completely absorbed in and directed toward revealing God's strength, and manifesting the light of God that can be found in Israel. For God created the world with the specific intent of fulfilling this purpose, of revealing the *Neshamah* of all creation, of all revelation. And a person who manifests in his inner being the supernal light that preceded all material existence and is a spark of prophecy, will find his whole body absorbed and transformed into holiness. And not only his body: the whole world will also direct itself toward his sanctification, until everywhere he looks, all he sees is light and holiness. In the future, when all of Israel reaches this level of holiness, all the peoples of the world will also see only the light of God when they look at the world. This is in accordance with the prophecy that states "And all the people of the worlds will see that God's name is called upon you" (Deuteronomy 28:10)—you, Israel, will be sanctified—"And the knowledge of God will fill the earth" (Isaiah 11:9). The earth and everything in it will adapt themselves to the task of being a means through which the essential holiness of the *Neshamah* of all revelation can become manifest. For is not the earth and its fullness a vessel for the manifestation of God's great power? And if the very flesh of a person changes, and his face shines with light when he begins to realize his purpose and manifest the consciousness for which he was created, as it says in Ecclesiastes (8:1): "The wisdom of man illuminates his face," how much more so will the holiness of God illuminate the whole world with the great light that is destined to be revealed in the future through Israel!

Our holy teachers have stated that the service of God accomplished by Israel, who possess the faculty of free will, is the purpose of all the upper worlds as well as the lower ones. Thus the revelation that reaches "from world to world," from the upper worlds down to the lower worlds, should also appear in the form and image of Israel, since the Jew is the vessel through which the purpose, the *Neshamah* of all the revelations, is manifested. For just as the soul of a human being, which is simple and unified at its source, takes on the form of all the vessels through which it is revealed in the world—it appears as sight in the eyes, hearing in the ears, and so forth—so too does the light and holiness of God. The simplicity and unity that exists in the higher realms is beyond compare. All the various vessels, including the world, which reveal His power, were created by God for the express purpose of allowing His light and holiness to become manifest in the heart and mind of Israel. Thus it is clear that the revelation will become manifest according to the form and the image of Israel.

Now the words of the *Pardes* are easy for even our small minds to understand. The *Pardes* said: "In actuality, in the highest spiritual realms there is no left and no right; everything is one undivided essence, united in a true and absolute unity." The *Pardes* then goes on to say: "Moreover, man as a whole and all his limbs have been created in the image of the supernal form . . . and the shadow of his right corresponds to the (supernal) right which is at the root . . . . Therefore man's right corresponds to the supernal right, etc." These two statements do not contradict each other, as we originally considered they might. In fact, they complement each other, and are both talking about the same phenomenon: Above, there is one simple unity; there is neither right nor left. However, since man is the vessel through which the higher light of God is revealed, the form of the revelation must be in accord with the form of the vessel. Since the form of the vessel has a right and left side here in the material world, so too the light, as it takes form in the spiritual worlds, also appears as having a right and left side.

You may ask the following question: Was not man the last creature to be formed? How could the *Sefirot* have already appeared in the spiritual worlds, with the *Sefirah* of *Chesed* on the right and *Gevurah* on the left before the creation of man? This question has no real foundation because what we are concerned with is the purpose and end that God intended when He thought of creating the world. The creation of man was the ultimate aim of God when He desired to create the world. Our holy masters commented on the liturgical passage that reads "because of our ancestors who did what You willed" as follows: It is as if God's desire to create all of the worlds was aroused by the patriarchs and all of Israel through their service of God. Past, present, and future are all the same to God, so that He could see their worship of Him before the creation of all the worlds.

We can perhaps understand in this manner, in a very limited way, the words of the prophet Ezekiel (in Ezekiel 1) who saw in a vision that "On the image of the heavenly throne was an image the likeness of a man above it." We cannot understand what Ezekiel saw—one would have to be a prophet of his caliber to really comprehend him. But the prophet is hinting that what he envisioned was not God Himself, in His utter simplicity—for it has already been said: "No man shall see Me and live" (Exodus 32)—but the manifestation of God as He is revealed in all the worlds, from the highest level to the lowest. For throughout all the levels of the unfolding of the worlds, God becomes manifest in the form of the vessel—which is man. This image of the spiritual form of man that exists in all the worlds is what Ezekiel saw. And this is the meaning of our earlier statement: that the process of contraction through which the various levels of the human soul—*Nefesh, Ruach, Neshamah, Chayah, Yechidah*—are manifested, does not affect only man. Rather, these contractions are the activating force that effects the manifestation of God, in general, throughout existence.

This will also help you understand a phenomenon you will encounter in the writings of the disciples of the Baal Shem Tov (may his memory be a blessing). The disciples of the Baal Shem Tov often explain kabbalistic concepts in accordance with their human correlative: what these concepts mean, how they appear in man. This is because man is the cause of their manifestation; they thus appear in his form—with a right side, a left side, and a center.

This is also the reason that different *tzaddikim* often have different approaches in their understanding of the concepts and phenomena of the spiritual worlds. They do not differ just in the depth of their understanding—which of course we have no way of measuring—but also in the way they perceive things. For example, the Kabbalah of the Ari is deeper than the Ramak's Kabbalah, and also explains more about what happened after the breaking of the vessels. But even when they both speak about the same thing, and in basically the same fashion, and in the same order, they still perceive things in their own distinct way. The same thing can be said of the disciples of the Baal Shem Tov. Among the disciples of the Baal Shem Tov, too, there are distinctions: the Rav (Rabbi Shneur Zalman of Liadi, the first Lubavitcher Rebbe) has an understanding of Kabbalah that is different from the understanding of the Maggid of Kozhnitz. Even though both of them are explaining the Kabbalah of the Ramak and the Ari, and both belong to the same school of thought, and there are no real disputes between them, the little that we understand of the Kabbalah of the Rav is not at all the same as that which we understand of the Kabbalah of the Maggid of Kozhnitz. The distinctions are even more apparent when they explain kabbalistic concepts according to Chasidism. Each teacher is so distinct in his way of thinking, that it is possible to hear how a concept has been explained and to be able to recognize, without being told, who is being quoted: the Ramak, the Ari, the Rav, or the Maggid of Kozhnitz. Now, the perceptions and teachings of these great *tzaddikim* are not the product of their own intellect, but are revelations that come from lofty heights. But since they caused the revelation to appear in this world, since they were the holy vessels through which it became manifest, this light took the unique shape characteristic of the *tzaddik* who drew it down into him from above. Just as all human beings have the same number of limbs and muscles and yet have their own distinct shape, so does everyone perceive things differently, even if they have the same basic beliefs and assumptions, and even if they are concerned about the very same thing. Perhaps the Talmud (*Berachot* 58a) is alluding to just this phenomenon when it states "Just as no two people have the same face, so no two people have the same way of thinking." The reason different people's ways of thinking changes, just as their faces change, is because what a person comprehends is revealed through his image. When a person's face and image are different, his thoughts and ideas will also be different.

And so it is with every Jew. By adding strength to your devotion to God, and continuing to expand your spiritual perception, you create a totality that has a certain form. Even when you are not saying anything particularly original, but are only explaining something written by our holy masters in an earlier generation, there will be a particular flavor and form to what you say, even if this form is perhaps not as distinct and unique as the thinking of the great people of earlier generations.

∿ V ∾

Now we have come to understand that the body, *Nefesh, Ruach, Neshamah, Chayah,* and *Yechidah* of a Jew are vessels for manifesting the level of *Neshamah* of the divine revelation, for through them and in them God's holiness is revealed in the world. Therefore, if a Jew works so hard at serving God that he exhausts himself—his body, *Ruach* and *Neshamah*—as he would in any kind of hard labor, and if he raises up all the parts of himself and binds them to God, then divine light will be manifested and revealed through every part of his being.

However, if he serves God in performing the commandments without the kind of effort that leaves you exhausted, if he does not

raise himself up and bind himself to God, there will be no revelation
and no light. For if the eye is not connected to the source of life,
can it be a vessel for the power of sight? And can the mind reveal
any new insight about anything with which it has not united in
deep, penetrating study?

A person who serves God with only superficial effort also does
damage to the *Sefirot*, in not serving as a vessel for their manifestation.
For the *Sefirot*—as we said in our explanation of the *Pardes*—are
revealed by man. "There is no right nor left above"; the various
levels of man's soul are a kind of vehicle through which, and in
whose form, God's holy light is revealed. "Know the God of your
ancestors and serve Him" (First Chronicles 28:9)—not through intellectual investigation, but only through service, can one know
God. And not through superficial service—only through service
that utilizes the full capacity of one's strength.

This insight can help us understand our earlier remarks about
song and prayer. The holy *Zohar* (*Pekudai* 268b) states, "The gifts
brought for sacrifice at the Temple are to arouse the holy spirit in
the will of the Kohanim, and the songs of the Levites and the prayers
of the Israelites." It seems that there are three revelatory levels here:
the holy spirit is the first and highest level; song is formed through
the contraction and diminution of the holy spirit, while prayer is
the contraction and diminution of song. As we have already discussed, song is itself a kind of vision because the inspiration for
song comes when the soul glimpses a spark from the supernal glory
and an illumination from a holy source and expresses what it has
seen in songs and praises. This is why only prophets and those who
possess the holy spirit are able to sing new songs, for their vision
is so clear and distinct that they are able to express what they have
seen. We, however, whose vision of God's light is limited, and
whose souls are not passionately aflame as the prophets and holy
men of past generations were, are not able to express what we have
seen of God's light by composing completely new songs, describing
and glorifying what we have seen. We infuse, instead, the songs of
our prophets with the small spark of prophecy that is within us.

And is this small spark awake within us at all times? Are there
not times when one of us wishes to arouse and express the purity
of our heart, our Jewish *Neshamah*, and yet is unable? At those times

it is as if he were lying in a dark pit, devoid of light and devoid of heart.

According to our explanation of the holy words of the *Pardes*, we find that it is not only our own soul that is sparking within us during our moments of arousal and upliftment. And it is not even just the portion of holiness that emanated downward to become our own *Nefesh, Ruach, Neshamah, Chayah*, and *Yechidah* that is seen by the soul during its periods of passionate arousal. Rather, "From faraway God has appeared to me." Since the shining of God's light is revealed through all the parts of a Jew's soul, and since they are thus the vehicle and the vessel through which God's light is manifested in the spiritual worlds (which therefore appear in a form that corresponds to man's image), he is able to gaze from afar on the light of God's holy glory that has, in a general and inclusive sense, been revealed through him. The great *tzaddikim* of former days transformed their entire body and soul into a vehicle for the revelation of holiness. But it is not only them, but every Jew, each to his own degree, who can become such a vehicle. If he guards his body and soul from, at the very least, the lower spiritual levels, he can create—from all the isolated points of goodness within his body and soul, the parts of himself that he has managed to elevate and sanctify—a vehicle for God's light. And the size of his vehicle depends on how much Torah he has learned and fulfilled; and on the manner in which he has fulfilled it—that is, either superficially or with hard labor. How hard has he worked at making his body and soul a vehicle for the manifestation of God's glory? To what extent has he guarded the other parts of his body and the strength God gave him from spiritual degradation? If he has guarded himself but has not made the necessary spiritual effort to draw the various parts of his soul out in the service of God, and has performed all his deeds with a kind of coldness, he will not be able to gaze at the divine light nor to be moved to song.

There are, however, people who learn and work diligently and are devoted to Torah, and yet still find it difficult to awaken within themselves the part of their soul that is a vehicle through which the supernal glory can be revealed, and can move and inspire them.

This we can also understand by using human life as a model. There are people whose bodies are weak, who are therefore not suited for physical combat of any kind. Then there is another kind of person, who is vigorous, strong, and heroic by nature, but has momentarily lost his courage, has lost heart, is unable to concentrate on the battle—the heroic part of him is napping. If he decides he wants to fight, he must awaken all the slumbering forces within him, gather up his strength with spiritedness and courage. A person who does not work hard at learning Torah and keeping the commandments, who does not even make part of himself into a vehicle for revealing divine light, is comparable to the weak person. For his soul to ascend, to glimpse the light of God, to sing of his vision, is impossible. Even if sometimes his soul becomes excited, he will never be sure that this excitation or passion is not just the result of fantasy or a kind of overstimulation of the nervous system. It is like foam upon the water that quickly dissipates. At times, a moment after he has become excited about something sublime, he is likely to become excited about something lowly. But a person who makes of part of his soul a vehicle for revelation is often like the reluctant hero—his soul, with the parts of it that are a vehicle for revelation, hidden and slumbering within him. He must bind together all the various parts of his soul that he has managed to fix until now and encourage, strengthen, and awaken himself until he is moved from within and becomes enflamed with passion for God, and feels his soul gaze upon and then unite with the divine light, each person according to his spiritual level.

And this is the relationship between prayer and song: song is one of the degrees of the holy spirit, and prayer is on a lower rung, along the same continuum as song. There is less illumination in prayer; when one is on the level of prayer and has not yet reached the level of song, one needs tremendous strength and effort just to sing and to see with spiritual vision, to become enflamed in passion for God in the midst of one's prayers. This is as it has been stated in the Talmud (*Sanhedrin* 44): "If one prays with strong inner effort below, no enemy (angel) has power against him from above." The task of the body and the *Nefesh* is prayer: one must strengthen oneself and awaken the spirit of song, which is the spark of holy spirit that is within one. The holy *Zohar* (*Terumah* 130b) says that there are six expressions for prophecy. *Masa* (burden) is the lowest. "That light is revealed only with great difficulty. There's the burden of the word upon him that cannot be revealed. . . . This is *Masa*. . . . It's a prophecy of a silent whisper. . . . " See the *Zohar* there. That is to say that since this revelation is the most limited degree of revelation that is still called prophecy, therefore it takes much effort and is very difficult to manifest. How much toil and how much effort must be needed, therefore, to reveal the small spark, the tiny gust of the spirit of song and passion that is within us now. When a Jew starts to pray, he must concentrate with great strength and create an image in his mind of how the whole world and everything in it is divine light, and how His glory fills the world. Imagine yourself in the middle, standing inside all this divinity. Concentrate some more, and think: "Is not God's desire to reveal His light in this world the foundation of the whole creation? And is not the aim of this desire that this light should be revealed within my heart and mind? For within the human heart and mind it is not only God's strength that can be revealed, but also the light shining from His very being, His holiness, His thoughts, His will. And moreover, I am the basis for the revelation of the supernal worlds as well; they unfold according to a pattern set by my form and image and that is how they appear in the spiritual realms. All of this is dependent on the hour of prayer I am about to begin. Should I be neglectful, and fail to arouse my soul, and thus cause destruction, God forbid, in all the worlds, and drive God's glory from this world and fail to fulfill His will?" The more deeply and strongly you think such thoughts, the higher your prayer will ascend.

But you should not only think such thoughts; you must also strengthen yourself within, and not only your mind, but your whole body. And it is especially important that you pronounce the words out loud, shouting not only outwardly, but in your heart as well. At the beginning of your prayers, you will have to force yourself, but then your *Nefesh* will awaken and pray passionately on its own, repeating the words of our holy prayers, the words of God, words hewn of fire.

Prayer is not just speech; it is work, as it states in the Talmud: "What is work (that takes place) within the heart?—Prayer." And it says in the holy *Zohar* (*Vayakhel* 201) as well: "There is a kind of service of God that the body fulfills, and then there is an inner service of God . . . that is a fixing of the *Ruach*. . . . people's prayers are the service of the *Ruach*." This means that there is a kind of service of God that is performed with the body, and there is also an inner service of God that is the core of all divine service. This is the service performed by the spirit, that is to say, prayer. And just as the service performed by one's body must not be superficial, but must be hard work, until one can rightfully say that the Torah has drained you of strength, so, too, one must pour one's strength and effort into the service of the spirit one accomplishes through prayer. Through this kind of effort, one will be able to reveal all the various parts of one's soul that have already been fixed, particularly on that day: its Torah, mitzvot, good deeds of thought, speech, and action. Then one will be able to bind all these parts together until they are a vessel into which the divine light can be drawn and made manifest, all in accordance with the kind of vehicle one has created within oneself. Then, as we have quoted the *Zohar* in saying: "Even if you don't see it, your soul at its root sees it." Your soul will gaze at the glory and the radiance of the divine, and will sing songs and praises to God. The author of the *Tanya* has written (in a letter printed in the *Siddur* he edited) that "the main concern and the essence of prayer is to know God, which is the foundation of the whole Torah: to realize His greatness, His beauty and all the other qualities emanating from Him, and thus to arouse the higher aspect of one's soul to the love of God and to the longing to cleave to God and to His Torah, and to fulfill His commandments. This we accomplish in our times by reciting the morning chapters of praise to God, and the blessings before and after the *Shma*, clearly and in a voice that awakens the heart to concentrate on the intention and meaning of the words." That is to say that the purpose of prayer is to awaken the soul to recognize the greatness and the beauty of the One above and to love God, to cleave to Him, and all this is accomplished through the recitation of the morning psalms of praise and the *Shma*. And even though the *Zohar* explains the various parts of prayer according to their esoteric meaning, and according to the fixing they accomplish in the spiritual worlds, it seems that the songs and praises contained in the morning psalms and in the blessings of the *Shma* and the *Shmoneh Esreh* (which are also songs and praises to God) are the means through which all these effects are attained. Even the middle blessings of the *Shmoneh Esreh*, according to the *Zohar*

(*Vayakhel* 200b), which contain man's prayers for the fulfillment of his needs, are effective only because of all the fixing and the mystical unifications accomplished by the songs and praises that preceded these requests. The songs create a "time of favor" on high, a propitious moment for the fulfillment of requests.

Therefore, do not let your heart fall within you, in the erroneous belief that since you have no knowledge of the secret meanings and intentions of the prayers, which cause fixing and repair in the higher realms, your prayers are ineffectual. Your evil inclination may bolster this argument, causing you to neglect your prayers even further, by quoting from *Midrash Tehillim*, Psalm 91, which states: "Why are prayers not answered? Because the petitioners do not know the explicit Name (of God)." And the author of the *Shaarey Orah (The Gates of Light)* states: "One who knows how to focus on the name of God, which is connected to each segment of the prayers, is like a person who has the keys to the gates in his hand." Therefore, you may decide, "What use is there in trying to pray with great effort since I don't know how to pray with the kabbalistic intentions anyway?" However, the following example should help you understand why this kind of thinking is mistaken. The artisan who fashions the inner workings of a watch knows all the details of its machinery. He is the biggest expert on watches and can fix a watch if it has been broken. Yet anyone is capable of winding the watch. You don't have to know why winding the watch makes it start ticking to make it work; the watchmaker has already set it all up so that all you have to do is wind it. And if you don't wind it, all the watchmaker's labors won't do a bit of good; the clock simply won't run. So it is with prayer. The truth is that a person who knows how to concentrate with all the proper kabbalistic intentions and unifications can accomplish more with his prayer. But all of his fixings and unifications depend on the arousal of Jewish souls, who cause the divine to become manifest through their songs. Moreover, the sages have already arranged the prayers in a certain order that functions like the key of the watchmaker, the key that unlocks all the intentions and unifications. A Jew who prays with all his heart and soul opens the gates on high and fixes what needs repair, since it is through his body and all the parts of his soul that the revelation of the divine in the upper worlds, and even the whole concept of left and right in the upper worlds, becomes manifest. Even a person who knows all the proper intentions cannot effect anything with his prayers, God forbid, if he does not awaken his soul and pray passionately. And perhaps the sages meant exactly this when they said that prayers are not answered because the petitioners do not know the explicit name of God. Perhaps the proper intention that they are hinting to is this kind of passion. The *Kedushat Levi* explained the biblical passage "And he called God, God . . . " (Exodus 34:6) as follows: "When a Jew arouses the divine holiness that is within him and cries out to God, it is really God calling God, that is to say that he is calling out to God with the Godly part of himself." Banish from your heart, therefore, your evil inclination, which tries to weaken your resolve. Strengthen yourself and repeat the following: "A person who prays with a dried-out soul, one who does not reveal the holiness that is within him, is the only person of whom it can be said 'he prays without knowledge of the Name'—that is, without the part of God that is contained within him. I, therefore, if I awaken myself, am praying with the Name; I cry out with the light of God that is within me. God will, therefore, surely answer me, will bring me close to Him and will save me, spiritually and physically."

Of course, as we have said earlier, a person must labor at the Torah and the performance of the commandments not only while he is praying. He must work hard and not just perform his duties superficially. He must prepare himself to become a vehicle through which divine light and holiness can be revealed. Then his prayer will truly be prayer. Even if he is not completely holy, but serves God, guards himself from sin, and labors every day to reveal at least part of the holiness that is within him, he will be able to pray— though not if he is completely neglectful and has abandoned all efforts to ascend spiritually. The passage (Proverbs 28:9) states: "One who turns away from hearing Torah, his prayer too becomes despised." This is because his soul has not become manifest; he therefore has no spiritual vision and consequently no song and no prayer. But just as prayer needs Torah, so Torah needs prayer, as the Rav said in his letter [mentioned on p. 190]: "Through the arousal of the soul that occurs in prayer, one's love of God and one's desire to cleave to God and to the commandments are aroused."

But Torah needs prayer not only because prayer awakens one's desire for Torah. Torah needs prayer even as it is being studied and absorbed. For a person who utilizes only his intellect in studying Torah will never be sure that this learning is connecting him to God. A person can try and understand the strategies his enemy may be thinking up to hurt him—this doesn't make him any closer to his enemy. They remain distant and opposed to one another. When we learn Torah, we need to draw into us the light of God, His wisdom, and His will, down from the upper worlds into our brain and heart. This can take place only if a person has fashioned a vehicle out of the various parts of himself, has labored with his soul, exerted himself in prayer, and caused the divine to become manifest in his image. Then, when he learns Torah, studying and concentrating for several hours on "the ox that gored the cow," he will find himself in a state of spiritual upliftment, the spirit of God ringing inside, for God is within him.

VI

During prayer, the soul is uplifted; the light of God is revealed and the soul gazes at and unites with Him. This is the cause of the spirit of purity, bliss, and spiritual joy that a person may experience during prayer or afterward, if the prayer was received and performed properly. Let your early mornings be a kind of holy time for you; learn Torah, recite psalms with strong focus and intention, and in general act with a modicum of seriousness. Don't speak unnecessarily; cultivate the feeling that you are preparing yourself to speak to the King. After praying, during the rest of the day, take care not to lose your prayer and destroy what you accomplished. The Lord, God of Israel, has come to you from the heights of heaven; don't drive Him away, God forbid. Yes, it is true that it is impossible to spend the whole day in the state of consciousness that you achieved during your prayers. But at least try to conduct yourself—in your thoughts, your words, and your deeds—as a Jew upon whom God's presence rests.

ESSAY 3

THE HOLY SHABBAT

~ I ~

The *Pesikta* on the Ten Commandments comments as follows: "Here (in Exodus), the commandment is recorded as 'Remember the Shabbat day to keep it holy' while in Deuteronomy the commandment reads 'Guard the Shabbat day to keep it holy.' " Rabbi Yudan and Rabbi Elazar in the name of Rabbi Shimon ben Lakish explained this discrepancy with a comparison. "Imagine a king who sent his son to the storekeeper with a coin and a flask. The boy broke the flask and lost the coin. The king punished him by pulling his hair and boxing him in the ear. He then gave him another flask and another coin and said, *'Be careful that you don't lose these like you lost the first ones I gave you!'* In the same way, because the Jews lost the commandment to 'remember' (through the sin of worshiping the golden calf, after which the first tablets were broken), they were

given the commandment to 'guard.' That is why the text of the
Torah records the commandment both as 'remember' and 'guard.' "

Let us try to understand why the second time the commandment is given, the Torah does not write "remember" as it does the
first time. The parable of the king and his son does not answer this
question; both times, the boy was given an identical flask and coin.
It is true that the word "guard" implies warning, as in "guard yourself
not to lose it this time as you lost it last time." But "remember" can
have the same implication, as in the Torah's warning: "Remember,
do not forget, how you troubled the Lord, your God, in the desert."
There the Torah is cautioning us about the very same sin, and yet
uses the word "remember."

We may perhaps clarify this matter through the words of the
Sifra in *B'chukotai,* which states: " 'Remember the Shabbat day to keep
it holy'—one might think this means to remember it in one's heart.
When the Torah says 'Guard the Shabbat day,' we realize that
guarding it in one's heart is what is implied. When the Torah says
'remember,' it is now apparent that what it requires is to repeat it
with your mouth." Guarding is thus with the heart, and remembering
is with the mouth. Both of them are necessary for the Shabbat—
the heart and the mouth. When the children of Israel lost the
commandment "remember," which was given to them first because
it was to be performed only with one's mouth, they were given
"guard," which also includes the heart, and this made their hold on
the Shabbat more secure.

In our generation as well, when, it is very sad to say, there
has been a terrible increase in desecration of the Shabbat, the destruction emanates initially from the abandonment of the guarding
in the heart. The Shabbat has become for many merely a day of
rest. Since, according to their foolish ideas, God gave them the
Shabbat for their benefit, to give them rest, if it is to their benefit
to continue doing business for fifteen minutes or so after the candles
have been lit on Shabbat eve, or to open their shop fifteen minutes
before Shabbat is over the next day, why should they deprive themselves? After all, the whole Shabbat was given just for their benefit.
Now this is what is to their benefit. In fact, why cause oneself undue
suffering? If it becomes important, why not keep one's store open
all of Shabbat?

This is the path of those bent on spiritual destruction. Yet how blind they are, and how closed their hearts are to reason! If the whole purpose of the Torah in commanding the Shabbat were for their rest, their pleasure, and their benefit, why would the Torah have said "And whoever desecrates her shall surely die"? Would it be logical to say to someone "Please eat because I love you; please enjoy yourself, drink wine, eat meat, because I have compassion for you," and then add, "if you don't eat meat and drink wine, I'm going to kill you with a sword"? The Torah explains very clearly the reason for the commandment of the Shabbat: "Because God rested on that day from all of His work that He had created to do." God kept— and still keeps—the Shabbat. The souls in the supernal world keep the Shabbat, and we, the Children of Israel, must keep it too, together with them. "The Shabbat is the bliss of the higher worlds and the lower worlds," according to the *Zohar* (*Beshalach* 47). "The Shabbat is the *Neshamah's* pleasure, the *Ruach's* bliss, the *Nefesh's* Eden, to delight in love and fear of You" (from a hymn written by Rabbi Aharon, the Great). When a Jew keeps the Shabbat, his *Nefesh, Ruach,* and *Neshamah* enter the Garden of Eden. Together with the pure souls and the souls of the righteous that inhabit that realm, they delight in the light of the Garden of Eden and feel the bliss emanating from the radiance of supernal love and awe. They do not only feel this bliss outside their body, nor does the delightful radiance of love and awe they experience remain in realms far away from this world. The supernal bliss and the radiance are drawn into this world, even into the body itself. Moreover, the flavor of Shabbat is absorbed even into the physical food of the Shabbat and is tasted by the physical palate. "We have a certain spice; Shabbat is its name. Whoever keeps the Shabbat is affected by it and whoever does not keep the Shabbat is not affected by it" (*Shabbat* 119).

Only we, the Children of Israel, are required to keep the Shabbat, and are able to enjoy the bliss of paradise the Shabbat brings. A non-Jew who observes the Shabbat is, according to the Talmud (*Sanhedrin* 58), committing an offense. The *Midrash* (*Beshalach* 25) compares this to a king who is sitting facing his queen. Whoever walks between them commits a capital offense. The essential nature of the Shabbat is hinted at in this parable. For who is the queen here—Israel or the Shabbat? If one says the queen is Israel, then what does this parable have to do with Shabbat? If one says the queen is the Shabbat, where do we find Israel hinted at in this parable? God and the Shabbat sit facing each other. Non-Jews must not pass through. But why should Israel pass through? They are not in the scene either.

The answer, of course, is that the queen symbolizes both the Shabbat and Israel. Israel is called "the Community of Israel," "the Queen," and *"Malchut"* many times in the *Zohar.* Shabbat is also called "Queen" in the *Zohar*—"Shabbat is *Malchut"* (*Zohar* Deuteronomy 272)—and in the prayer service—"Approach us, bride, O Shabbat queen."

For you to understand all this better, we must first explain to you something about the concept of *Malchut* and the Community of Israel. As we have already cautioned, when learning or hearing any of the teachings of the esoteric tradition, you must not come to think that you now know the matter or concept in question as it actually is. In Section I of Essay 2, we explained that it is impossible to understand spiritual concepts with the intellect alone. In our discussion there, we made a distinction between what can be known through the intellect and what can be known through the soul, which is a kind of knowing that is very different than the knowing of the intellect. For example, one may know the whole order of the emanation of the worlds, and know that the world of *Beriah* exists between the worlds of *Atzilut* and *Yetzirah,* and yet have no understanding of what *Beriah* or *Yetzirah* actually are. At this point we'd like to make it clear that our intention in what follows is not even to provide a simple intellectual understanding of the concepts we will discuss, but to open up the student's mind and heart a little at a time, as much as a pinprick. This will enable the students to study the sources that speak about these matters with greater understanding, with the help of God. Yet the explanations we will provide, even if they are not complete, are consistent with what the holy sources write about these subjects.

This can be compared to a man who sees a range of mountains, some larger, some smaller. Holes and windows were drilled into the mountainside, and buildings and towers stood on its various peaks.

"What is this whole complex?" the man questions. He is told that it is a great fortress, that the mountains have caves and rooms within them where soldiers could gather during times of war. Through the holes and windows they could shoot at the enemy. Hearing this explanation does not make the man an expert on the fortress like the officer in charge of it is. The officer knows each and every detail of the fortress's structure; he knows where the food is, where the ammunition is, where all the camouflage equipment and all the other tricks for deceiving the enemy—the traps, the pits, and the mines— are located. Both the man and the officer have the same basic picture of what the fortress is. The difference is that the officer knows what's inside the fortress, every particular, while the man has a very general notion: he knows merely that this is a fortress prepared for war. However, because his knowledge is incomplete, even what he does know is vague and sketchy, so that his idea of what a fortress is, is less clear and developed than the officer's. The way he understands it, any hidden place with a strong cellar should be considered a fortress. If he knew all the secrets of the fortress and all the wisdom that went into building it, his whole concept would change, and he would realize that he had not, until now, had any real understanding of what a fortress truly is. At this point, since he has only a very general, inexact understanding of the fortress, he remains with many unanswered questions: he does not know why this particular tree was planted over there, or why a pit was dug over here, and so forth. However, if he is intelligent and realizes that he is missing the completed picture, he won't be disturbed by all the mysterious things he sees.

The same is true of what we have come to explain. The concepts of *Malchut* and of the Community of Israel that we will describe is the same as is found in the *Zohar* and in all the holy books. But what we will envision are only the outer edges. Therefore, when we explain some of the passages of the Shabbat hymn "A Woman of Valor" or some of the meaning of *"Kegavna"* (a passage from the *Zohar* [2:134a] recited Friday night in the prayer service), we will not be able to clarify every word or every sentence. But what we do explain will be true, according to the opinions of all the sages, elders, and scholars of Torah—just as the general answers given to the man in the parable were true.

II

In the first essay, we explained a little bit about the process of contraction—the contraction of His light—through which God created this world. Although numerous contractions took place during creation, we discussed only the four worlds of *Atzilut, Beriah, Yetzirah,* and *Asiyah,* because they parallel the process of contraction within man's soul. We used the funnel as a model for this process and explained how the funnel must grow progressively more narrow in order to serve its purpose, allowing wine poured from a barrel, say, to enter the narrow mouth of a flask. But we did not explain why the worlds are divided into four. The funnel we used as a model slopes down, becoming narrower and narrower, but always remains one continuous surface. One can't make distinctions within the funnel or divide it up into four separate parts, giving each part a different name, as we do with the worlds.

However, we cannot question whether or not such a division exists, for we have a tradition, handed down to us from Abraham through the prophets to the Tannaim and on, asserting that it does. Nor can we question why God divided them, for this was His will. Nor is it our intention to fully explain, even as much as is humanly possible, the actual differences between each of the worlds; our sages have done this already in the holy books they have composed. We want instead to show you an example from this world that will make the distinctions between the various worlds more clear. The human mind is helped in its understanding of spiritual concepts when it can see a parallel phenomenon in this world. If we can show how the various life forms are divided in this world, and called by different designations, the divisions between the four worlds will be better understood.

There are four simple categories of life in the world: inanimate objects, plant life, animal life, and beings who have the capacity for speech. As we have said earlier, all of these have an existence in the spiritual worlds as *Nefashot.* The inanimate *Nefesh* that God made becomes manifest in this world through all the different kinds of inanimate material God created. The plant *Nefesh* that God made becomes manifest in the world through all the various species that God created, which are each divided into thousands and millions of individual plants. The same is true of the animal *Nefesh*. Each individual member of a species is subordinate, without even being fully conscious of it, to the species as a whole; and the species is subordinate to plant or animal life as a whole. Through all the various species and all their individual members, the *Nefesh* of plants and the *Nefesh* of animals fulfills the commandment with which God entrusted it: to become fully manifest with the single purpose of revealing God's great power. For every form of life is a spark of God's power; the whole earth is filled with His glory.

Even though in this world we see all the various forms of life as separate and individual physical entities, their *Nefashot* all come from one source, a source in which they are all included in one another. And just as the four worlds are the result of one continuous process of contraction and diminishment, until the creation of the world of *Asiyah*, so too in the world of *Asiyah* itself, the power of God that is manifest within this world contracted itself into various levels: speaking beings, animals, plants, inanimate material. This is discussed in detail in the *Etz Chaim* (Gate 50: 1). And all of life comes from a single source, in the same way that all the animals of one species are a subcategory and a small part of the collective *Nefesh* of that species, and all the species are part of the collective *Nefesh* of animal life in general, and all trees are a subcategory of the general *Nefesh* of all plant life. Through subdivisions and further contractions, the *Nefesh* of life and the different forms of life are broken down into smaller parts.

We can now see a comparison between the various forms of life in this world and the four worlds contracted from God's light. For although, in general, the forms of life all come from one source that undergoes a contraction, becoming smaller and smaller, like the funnel, still each form of life is distinct, with its own *Nefesh* and its own name. Moreover, just as the process of contraction is so effective that when life does become manifest it does so in various forms and guises, each one distinct and different from the other, something similar happens as the worlds unfold, and as the five parts of a Jew's soul are revealed. And since we can see this in our world, in the various forms of life, our intellect can begin to imagine the way it must occur in the unfolding of the four worlds. God exists above all the various worlds, contractions, and manifestations. The worlds all appeared through the contraction of just a part of His radiance. What is actually manifested depends on the nature of the contraction that the simple light of God has undergone. One cannot compare the abundant light that is revealed in the world of *Yetzirah*, with all its angels, to the scanty light that appears in this world, the world of *Asiyah* and its inhabitants. Similarly, one cannot compare the part of the collective *Nefesh* that is revealed in a single speaking being to the smaller part of *Nefesh* that appears in animal life, plant life, and inanimate material. Each variation in the quantity of divine light reveals a different kind of world or *Nefesh*. Therefore, every modification of the process of contraction is distinguished by a *Nefesh* and a name of its own. This is different than in the example of the funnel because, in the funnel, the wine remained the same as it passed from the wide to the narrow end; it changed only in volume.

In Section II of Essay 2, we explained the difference between the way God is revealed in the world and the way He is revealed in Israel. Although God's divinity is revealed throughout the whole world, and the whole earth is filled with His glory, what is revealed is only God's power. All the *Nefashot* of all the different kinds of beings in the entire world are all sparks of the light of God's power. The radiance emanating from God's essence, from His holiness, is revealed only in Israel. It is true that God's holiness and wisdom are to be found in the world as well; however, it takes study and meditation to reach this realization, and without such reflection one will not reach this knowledge. This is because, on the face of it, the world is physical; it reveals only God's power. The knowledge and holiness of God are like the great light that the traveler tells us is burning far away in the distance. But within a Jew's mind and heart, there already exists a ray of God's essential holiness and knowledge. This is because he thinks about Torah, which is Godly knowledge, and because he is filled with holy and spiritual thoughts about God and how to serve Him. He has a memory of God, and longs to draw close to Him. All of these desires and holy thoughts are a revelation of God within him. A Jew is like Mount Sinai, on which an illumination from the essence of God's holiness and knowledge was revealed (see *Tikunnei Zohar, Tikuna Tannina*). And since we have already shown that the four worlds and the various divisions of life forms on this planet are the result of an illumination from God that became manifest in different distinct bodies, it is certainly apparent that this is true in regard to Israel as well. Above, there is one collective *Neshamah*, the *Neshamah* of the Community of Israel. The manifestation of this *Neshamah* is distinct from the manifestation of the divine, which the *Nefashot* of the other forms of inanimate, plant, animal, and human life bring into the world. It takes on form and appears in individual Jews. In the spiritual worlds this collective *Neshamah* is known as *Knesset Yisrael*.

And since the *Neshamah* of *Knesset Yisrael* reveals not only God's power, but His essential holiness and wisdom, our holy sages called it "woman," because of the passage in Genesis that relates that woman was created out of man's body and is "bone of his bone and flesh of his flesh." In this world, a woman brings children into the world who contain aspects of her husband's intelligence and wisdom—his actual brain. So, too, the collective soul of Israel on high—God's queen—reveals the essence of the king through the individual Jews who emanate from her. All of the souls and all of the manifestations of this world all serve her purpose—the revelation of God's essence, which is the central purpose of all creation, all revelation.

With this knowledge, the whole nature and character of the Jew—which has been a riddle for the whole world—is now comprehensible. The *Midrash* in *Eichah* (Chapter 1) states that the nations of the world are amazed at the willingness of Jews to die all kinds of terrible death for the purpose of sanctifying God's name. Yet that this should be the only thing about the Jews that astonishes the nations is in itself a cause for amazement. For the entire life of a Jew is one of devotion and self-sacrifice. It is not only when called upon to, God forbid, renounce his God, when a Jew goes skipping to the altar like a young ram, that a Jew is tested. His whole life is a series of tests. He is oppressed from the moment he leaves his mother's womb until his last breath; persecution addles his mind and makes him heartsick—yet he refuses to budge even a hairsbreadth from the Holy One of Israel. This is the whole nature of a Jew. Even his heartbeat and his breathing are full of self-sacrifice. He studies Torah, keeps the Shabbat, educates his children in Torah, and devotes himself to God not in a superficial manner, but with tremendous devotion and sacrifice. But the nations of the world, in reality, should not be perplexed or amazed. The power that is manifest within us is not of this world. The supernal *Matronita*, the woman of valor who is the crown of her divine husband, is manifest through us and works through us. She transcends the world, and thus all the trials of this world and all the suffering they bring in their wake have no effect on her and cannot impede her godly actions. The day approaches when her husband will save her, will raise her from her sickbed and shake the dust from her garments. Her light will then shine from one end of the world to the next. The whole population of the planet will be ashamed and afraid, and will say: "Woe unto us, for we have trampled on the supernal *Matronita;* we have sinfully reproached part of the inner soul of God, of His holiness."

There are times—perhaps on Shabbat at night, when you are thinking about the holiness of God and Israel—that you suddenly stop seeing Israel as a group of individuals and see them instead in totality, as the supernal queen, as light shining from the essence of God's holiness enclothed in the physical garments of individual bodies. With the additional measure of *Neshamah* one receives on Shabbat you see all of Israel in one glance. You see them bent over from all their suffering, shaken and distressed, blackened from poverty, suffering and sighing, and at the same time full of joy and song. They are saying: "Master of the world, we are Yours, and our suffering is for Your sake. With our whole lives and with every breath we devote ourselves to making You King over all the earth. We will fill the whole world with the glow from the part of Your holiness, Your knowledge and will, even Your essence, that You have chosen to shine toward us." This vision moves you, inflames you. Instead of feeling broken and depressed at the sight of the suffering, you feel uplifted, raised high, proud of the aspect of royalty that the Community of Israel on high and in this world embodies—and that exists even within you. Your soul longs to sing a song before God dedicated to her, the royal queen, Israel. You have already recited "Woman of Valor" (*Ayshet Chayil*) and sanctified the Shabbat with Kiddush over wine. But your mind is still on fire. You walk over to the window, you raise your eyes to God and feel

your soul spontaneously begin to sing from within you: "Master of
the world, who can find a woman of valor" (Proverbs 31:10) such
as this? "Her value is far above pearls. Her husband trusts her with
his heart" (Proverbs 31:10, 11), for she serves him in faith and with
sacrifice, and does His work in the world. She bends the whole
world to His will, bringing them toward Him as one brings tribute
to a king. "She repays His good, but never His harm all the days
of her life" (Proverbs 31:12)—that is, she is good to Him, not only
when things are right for her but always. "She awakens when it is
still night"—that is, even during the bitterness and darkness of
exile—"to give food to her household" (Proverbs 31:15)—she dis-
tributes holiness to all of Israel and to the whole world, not in a
superficial or offhanded manner, but "with strength she girds her
loins, and gives power to her arms" (Proverbs 31:17)—that is, her
Torah and her devotions are all performed with self-sacrifice. Her
worship of God is not arid and lifeless, but is filled with illumination
drawn from the essence of the divine. "She realizes the goodness
of her enterprise" (Proverbs 31:18)—she, too, tastes His holiness,
and the delightful flavor that accompanies true service of God. "And
her lamp is not extinguished at night" (Proverbs 31:18)—this is her
strength in the darkness of her suffering and exile. "Her husband is
known at the gates" (Proverbs 31:23)—who acknowledges Your
name in the world if not Israel? And who makes Your holiness holy
if not us, your children? We carry your burden voluntarily, we suffer
for the sake of your holiness without sadness, but with joy and with
strength. "Strength and majesty are her raiment, she joyfully awaits
the last day" (Proverbs 31:25) of her life, knowing that she served
God faithfully and sanctified His name. "She opens her mouth with
wisdom (the wisdom of God), and the Torah of loving-kindness
(God's Torah) is on her lips" (Proverbs 31:26). And at this point, I
cannot hold myself back any more. My soul sings out to her: "Her
children rise and praise her" (Proverbs 31:27) and not only we but
"her husband" in the lofty heights "lauds her" (Proverbs 31:28).
"Many daughters have accomplished great deeds" (Proverbs
31:29)—all the souls that God created reveal His glory— "But you
have surpassed them all" (Proverbs 31:29)—because all the others
reveal only the shining of His power, while you reveal light whose

source is God's self, His knowledge and His holiness. "A God-fearing woman is to be praised" (Proverbs 31:30), and therefore, Master of the World, "give to her from the fruit of her hands" (Proverbs 31:31)—raise her up from the dust, and hurry to save her from her suffering and her exile.

Your vision is now not of the downtrodden state of the Jewish people; it is not out of pity that from the depths of your soul the song of *Ayshet Chayil* rises up. All you see is greatness; you no longer see the material world at all. "The whole world is filled with His glory"—that is all that exists. The *Shechinah* and all its limbs—the souls of Israel—are the center, are everything. At this hour, you feel yourself as one of the children of God. The *Shechinah*, the Community of Israel, dwells within you—and you within it. You no longer feel merely joy or bliss, but the absorption of your self into the divine, to the degree that your spiritual level will allow, and purity and ascension beyond your level. Your lot is a happy one, in this world and the next.

You certainly will not understand all the secrets that each passage in "Woman of Valor" is hinting at, because you still do not know everything there is to learn about the *Sefirah* of *Malchut* and the Community of Israel. However, as in the parable of the fortress, even though you don't have a complete understanding, the little that you do know is true knowledge. And when you recite the words of praise from the song with your whole heart and soul, you are performing an act of great unification in the spiritual worlds above. Because the aspect of *Malchut*, the Community of Israel, which is manifested in this world through each and every individual Jew, is dependent on the devotions of the Jews in this world. By serving God with all the limbs of their body, and sanctifying His name among them, they cause God's holiness to become manifest in them, and they thus effect the unification of the collective pure *Neshamah* of Israel on high with God. His light emanates into it, and through it into each individual Jew.

But if, God forbid, individual Jews do not fulfill the will of God, and do not cause divine holiness, knowledge, and desire to become manifest through Israel, it is not only themselves and their own soul that they injure. They also damage the collective *Neshamah* of Israel on high, *Malchut*, the Community of Israel, and cause a breach in the unity of God and the Community of Israel. And this is what is known as the exile of the *Shechinah*.

Now you can begin to understand a concept you may have come across in the holy books: the idea that the forces of evil *(sitra achra)* damage the aspect of *Malchut* through the sins of Israel. Moshe Rabbainu says (Numbers 10:35), "Rise up, Lord, and scatter your enemies, and cause those that hate you to flee from before you." Rashi comments on this passage that all those who hate Israel hate the One who spoke and brought the world into being. To hate Israel is equivalent to hating God, and all the suffering and trouble that Israel is subjected to actually serve to conceal the light of God. To the extent that a person is devoted to revealing the light of God, he will be persecuted and mistreated. In the future, when the forces of evil pass away, "There will be no evil and no destruction on my entire holy mountain, for the knowledge of God will fill the earth as water covers the sea" (Isaiah 11:9). There will be no concealment and thus no evil.

To put it simply: God's will is that we serve Him of our free will, that we choose to do good and not evil. If God were to be revealed in this world to the same degree that He is revealed in the higher worlds of *Atzilut*, *Beriah*, and *Yetzirah*, no sin, nothing that contradicted the will of God, would be possible. That is why God contracted His light to such an extent that doing evil became possible; nevertheless, man should not do evil and should choose only good. Not only did God cause the contraction of the light, He also made the evil inclination, whose task is to seduce man to evil, though in doing so His intention is to do good—He wants man to resist seduction and not bend to evil. It can be rightfully said that at their origin, both evil—the concealment of God—and the inclination to do evil, were good. Only their outer garments were evil. They were not evil in their essence, they were just disguised in garments that looked evil. But because of the sin of Adam, and the sins of each individual—which are in reality evil, as they are in opposition to the will of God—and for certain other reasons which the Ari Zal discusses, the forces of evil *(sitra achra)* became truly evil. In the Messianic future, the additional dimension of evil that accrued to the forces of evil and to the evil inclination will be wiped away and slaughtered, while what is good within them will ascend.

The whole desire of the forces of evil and the evil inclination is to conceal the light of God, and to persecute individual Jews who have the capacity to make God's light manifest. They use all kinds of things to carry out their task. Sometimes they use one of the other nations, God forbid, to oppress Israel and especially oppress those Jews who are serving God. Thus those who hate Israel hate God. And every time a Jew does himself spiritual damage, and causes greater concealment within himself, the forces of evil gain in strength and injure the aspect of *Malchut*, the *Matronita*, whose purpose is directly opposed to theirs: to cause the revelation of the light of God in Israel. All of our devotions are for the purpose of purifying her and causing her to be revealed—both that aspect of the *Matronita* that is within us, and also the main center that exists on high. We wish to unify her in supernal unity, so that the light of God should be revealed in her and in the midst of Israel, in the form of holy thoughts, desires, and devotions. And all of the revelations we have been speaking about and describing throughout this book are all revelations of the aspect of *Malchut*. *Malchut* is called "a looking glass" in the *Zohar* because all the holy sights and supernal sparks that are seen within a Jew, which cause him to become awakened to the love and fear of God and arouse him to song, all appear through her, for the revelation of God's holiness in the souls of Israel in these matters is indeed the holy sight.

Concerning the subject of unification, it is known that there are two kinds of unification: unification above and unification below. Unification below is the unification that must take place within *Malchut* itself. This kind of unification is mentioned in the passage from the *Zohar*, which is read as part of the Friday evening services ushering in the Shabbat: "The Holy One, blessed be He, who is One above, will not sit on His throne until the throne itself has become one." The collective *Neshamah* of Israel above is called God's throne, for God's Kingship is revealed through it. But God will not reveal Himself through it [the collective *Neshamah*] until it is itself in a state of unity.

Our concern, however, is not with the various aspects and

polarities within the supernal *Sefirah* of *Malchut* that must be united, but with the individual Jew and his devotions, with the aspect of *Malchut* and the *Neshamah* that are to be found within him. What is important is for a person to be able to understand himself, and to create in himself a unity. If he can accomplish that he will be able, through his devotions in this world and through the unity of his own being, to cause healing and repair to occur above, which will create unity in the section of the Community of Israel—the *Sefirah* of *Malchut* as it exists above in the heavenly realm—that corresponds to his soul below. He will accomplish this regardless of what he understands about the concept of unification below, in the level of the supernal *Malchut*. (This is according to the principle we quoted from the *Pardes*, which describes the correspondence between our form and actions below, and the manifestation of the divine light above—we have right and left sides, therefore there are right and left in the spiritual world above us, etc.) And by causing unification below (within *Malchut*), he eventually helps cause unification above (the unification of *Malchut* and the Holy One, Blessed be He).

For the purpose of knowing how to create unity within oneself, we must understand the pronouncement our holy sages instituted for us to recite before the performance of every commandment: "For the sake of the unification of the Holy One, Blessed be He, and His *Shechinah* "(that is to say, the above-mentioned unification of God and *Malchut*). From this pronouncement it seems clear that every Jew, including those who have not yet fixed their whole soul, is also able to cause unification with his devotions. For the sages' intention was that not only the *tzaddikim*, but all of Israel, recite this phrase. What does the accomplishment of this unification depend on?

Twice before we have emphasized that even a person who has not yet fixed his whole soul is capable of uplifting, through his devotion, the parts of his soul that are already fit. They then can serve as a chariot for the manifestation of the *Shechinah*. This can be accomplished if the person guards himself with all his might against sin and spiritual lowliness.

Now that we have begun to discuss unification, we must define this term more precisely. We have learned that a person is capable of causing unification below and above, even though he has not completely fixed himself yet. Even if he has weaknesses that are definitely to be considered flaws in a person of his spiritual stature, he can bring about these unifications. Yet in the case of some people, their flaws, or even their lack of spiritual stature—matters which are not really clearly sins—may cause them to become distant from God. Why is this so?

In the fourth part of the second essay we discussed the fact that every entity has a purpose toward which its entire being, even its physical body, is directed. All of its manifold parts shape themselves toward the aim of realizing and revealing this essence, which is a spark from the light of God's power. The purpose of a Jew is to reveal God's holiness. Whether he fulfills this goal or not is up to him. To the extent that he decides to devote himself to God and to divine service, to that extent will all the parts of his *Nefesh, Ruach,* and *Neshamah,* and even the limbs of his body, become absorbed and united in God's holiness. This is the crucial point: if a person unites himself toward this one purpose, so that all his thoughts, words, and deeds are directed toward the one goal of serving God— including his eating and his business activities and so forth—then even his faults and flaws will be considered exceptions to the rule, and will not affect his essence, even if he is punished for them. Since his whole self is devoted to holiness, this has become his essence. All his faults, whatever damage he has done, are to be considered unintentional, for his whole being is absorbed in its collective purpose.

This then is the reason one person may be distanced from God by his faults while another is not affected by them. A person who, of his own free will, discovers his purpose in life and devotes his mind and thoughts and will to fulfilling this goal, the goal of a Jew, gains an identity. We can say what he is in his essence—one who serves God. This remains true even if he has not yet fixed his desires, even if he still feels lust and cravings within himself for forbidden things. If he is at least working on these desires, trying to uplift them, we can still truthfully define him as a servant of God. All of the parts of his soul, which spread and extend through the various limbs of his body and into his actions, are united in this one central quality. This is the "unification below" that takes place in the Community of Israel that is within him.

Then there is another kind of person, one who has not defined himself, who has no central purpose or intention that unites his thoughts, words, and deeds, but acts haphazardly, and thinks and says whatever crosses his mind. Even if such a person performs various commandments—when they cross his path—one cannot define his essence in any way, for his essence is not united in devotion to anything, but is disparate, made up of isolated parts. Even if such a person does experience, at times, the arousal of part of his soul into a state of spiritual excitement, this arousal is a kind of desperate flapping or paroxysm rather than a true ascent. This can be compared to a person trapped under an avalanche of rocks. He desperately waves one limb and then another as he tries to lift himself out from under the rocks. Limbs from the carcasses of freshly killed animals, which have already lost the fullness of life from within their hearts and brains, sometimes twitch and convulse for some time after their slaughter. This is the nature of the spiritual arousals of a person who is not devoted to God. He possesses neither fullness of soul nor fullness of vision. In order to perform unification above— the unification of God with *Knesset Yisrael*—one needs first to have performed unification below, the unification of the part of *Knesset Yisrael* immanent within the self.

But it is necessary not only to unite all the various parts of one's *Nefesh, Ruach*, and *Neshamah* within, but to unite one's *Neshamah* with all the different *Neshamot* that together form the collective whole of Israel. One's own *Neshamah* is, after all, just a branch or a limb of the aspect of the Community of Israel that is spread and diffused throughout all of Israel. It is impossible, therefore, for an individual to perform a unification above, in the Community of Israel, if he is filled with hatred for his fellow Jew here below. His hatred causes his soul to become like a limb torn away from its source, the Community of Israel. The pronouncement our sages advised us to recite before every commandment, therefore, ends with the words "in the name of all of Israel."

Thus, both parts of the unification are performed within us— the unification of the *Shechinah* that abides in us, and our unification with the collectivity of Israel.

When you merit to study further in the holy books, you will

now understand with greater ease how these two unifications—above and below—are also performed through the recitation of the passage "Hear, O Israel," when accompanied by your inner devotions. You should also be able to better understand what the *Zohar* is hinting at in the *Kegavna* section from the Friday evening services we mentioned earlier: "This is the Shabbat, who unites in the secret of One so that the secret of One can dwell upon her." First comes her union in "the secret of One"; then the one God can come to dwell upon her. "And all the harsh judgments pass away from her, and He dwells in the unity of the holy light." We have already discussed what the *sitra achra* is, and how it attempts to reach and disrupt the aspect of *Malchut*, the holy *Matronita*. On Shabbat, God's holiness is revealed to a greater extent, and this light drives away the darkness and the concealment, "and all the judgments pass away from her," and "she is crowned below among the holy people, and they are all crowned with new *Neshamot*." When she is enclothed in the revelation of her holiness among the people of Israel, new *Neshamot* are added to them. There is much more to know, but this is enough right now. The main thing is to devote yourself. On Shabbat, when you serve God and have prepared yourself for the Shabbat, and have sung her praises with the song "Woman of Valor," know that you will have performed a unification on high.

❧   III   ☙

To review what we have said: The light of God is revealed in the world "and the whole earth is filled with His glory." But what is revealed is only God's power—His essence and His holiness are hidden. Within a Jew, the light of His holiness and His essence can also be revealed by way of the collective *Neshamah* of Israel on high, which is also called *Malchut* and *Matronita*. This is the spiritual structure of the world; we find a corresponding structure in time. During the six days of the week, God reveals His power, while His essence and holiness remain concealed. For during the six days of the week, He created the world, which is the revelation of His power; while on Shabbat He rested, "for on that day He rested from all the work that He had done." He did not rest completely—He rested only from His work. The purpose of creation was revealed on Shabbat—precisely because it was Shabbat.

Since one God created the totality of existence, He is revealed in every dimension in the same fashion. His power is revealed in the world as a whole, and the holiness of His essence, the aspect of existence known as *Malchut*, is revealed in Israel. His power is revealed in all the countries of the earth, and His holiness in the land of Israel, which is similarly part of this same aspect: *Malchut*. And in time: there are the six days of the week, and the seventh day, Shabbat, is a manifestation of *Malchut, Matronita*. This then is the meaning of the midrash we quoted, which explains why only Israel is to keep the Shabbat. The parable is told of a king sitting with his wife facing him—whoever walks between them commits a capital offense. Israel and the Shabbat are this *Matronita*, this woman of valor, and on Shabbat she unites with the Holy One, blessed be He, and no stranger has a place between them.

The difference, however, between the revelation of holiness on Shabbat and in the land of Israel, and its revelation within a Jew, is that the dimensions of time and space—Shabbat and the land of Israel—have no free will. Even though they remain holy forever, they can be blemished by desecration. The holiness of a Jew depends on him—it is his choice. If he wants to, he can sanctify himself, can draw down the *Neshamah* of Israel and reveal it within him. If he does not, God forbid, he darkens both himself and his fellow men.

When Shabbat comes, an extra measure of *Neshamah* is added to each Jew, both within him and within the dimension of time. The Holy, supernal *Matronita*, the throne of God's holiness, is revealed more abundantly. A Jew actually feels—even with his body—the arrival of the Shabbat. If you wanted to take off a day during the middle of the week, and to forget all your profane thoughts and all your worries, you would find it extremely difficult. To disengage yourself from the world and its problems when you're right in the middle of them is hard. But at the approach of the nightfall that brings Shabbat, you feel all the dust and dirt of the week leave your mind and heart as if forcibly shaken away. The light and the shining from *Malchut* on high fills you now, drives away the darkness from within you—both you and the whole world are transformed. Shabbat is not a composite, consisting of a normal day that has holiness grafted onto it: its essence is its holiness, and its holiness is its essence. The Shabbat is a guest whose presence is not familiar to us from the other days of the week. A person, too, is not the same person on Shabbat that he was the rest of the week. Everything has changed, even the world has been transmuted. A world of holiness has been drawn down for each person, and he enters into it. Just as the souls who are about to enter the Garden of Eden immerse themselves in the river of fire, so too, on the eve of Shabbat, a person immerses in the mikvah and emerges feeling a greater sense of closeness to God and longing for Him. He feels the aspect of *Malchut* within him longing for God, and he recites the Song of Songs. He may not be able to understand with his mind what he feels when he reads each passage; still, he has already learned the allegorical significance of "Woman of Valor" and moreover, he can already feel flashes and quivers of longing for God moving inside him: "Kiss me with the kisses of Your mouth, for Your love is better than wine . . . draw me after You—I will run . . . the King has taken me into His chambers." He is no longer involved only with the glories of the past—with how at one time God's dwelling place was in the midst of Israel. His prayer and longing are for the present: "Master of the World, draw me after You and I will run." And just as in the past, "The King has taken me into His chambers"—the chambers of His holiness—so too, take me now, and I will celebrate and rejoice in You.

From where do these passionate feelings emanate? What is the nature of these transformations that affect even the body, even the surrounding environment? The human intellect is unable to fathom the essence of holiness as it exists in the spiritual fixings he effects, the unifications and illuminations he causes above through his fulfillment of the commandments and through his devotions—all of these are beyond the grasp of the human intellect. . . .

We have given you a slight bit of insight into the aspect of God's light called *Malchut*, the Community of Israel, and have explained a little bit, here and there, about the words of the passage *Kegavna* from the *Zohar*. But even if you were much greater and more advanced spiritually, you would still be unable to apprehend with

your mind the true nature of *Malchut*, its actual reality on high. Nor
could you really comprehend the joyful noise and the fixing caused
in the heavens by your sanctification of the Shabbat on Friday night.
Is it possible for an earthbound being to imagine even a little of the
unification and holy joy that fills the heavens when the people of
Israel recite *Kegavna* in awe, love, and joy?

"If only the Jews would keep two Sabbaths properly, they
would immediately be redeemed" (Talmud *Shabbat* 118). Every Shabbat, as night falls, all the supernal worlds are in an uproar, everyone
hoping that "perhaps now Israel will keep the Shabbat and the
redemption will be revealed. The *sitra achra* will be obliterated, and
His great name will grow and be sanctified. God will be King over
heaven and earth; one unity and one holiness, emanating from the
one God, will prevail everywhere." The truth is that even though
all of Israel does not yet observe the Shabbat properly, individual
Jews operating at their own level bring the time of redemption closer
through their own observance of the Shabbat. Can the human mind
comprehend this? And is it possible for us to see the spark of redemption that we ourselves have brought into the world? "No eye
can see it, God, save Yours, alone."

"The secret of Shabbat . . . the prayer that ascends on Shabbat . . . is the secret of the One." The Shabbat is a secret, and even
the prayer that he prays on Shabbat is itself a secret. The eve of
Shabbat is unified with *Malchut* together in their unification with the
one God whose name is One. She crowns herself below with the
holy people; above there is God, and below, His children, the holy
people, and everything unites together in one holiness.

What is so astonishing, then, about the transformation of a
Jew's body and even his surroundings on Friday night, or in the
passionate feelings that move him? Even a stone would be transformed if exposed to this abundance of precious light and to the
spirit of the Messiah.

And even within the Shabbat itself, the special quality of each
time keeps changing. The flavor and sight and holiness of Friday
night is different from the flavor and sight and holiness of Shabbat
day, and the third meal at the conclusion of Shabbat is different
again. Just as souls in the Garden of Eden keep ascending, growing
stronger, reaching new levels of beauty and holiness, so too does

the soul on Shabbat. And during the third meal, as the Shabbat ends, your heart breaks within you as you pray for what your soul and body need—but this heartbreak is not one of sadness or spiritual descent. To the contrary, it is a heartbreak of yearning, the yearning of the child for his father. We can compare this to a prince who has been sent far away from his father and remains bereft of everything. What he really is missing, what he really needs, is to be with his father—but he is so beset by troubles, so oppressed, he is unable to distinguish between all his various miseries and afflictions. A web of misfortunes burdens his heart; his soul is bitter. He returns for a visit to his father's house, sees his father, and suddenly all his worries are forgotten. His troubles melt away and his heart is filled with light, security, and salvation. After a short time, though, realizing he will have to leave soon, he falls into his father's arms and weeps, pours out his heart to his father and cries "Father, it is so hard for me to be so far away from you! My heart becomes closed from all the suffering, and my whole being is surrounded by darkness. I have nothing that I need, not even food or water, and I become so deranged from the complexity of all my troubles that I forget my true nature, I forget that I am the son of a king, and I even forget your holiness, your glory, and your devotion."

True, after having ascended spiritually from level to level throughout the whole Shabbat, it's a shame to waste any of the precious moments of the third meal praying for one's material sustenance. But imagine a child, held in his father's embrace, clinging to him and sobbing. Is such a child capable of hiding anything from his father, holding back any of his worries or fears? When you pour out your soul, all its cracks and fissures become visible.

A Jew continues to feel the Shabbat and its holiness the whole week long. The supernal light was revealed within him; through him, the Community of Israel, the supernal queen, is united with God on high. It is impossible that his body would not be changed—at least a little bit—by this experience. If he takes care during the week not to lose or destroy the little bit of holiness he absorbed on Shabbat, if he keeps Shabbat and guards it during the week, the whole year, and then for his whole life, he will eventually become completely holy. Perhaps the Talmud (*Shabbat* 118) is alluding to this process when it makes the statement that if all of Israel "would

keep two Sabbaths properly, they would immediately be redeemed."
That is to say: if you don't feel the holiness of the previous Shabbat
during the week, because what remained transformed in your body
was an insignificant amount, keep the following Shabbat properly
again, and more holiness will be added to you during the week,
until you find you have become a storehouse of holiness, and you
will find redemption as well.

And from now on, diligent students, let our words be at least
a beginning for you, an opening the size of a pinprick. You have
already been shown and have come to understand at least the first,
primary steps of Chasidism and Kabbalah, and particularly their
relevance to devotion. Now nothing is beyond your power.
Strengthen yourselves, devote yourselves to God, and He will open
your heart like the entranceway to the Temple; and through the
gates of the chambers of holiness you will now enter, rising from
strength to strength until you see God in Zion, speedily in our day,
bringing joy and salvation for all of Israel as a whole and for each
individual. Amen.

This book was translated from the original Hebrew text of *Chovat HaTalmidim* by Rabbi Micha Odenheimer. He studied in Yeshivah Gush Etzion in Israel and Tifereth Yerushalaim in New York City, where he received Smichah (rabbinic ordination) from HaRav Moshe Feinstein in 1984. He had previously graduated *cum laude* from Yale University in 1980. Rabbi Odenheimer is a writer and teacher in Jerusalem, and has recently been covering news stories in Ethiopia for the *Jerusalem Report* and UPI. He lives with his family in Jerusalem.

⚬⚬⚬⚬⚬⚬

Aharon Sorasky is a prolific author and scholar, and a frequent contributor to such Hebrew-language publications as *HaModia*. He has written biographies of many prominent Jewish leaders including chasidic rebbes, great scholars, and noted rabbis. His books include *HaRebbe MiKotz VeShishim Giborim Saviv Lo*, a biography of the Kotzker Rebbe; *Pe'er HaDor*, a biography of the Chazon Ish; and *Marbitzei Torah Me'Olam HaChasidut*, which is about nine chasidic rebbes and rabbinic leaders of Poland who perished in the Holocaust. Aharon Sorasky lives in B'nei Brak, Israel, where he is a respected member of the Slonimer chasidic community.